SIMONE DE BEAUVOIR

This one's for Peg

SIMONE DE BEAUVOIR

A Critical Introduction

Edward Fullbrook
and
Kate Fullbrook

Polity Press

Copyright © Edward Fullbrook and Kate Fullbrook 1998

The right of Edward Fullbrook and Kate Fullbrook to be identified as authors of this work has been asserted in accordance with the Copyright, Designs and Patents Act 1988.

First published in 1998 by Polity Press in association with Blackwell Publishers Ltd.

2 4 6 8 10 9 7 5 3 1

Editorial office:
Polity Press
65 Bridge Street
Cambridge CB2 1UR, UK

Marketing and production:
Blackwell Publishers Ltd
108 Cowley Road
Oxford OX4 1JF, UK

Published in the USA by
Blackwell Publishers Inc.
Commerce Place
350 Main Street
Malden, MA 02148, USA

ISBN 0-7456-1202-4
ISBN 0-7456-1203-2 (pbk)

A CIP catalogue record for this book is available from the British Library and has been applied for from the Library of Congress.

Typeset in 10.5 on 12 pt Palatino
by Best-set Typesetter Ltd, Hong Kong
Printed and bound in Great Britain by MPG Books Ltd, Bodmin, Cornwall

This book is printed on acid-free paper.

Key Contemporary Thinkers

Published

Jeremy Ahearne, *Michel de Certeau: Interpretation and its Other*
Peter Burke, *The French Historical Revolution: The Annales School 1929–1989*
Colin Davis, *Levinas*
Simon Evnine, *Donald Davidson*
Edward Fullbrook and Kate Fullbrook, *Simone de Beauvoir*
Andrew Gamble, *Hayek: The Iron Cage of Liberty*
Phillip Hansen, *Hannah Arendt: Politics, History and Citizenship*
Christopher Hookway, *Quine: Language, Experience and Reality*
Sean Homer, *Fredric Jameson: Marxism, Hermeneutics, Postmodernism*
Douglas Kellner, *Jean Baudrillard: From Marxism to Post-Modernism and Beyond*
Chandran Kukathas and Phillip Pettit, *Rawls: A Theory of Justice and its Critics*
Lois McNay, *Foucault: A Critical Introduction*
Philip Manning, *Erving Goffman and Modern Sociology*
Michael Moriarty, *Roland Barthes*
William Outhwaite, *Habermas: A Critical Introduction*
John Preston, *Feyerabend*
Susan Sellers, *Hélène Cixous: Authorship, Autobiography and Love*
Georgia Warnke, *Gadamer: Hermeneutics, Tradition and Reason*
Jonathan Wolff, *Robert Nozick: Property, Justice and the Minimal State*

Forthcoming

Alison Ainley, *Irigaray*
Sara Beardsworth, *Kristeva*
Michael Best, *Galbraith*
Michael Caesar, *Umberto Eco*
James Carey, *Innis and McLuhan*
Thomas D'Andrea, *Alasdair MacIntyre*
Eric Dunning, *Norbert Elias*
Jocelyn Dunphy, *Paul Ricoeur*
Graeme Gilloch, *Walter Benjamin*
Adrian Hayes, *Talcott Parsons and the Theory of Action*
Ian Holliday, *Michael Oakeshott*
Christina Howells, *Derrida*
Simon Jarvis, *Adorno*
Paul Kelly, *Ronald Dworkin*
Carl Levy, *Antonio Gramsci*
Harold Noonan, *Frege*
David Silverman, *Sacks*
Wes Sharrock and Rupert Read, *Kuhn*
Nick Smith, *Charles Taylor*
Geoff Stokes, *Popper: Politics, Epistemology and Method*
Nicholas Walker, *Heidegger*
James Williams, *Lyotard*

Contents

Acknowledgements   ix

Introduction   1

1 *The Education of a Philosopher*   7

2 *Writing for her Life*   30

3 *Literature and Philosophy*   37
   'A New Dimension of Investigation'   37
   All Men Are Mortal   44

4 *Narrative Selves*   52
   The Philosophical Background of Existentialism   52
   Consciousness as a Relation   55
   Two Dimensions of Human Reality   60
   The Theory of the Narrative Self   63
   Bad Faith   67
   The Philosophy of Joy   70

5 *Embodiment and Intersubjectivity*   75
   She Came to Stay   75
   The Body   77
   Social Solipsism and Holistic Union   82
   Subjects and Objects   85
   The Internal Relation   88
   The Blood of Others   92
   Intersubjective Social Theory   94

6 *The Ethics of Liberation*   100
   Introduction   100

The Origin of Value   101
The Structure of Freedom   105
Social Ethics   109

7 *Applied Ethics I:* The Second Sex   116

Introduction   116
The Second Sex   118

8 *Applied Ethics II:* Les Belles Images, The Woman Destroyed
   and Old Age   135

Les Belles Images   136
The Woman Destroyed   138
Old Age   141

Notes   149

Glossary   165

Works of Simone de Beauvoir   169

Index   173

Acknowledgements

This introduction to Simone de Beauvoir's writing and philosophy is a contribution to what has been called the current renaissance in Simone de Beauvoir studies. This renaissance necessarily depends on the dedicated work of a number of fine scholars, and we want to thank some of those who have been most important for us. First, the new interest in Simone de Beauvoir would not be possible without the editorial work of Sylvie le Bon de Beauvoir, who has been instrumental in publishing Beauvoir's posthumous papers in ways that continue to be of the utmost importance. Secondly, we particularly want to thank Margaret A. Simons, both for her personal encouragement and for the exemplary standards set by her own foundational work on Beauvoir's philosophy. Her energy and commitment to the serious analysis of women's achievement in philosophy is of immense value for a generation of scholars. We also want to thank Eleanore Holveck, Debra Bergoffen and William McBride for kindly allowing us access to their own research on Beauvoir. Alice Schwarzer's response to our previous study of Beauvoir, *Simone de Beauvoir and Jean-Paul Sartre: The Remaking of a Twentieth-Century Legend*, gave us enormous pleasure, and we want to record our thanks to her here. Yolanda Patterson's dedication to Beauvoir deserves special thanks from all who value the philosopher's legacy. We are grateful to the British Academy's Humanities Research Board and the University of the West of England's Faculty of Humanities Research Committee for providing funding for aspects of the work which went into this project. We also want to thank Geoff Channon, Roger Gard, Bill Greenslade, Jean Grimshaw, Sue

Habeshaw, Robin Jarvis, Renee Slater and Helen Taylor for kinds of support that it would have been difficult to do without. Like all scholars, we owe an immeasurable debt to the librarians who helped to secure the documents that made our work possible, in this case the more than patient librarians at the University of the West of England. Finally, thanks must go to our editor, Andrew Winnard, for his help, patience and encouragement.

The authors and publishers are grateful for permission to reproduce material from the following works: Debra Bergoffen, 'Contesting Intentional Anxieties', Silverman Phenomenology Series, Dusquesne University Press, Pittsburgh; Margaret A. Simons, 'Joining Another's Fight: Beauvoir's Post-Modern Challenge to Racism in *America Day by Day*', paper delivered at the Midwest Division, Society for Women in Philosophy, October 1994.

This problem . . . of the other's consciousness, it was my problem.
Simone de Beauvoir

Introduction

This book provides a new kind of introduction to one of the greatest twentieth-century philosophers and writers, Simone de Beauvoir. While Beauvoir's importance as a major contributor to the development of modern thought can scarcely be contested, the ways her work has been received do only partial justice to her achievement. This study's central concern is to draw a coherent map of Beauvoir's philosophical methods, interests and originality in ways which augment and clarify various other significant ways of reading her work. For despite continuing interest in Beauvoir as a novelist, as an autobiographer, as a female intellectual icon and as the pre-eminent foundational theorist for contemporary feminism, her accomplishment as a philosopher still has not come clearly into focus. This study aims to present the first comprehensive introductory guide to the major substantive elements of Simone de Beauvoir's philosophy.[1]

Although the situation is now changing, there are numerous reasons why Beauvoir has been undervalued, and even ignored, as a philosopher by almost everyone, with the all-important exceptions of her immediate colleagues. Many of these reasons derive from misapprehensions regarding accounts Beauvoir gave of her own activities, from false stories which tend to accrue to women who work as philosophers, and from Jean-Paul Sartre's willingness to take credit for her ideas and Beauvoir's willingness to allow him to do so. Indeed, the single major obstacle to understanding Beauvoir's philosophical ideas has been the impact of her lifelong and highly productive association as Sartre's friend, lover and colleague. This partnership, with its joint commitment to many shared philosophical ideas, means that Beauvoir has been cast repeatedly (and merely) as Sartre's philosophical disciple and follower. That Beauvoir, and not Sartre, was the intellectual force behind some of the key ideas which characterized French Existentialism in its most influential phase is a circumstance which has only recently become demonstrable. Beauvoir is, in fact, the least docile or derivative of thinkers. The elements of her philosophy which she shared with Sartre are precisely that – positions held in *common* in the full sense of the word by two philosophers who found themselves in agreement on certain counts, and who critiqued and helped to hone each other's ideas. Furthermore, and in crucial aspects, Beauvoir's thought differs from Sartre's. She followed philosophical avenues which were very much her own.

Another of the greatest obstacles to a coherent evaluation of Beauvoir's achievement as a philosopher is the writer herself, who often denied her right, and indeed any wish, to be placed in this category. However, what Beauvoir meant by her persistent rejection of the title 'philosopher' was idiosyncratic and pragmatic, and demands careful examination. That a major philosopher should deny being one is, without doubt, peculiar. But the fact that such a curious case should indeed *be* the case is, in many ways, not overly surprising. 'Philosopher', as Michèle Le Doeuff (among others) points out with blinding obviousness, is itself a strange category which does not easily admit that other awkward category, 'women'. It is crucially important to note that Beauvoir herself explicitly linked her rejection of the title of philosopher with her views on her position as a woman.

In 1960, in the second volume of her autobiography *The Prime of Life*, Beauvoir looked back on herself in 1935 and gave the following account of her decision not to devote herself to philosophy, despite her clear talent as a philosopher. Margaret A. Simons provides a new translation of this curious aspect of Beauvoir's autobiographical self-presentation:

> 'Why not try my hand at philosophy?' she asks herself in 1935. 'Sartre says I understand philosophical doctrines, Husserl's among others, more quickly and more exactly than he . . . In brief, I have . . . solid powers of assimilation, a developed critical sense, and philosophy is for me a living reality. I'll never tire of its satisfactions.'

> 'However, I don't consider myself a philosopher. I know very well that my ease in entering into a text comes precisely from my lack of inventiveness. In this domain, the truly creative spirits are so rare that it is idle of me to

ask why I cannot join their ranks. It's necessary rather to explain how certain individuals are capable of pulling off this concerted delirium which is a system, and whence comes the stubbornness which gives to their insights that value of universal keys. I have said already that the feminine condition does not dispose one to this kind of obstinacy.'[2]

The statement exemplifies many Beauvoir made throughout her public career to distance herself from the title of 'philosopher'. Her readers have tended to read Beauvoir on this matter rather unproblematically, without analysing the very particular (even peculiar) definition she gives this term. A clue is given in her comment, just noted, of philosophy consisting of a 'concerted delirium which is a system'. Another clue emerges in her remarks in an interview with Margaret Simons in 1985, where the topic under discussion is the omission of much of the philosophical apparatus from H. M. Parshley's English translation of *The Second Sex*:

'Well, I think it's very bad to suppress the philosophical aspect because while I say that I'm not a philosopher in the sense that I'm not the creator of a system, I'm still a philosopher in the sense that I've studied a lot of philosophy, I have a degree in philosophy, I've taught philosophy, I'm infused with philosophy, and when I put philosophy into my books it's because that's a way for me to view the world and I can't allow them to eliminate that way of viewing the world, that dimension of my approach to women, as Mr Parshley has done. I'm altogether against the principle of gaps, omissions, condensations which have the effect, among other things of suppressing the whole philosophical effect of the book.'[3]

It is important to note carefully what Beauvoir is doing here. She uses the term 'philosopher' in several senses, and agrees, even insists, that in most of these senses she must be read in philosophical terms. While she denies the title of philosopher in the sense that she does not regard herself as 'the creator of a system', she claims it on all the other counts she mentions. 'Philosopher' is a term which Beauvoir only uses in what she regards as its fullest force, with extraordinary precision and idiosyncratic limitations (and the shelves of library philosophy sections would be thinly stocked indeed if Beauvoir's definition of the term was generally accepted: Wittgenstein and Merleau-Ponty, for example, and all the postmodernists, would simply have to go). We want to cite one more statement by Beauvoir to make it quite clear what she was doing in rejecting the systems-making version of this term for herself.[4]

In another interview with Margaret A. Simons and Jessica Benjamin, this time in 1979, after insisting that her 'field is literature'

and that she never 'created a philosophical work', she explains
further, after *The Ethics of Ambiguity* has been mentioned by her
interviewers as an indubitably philosophical production, that

> 'For me it is not philosophy; it is an essay. For me, a philosopher is
> someone like Spinoza, Hegel, or Sartre; someone who has built a great
> system, and not simply someone who likes philosophy, who can teach it,
> understand it, and who can make use of it in essays. A philosopher is
> somebody who truly builds a philosophical system. And that, I did not do.
> When I was young, I decided that it was not what I wanted to do.'[5]

After this further instance of clarification, and while honouring
her own qualifications, Beauvoir's rejection of the title of philosopher must, simply, be set aside. Beauvoir's primary usage of the
term is a strikingly limited definition of philosophy, and one which
she herself is careful to qualify. (It is helpful, too, to note that the
division sometimes made in French between the kind of essay to
which Beauvoir refers and philosophy does not operate in English.
Further, it is just as well to note Beauvoir's utter confidence in her
own philosophical abilities, signalled by her insouciant statement
that she simply 'decided' not to devote her life to the kind of philosophy represented by systems-building). What Beauvoir *did* think
she was doing as a writer 'infused' with philosophy is suggested in
the introduction to *Force of Circumstance* (1963), the third volume of
her autobiography, where she suggests that her text might be bracketed with those of Rabelais, Montaigne, Saint-Simon and Rousseau,[6]
in effect, precisely where we locate her philosophical work, as part
of the great stream of politically and socially engaged continental
philosophy. But there is the difference that Beauvoir the philosopher, unlike these important philosophical predecessors, also
displays the academically trained philosopher's precision and discipline with work which is heavily inflected with the rigour and close
reasoning of the phenomenology of her day.

If Beauvoir's philosophy has suffered, with certain admirable
(and mostly feminist) exceptions, from an absolute lack of attention
from mainstream academic philosophers, for the reasons noted
above, another factor inhibiting such interest is the unfamiliarity of
her methods. The fact that Beauvoir treated literature and philosophy as a unitary practice, and developed and tested many of her
most original philosophical ideas in her fiction, has tended to make
what she was doing either opaque or incomprehensible to philosophers trained in, and at times limited by, academic traditions which
do not admit the work of precisely those thinkers whom Beauvoir

claimed as some of her most important forerunners. To read Beauvoir adequately requires knowledge both of literary analysis and of philosophy. Further, because Beauvoir, when she is treated as a philosopher, usually is viewed as working solely in the context of her immediate, contemporary circle of male colleagues, her originality and her singular orientations tend to be concealed behind Sartre's adaptations of her ideas, which are, at times, incomplete or confused or simply different in their final formation. From this point of view Beauvoir becomes a footnote to an existentialist era whose major players were Sartre, Albert Camus and Maurice Merleau-Ponty. Almost exclusively, she has been read philosophically only with an eye to how her male colleagues influenced her. Yet to a remarkable extent the influence ran in the other direction. In addition, insufficient attention has been given to the fact that Beauvoir's philosophical interests diverged from those of her male colleagues as much as they converged with them. A different kind of historical account is needed to address Beauvoir's philosophy. To understand her work she, like all significant philosophers, must be seen not just in terms of her own era, but in terms of the long view which is the history of philosophy.

The need to address all these issues regarding Beauvoir the philosopher shapes the structure of this book, which also provides an introduction to Beauvoir's major texts. We begin where any serious account of any philosopher must, that is, with an overview of Beauvoir's education which identifies the philosophical traditions within which she was first trained, and the philosophers and philosophical lineages to which she responded most strongly during this formative period. The pressing need to clarify Beauvoir's views regarding the relationship between fiction and philosophy sets the direction for chapters 2 and 3, which survey the history of Beauvoir's publications and which give a detailed account of her literary-philosophical method. The next three chapters are devoted to giving accounts of the most important fundamental principles in Beauvoir's philosophy. We have organized this analysis around the topics of narrative, of embodiment and intersubjectivity, and of ethical theory. Chapters 7 and 8 are concerned with Beauvoir's applied ethics. Chapter 7 considers *The Second Sex*; chapter 8 examines *The Woman Destroyed*, *Les Belles Images* and *Old Age* as examples of Beauvoir's mature textual exploration of applied ethics. In order to help readers who may be considering Beauvoir as a philosopher for the first time, we have provided a glossary of some of the most common philosophical terms used in the book. It has been our hope and intention, throughout the composition of this introduction to the intellectual structures of Simone de Beauvoir's writing, to provide an accessible guide to the major features of the philosophy and texts of a woman who more than merits her place as a key contemporary thinker.

1

The Education of a Philosopher

> I've studied a lot of philosophy, I have a degree in philosophy, I've taught
> philosophy, I'm infused with philosophy, and when I put philosophy into
> my books it's because that's a way for me to view the world.
>
> Simone de Beauvoir

The major source of information about Simone de Beauvoir's early
training as a philosopher are the first two volumes of her four-
volume autobiography, *Memoirs of a Dutiful Daughter* and *The Prime
of Life*. Beauvoir's kaleidoscopic and extraordinarily multivalent accounts of her life tend to attract readings which construe them in a
number of familiar ways, none of them focused on her philosophical development. One favoured interpretation of her multifaceted
narrative of the evolution of her self is that of a determined bourgeois girl's escape from her gendered class destiny into an adult life
of adventure, independence, work and intellectual celebrity. Another, perhaps the most common, is a variant on a traditional
enough love story, in which one of the most intelligent women of
her generation becomes the lifelong companion of a man who was
one of his era's most influential thinkers. Another is a case history of
an exemplary life which reflects the development of twentieth-
century history dominated by war and by the struggle for political
and cultural freedom. Yet another has to do with Beauvoir as an
instructive case of the slow emergence of a powerful feminist consciousness. None of these readings is unsupported by Beauvoir's
volumes of memoirs: her autobiographies are compendious and
simultaneously tell many stories, each with its own structure, recur-
rent themes and muted subplots. In addition, each interlocking

strand of her narrative of herself as a historically located subject is fashioned with a novelist's skill, and the proprieties Beauvoir observes in her composition, as she changes dates and elides or covers or misrepresents her experience, often owe as much to the demands of her craft as to her more complex needs (or desires) to present her life coherently in certain selected lights.

For the themes which Beauvoir pursues through her autobiographies all designedly illuminate other themes, and therefore stand in a complex illustrative relation to each other. For example, the overtly trivial recurring theme of Beauvoir the walker/cyclist/skier/tourist, which takes up many pages of her memoirs, is enmeshed with the profound idea of the need for women's enactment of freedom in public and open spaces as well as with ideas of pleasure through the body, in addition to carrying views on nature, otherness and knowledge. The theme of food and the sense of taste, which Beauvoir foregrounds in the opening pages of the first volume of her memoirs, transmutes into a favoured trope: the opposition of repletion and hunger which Beauvoir uses in her fiction as well as her non-fiction as one of the main marks of history when power is expressed as the granting or withholding of food, and therefore control of life and death.

As we have noted, in the past Beauvoir's place as a philosopher in the existential and phenomenological tradition usually has been seen as strictly that of a disciple of Sartre. Even many of her most sympathetic readers have tended to analyse her writing against a Sartrean grid. And there is no doubt that Beauvoir, often but not always, encouraged this reading. However, as in so many areas of her narrative presentation of herself, she tells alternative stories. (And it is undoubtedly important to recall the importance of the concept of ambiguity for Beauvoir when considering the shifting yet linked accounts she gave of her life.) One of the strands of her autobiography is deeply concerned with the history of her maturation as a philosopher, and in this Beauvoir traces a trajectory of development which, while it coincides with Sartre's at some points, moves at others in significantly different directions. The story of her education and then assumption of authority as a philosopher forms one of the crucial recurring themes in Beauvoir's memoirs: it is a facet of the narrative to which she returns again and again. And it is an aspect of her representation of herself which must be comprehended if her later philosophical originality is to be understood.[1]

Beauvoir's birth, in January 1908, to Françoise (née Brasseur) and Georges Bertrand de Beauvoir not only placed her as the daughter of a French *haute bourgeoise* family on the slide, but also positioned her between the two philosophical traditions represented by her mother and father. From her mother came the insistence that Beauvoir's educational grounding and moral instruction, from infancy through to late adolescence, should be based on the diluted, but highly conventional version of the Roman Catholic theology which was deemed appropriate for the females of her class. From her father, who was trained as a lawyer, came the counter-influence of educated but also demotic forms of extreme religious scepticism, with attendant ethical values, and right-wing political principles, coupled with an aristocratic sense of aesthetic values. What both parents shared, in different ways, was the cult of the family, specifically the patriarchal family as organized by their class, place and time, which not only allowed for, but encouraged the kind of intellectual split displayed by Georges and Françoise de Beauvoir. The paradigmatic contrast between her parents' views was itself important for Beauvoir, and she underlines this in *Memoirs of a Dutiful Daughter* when she cites her own precarious position as a child caught between her parents' ideological differences as 'the main reason why I became an intellectual'.[2]

This polar opposition, which Beauvoir herself too schematically characterized as that between the intellectual, represented by her father, and the spiritual and moral, governed by her mother, was in fact more blurred than clear, with areas of overlap which Beauvoir was to carry, in transformed ways, into the philosophical commitments of her maturity. While this bifurcation in Beauvoir's familial intellectual background is often crudely analysed as an instance of a masculine/feminine divide, with Beauvoir choosing the traditional masculine set of scepticism and intellect over the traditionally feminine one of spirituality and body (construed variously as family, reproduction, sexual pleasure, etc.), the case is more tangled than this analysis suggests. The theologically based training Beauvoir received at her mother's instigation was, without doubt, linked in important ways to her later philosophical orientation, with its necessary attention to logic and disputation, while her father's scepticism had equally important effects on her ethics and on her political philosophy. By parentage, Beauvoir found herself the inheritor of two great philosophical traditions: late medieval theology and modern scepticism. Each played a significant part in the youthful formation of her mind.

Beauvoir's theological background is often forgotten, or completely elided with her religious affiliation and therefore dismissed as irrelevant after her adolescent loss of faith at the age of fourteen. While it is clearly the case that the major elements of Beauvoir's religious training that had to do primarily with belief in the divine and with the Church's role in the surveillance and policing of appropriately docile and obedient behaviour (especially for children and women) were rejected early by her, it was nevertheless the case that both certain habits of mind and a certain range of knowledge inculcated by her early religious education were important first steps in Beauvoir's philosophical education.

From October 1913, when Beauvoir was enrolled in the private girls' school, Le Cours Adéline Désir, until 1926, when she completed her teaching certificates in Latin and literature at the Institut Sainte-Marie and in mathematics at the Institut Catholique, Beauvoir was educated in a determinedly religious milieu. Le Cours Désir was run by pious Catholic laywomen who were affiliated to the Jesuits. In teaching their students – girls from privileged backgrounds who came from families who could not afford a better private education – there was a heavy emphasis on Catholic piety, doctrine and theology. While Beauvoir later deplored the weakness of this early schooling, especially in comparison with that of the privileged intellectual men of her generation who became her closest associates, she also recalled the rapture with which she had taken to it as a child.

After outgrowing the excesses of religious devotion triggered by the overwhelmingly pious atmosphere at her school, Beauvoir settled into a primary education dominated by the catechism, Thomas à Kempis's *Imitation of Christ*, and ideas generally tested against the teachings of Thomas Aquinas. This background was more important for Beauvoir than is usually noted, and the religious principles in which Beauvoir was schooled as a child contributed to the formation of her ethical philosophy in maturity. The transmutation of the religious ideas inculcated in her early life into other, non-religious forms is sometimes surprisingly direct. For example, Beauvoir notes that her first declared rejection of marriage was linked to her religious convictions. Like many Catholic girls she went through a phase when she thought she would become a nun, but it was this phase which first allowed her to imagine a woman's life without marriage and children, and one dedicated above all to work.[3] Equally, her first serious conviction of the 'absolute equality of human beings'[4] was intellectually grounded, she says, in the teachings of the Gospels. It may be a truism to note that both the ethics and political philosophy of the West since the Renaissance find their roots in the theological disputations of the medieval period. However, even when religious considerations are completely replaced by strictly secular terms (such as those adopted by Beauvoir as an adult), there is no doubt that the intense attention, particularly to ethical questions, demanded of Beauvoir by her Catholic schooling turned her rigorously logical mind early to issues which would shape the core of her philosophical work, if in transmuted forms.

Far from achieving its aim of turning its star pupil into the docile and pious upper-class Catholic French wife and mother for which its syllabus was designed, Le Cours Désir produced one of the century's paradigmatic, if ambiguous, rebels. While Beauvoir's extensive private reading was undoubtedly also important in her intellectual formation (in *Memoirs of a Dutiful Daughter* she particularly stressed the impact on her of George Eliot's *Mill on the Floss* and Louisa May Alcott's *Little Women*, in which she found the first secular models of the heroic and intelligent girls with which she identified), she gave her formal studies the enormous attention of the academically brilliant and ambitious child. Amid the dross of the curriculum of Le Cours Désir, training in certain skills and habits of mind which would be of enduring use to Beauvoir can be discerned. *The Imitation of Christ*, which was read in a version translated and abridged for children,[5] was one of the staple texts at the school, with the little girls being given more advanced versions of the book as they grew older. This famous, early fifteenth-century devotional text fostered intense scrutiny of the self and deep meditation on the personal relationship of the self to God. While the work is linked to the mystical traditions of the late Middle Ages (and is often seen as a compendium of its practices), it also inculcated habits of mind attuned to the examination of subjectivity which would be of great use for the phenomenological philosopher and autobiographer Beauvoir was to become.

Equally important was the effect of the teaching of Thomas Aquinas on her early schooling as a whole. As in all Catholic educational institutions since 1879, when Aquinas's philosophy was officially designated as the 'correct' one and the required base for any Catholic teaching of philosophy itself,[6] the general outlines of the teachings of the great thirteenth-century scholastic philosopher made their mark. Indeed, late in her education at Le Cours Désir, when she began studying philosophy for the first time as a discrete subject – working for four hours a week on psychology, logic, moral philosophy and metaphysics under the tutelage of the safe, but not particularly philosophically adept Abbé Trécourt – Beauvoir was taught (under chaperonage) from a textbook based on the teachings of Aquinas. It was under this regime that she first 'conceived a passion for philosophy'.[7]

What Beauvoir might have gained from Aquinas seems as startling a question as what she gained from à Kempis, but, again, certain areas of possible indebtedness can be distinguished. The first of these is the anti-idealism of Aquinas, which may have provided Beauvoir with an initial balancing influence to the Cartesianism which tends to dominate all forms of French philosophy after the seventeenth century. Aquinas's defence of Aristotle, his respect for natural reason, his formidable logical rigour and his exceptional clarity in argumentation were all aspects of his work which must have appealed to Beauvoir, whose philosophical writing is marked by precisely these qualities. Further, Aquinas's notable fairness in stating his opponents' cases could only have been welcome to Beauvoir as she began to get philosophy into focus as being, for her, the primary means by which one turned from certainty to doubt, from dogmatism to questioning in ways which could only be answered by each individual. She felt philosophy addressed *her* in a way no other discipline had done. Further, philosophy appealed to her intellectual ambition: it addressed the essentials; it seemed the way to 'the heart of truth', while all other disciplines seemed secondary to philosophy, which dealt in 'order', 'reason', 'necessity'.[8]

Beauvoir's Catholic schooling was meant, of course, to foster anything but the passion for reason over doctrine and the welcoming of doubt over faith which Beauvoir took from it. The illustrated magazine which devoted a feature to a successful woman philosopher, Mlle Léontine Zanta, one of a scant handful who had achieved such a position in the France of Beauvoir's youth, gave her the living model she needed to form the resolve to become a similar female 'pioneer' in the field (Beauvoir herself returned the oblique favour many times over in serving as just such a model for young women who have followed her into a formal education in philosophy).[9] Both Beauvoir's parents and her teachers met this ambition with extreme disapproval: studying philosophy at the Sorbonne, they felt, with the express aim of gaining qualifications to teach in a public lycée was tantamount to taking a place among the damned. Beauvoir initially bowed to family pressure and declared herself ready to study literature instead of philosophy as her specialist discipline in her higher education. But her determination to teach outside the Catholic school system was unshakable, and given that she would have no dowry and so would need preparation to earn her own living, and given the relative prestige attached to secondary school teaching as a profession in France, her parents gave way to her determination.

So she turned again to the formal study of philosophy as soon as she could. Supported by the enthusiasm of Mlle Mercier, one of the first female *agrégées* in philosophy and her teacher at the Catholic Institut Sainte-Marie at Neuilly, run by Mme Charles Daniélou, a crusader for the highest educational standards for women, Beauvoir began reading for her second *licence*, in philosophy, at the Sorbonne in 1926. She passed two of the four *certificats* needed for the *licence*, in history of philosophy and in general philosophy, in 1927. In 1928 she passed two more, in ethics and psychology, and began her teaching career by instructing classes in philosophy at the Institut Sainte-Marie. She chose not to complete the final *certificat* needed for her *licence* in classics (she passed *certificats* in literature (1926), Latin (1926) and Greek (1927) for this qualification, but decided not to complete it with the necessary *certificat* in philology; she also passed the *certificat* in mathematics (1926)). Instead she turned to simultaneous preparation for her secondary teaching diploma (for which she wrote her dissertation on Leibniz under the supervision of the distinguished neo-Kantian Léon Brunschvicg) and for the *agrégation* in philosophy, both of which she passed in 1929.[10]

Before examining the kind of formal training in philosophy Beauvoir received as an undergraduate, one more significant area of her education needs to be noted. The area in question is mathematics, in which Beauvoir was not only able, but, at least for a time, seriously interested.[11] Although this interest was to wane with her increasing immersion in literature and philosophy, there is no doubt that this early talent and relish for mathematics is yet another sign of her passion for logic and order which was always to characterize her thought.

From the autumn day in 1925 when she began her higher education by taking her seat in the 'ladies only' section of the Bibliothèque Sainte-Geneviève opposite a middle-aged woman wearing a gigantic plumage-covered hat and muttering to herself,[12] until her triumph in 1929 when she became the youngest student ever to pass the *agrégation* in philosophy, Beauvoir herself lived through the contradictions of turning herself into that eccentric thing for her time: a thoroughly educated woman. Beauvoir opens the section of her autobiography dealing with this crucial period in her life with a highly gendered (if coded) account of a woman's entry into the most sophisticated realms of higher education. She stresses female separation from knowledge, continuities as well as divergences from her earlier schooling, sexual knowledge, public announcement of her loss of faith, and the ever-present danger of the eccentricity, loneliness, depression, and yet exhilaration of the woman who transgresses the gender boundaries metaphorically signalled by the eccentric woman sharing Beauvoir's library table on her first day as a university student. The sharing of tables is used as a constant metaphor of commonality in Beauvoir's fiction and non-fiction, and it is no accident that Beauvoir represents her entry into student life through a table, covered with the same ersatz leather as those at Le Cours Désir, in a segregated section of the library, shared with a woman who is slightly mad. What Beauvoir brings to the table are two books: *The Human Comedy* and *The Memoirs of a Man of Quality*. Accompanied by Balzac's and the Abbé Prévost's fictional chronicles of lust, greed and human folly, as well as by the woman who embodied the dangers faced by even the most privileged of female pioneers, Beauvoir set out on her intellectual adventure.

As a student, Beauvoir, famously, succeeded with utmost brilliance. She worked her way through the required curricula of her various qualifications at extraordinary speed and with enormous success. As Toril Moi points out, when she completed her formal studies Beauvoir was not only the ninth woman to be awarded the *agrégation* in philosophy, but, as has been mentioned, the youngest person of either sex to pass.[13] (She was, for example, three years younger than Sartre when they both passed the *agrégation*.) Her contemporary, the philosopher Maurice de Gandillac, one of the group of student friends, all destined for fame, which included Beauvoir, Sartre, René Maheu, Maurice Merleau-Ponty, Raymond Aron and Paul Nizan, later discovered how the examining panel had hesitated before awarding the second place in the *agrégation* to Beauvoir in 1929, and the first to Sartre. (The vote of the three-man jury was one to two for the final top two placings: only thirteen of the seventy-six students who sat the exam passed).[14] While the examiners agreed on Sartre's intelligence and culture (as well as his tendency to inexactitude), they agreed that 'of the two, she was the real philosopher.'[15] In addition, it should be noted that Beauvoir passed this, and all of her exams, at her first attempt, unlike the three young men who were most important to her in her late adolescence and early adulthood. Jacques Champigneulle, the cousin around whom Beauvoir wove her first fantasy of heterosexual attraction, failed his law exams twice; René Maheu, her first lover, failed the same *agrégation* which Beauvoir triumphantly passed; Sartre passed the examination only after failing in 1928, and there is evidence to support the idea that he was awarded the first place in 1929 over Beauvoir, first, because he was a student at the elite and all-male École Normale Supérieure (while Beauvoir was simply a student at the Sorbonne), and secondly, as compensation for his previous year's failure.[16]

The brilliance, confidence and high success which characterized Beauvoir's student career were not to return to her life until she established herself as a writer in the mid-1940s. For roughly a decade between these two periods, Beauvoir remained immersed in philosophy, earning her living as a full-time philosophy teacher in lycées in Marseilles, Rouen and Paris. Then, as a novelist, she intertwined philosophy and fiction in radical ways. For a decade and a half, first as a student and then as a teacher, philosophy, in pure and academic forms, occupied the central place in Beauvoir's professional life. This period was then followed by the intense evolution of her own philosophical principles as the force driving her second career as a writer.

The formative philosophical influences which Beauvoir cites in her memoirs as being of most interest to her during her student years are important to note as the foundations of her own philosophical edifice. Equally, Beauvoir should be taken seriously when she says that at the beginning of her higher education, and like most students, she had very few ideas of her own: she saw her task as absorbing those of others, of training herself to think, of sharpening her critical powers.[17] With her capacity for quick absorption of intellectual material (a skill which would serve her well in her research for *The Second Sex*, *Old Age* and *America Day by Day*, as well as her later studies of Hegel and Husserl), Beauvoir's student years provided her with a compendium of philosophical knowledge which proved invaluable to her own developing thought.

Philosophy in Paris in the late 1920s was dominated by a number of influential teachers. One of these was the philosopher and popular essayist Alain (Émile-Auguste Chartier), who taught at two prestigious schools: the Collège Sévigné for girls, and the Lycée Henri IV, the boys' secondary school which Sartre and most of his friends attended. All of them had been significantly influenced by Alain. His ex-students (who also included Simone Weil) were a significant presence in the student cohort to which Beauvoir belonged (in her memoirs she records having long conversations about him with a

fellow student).[18] Alain's left-wing humanism, grounded in the tradition of Descartes, along with his lucidity, his interest in art, music,
literature and politics, and his encouraging of his students to re-
think inherited ideas and practices, made him an attractive source
of influence for the young philosophers of Beauvoir's generation.
Alain's insistence on a position of pacifism during World War II (a
position that Beauvoir, as a young woman, first adopted for herself
partially under the influence of his ideas) so damaged his prestige
that the group with which Beauvoir allied herself after the war felt
both betrayed and obliged to fill the gap his loss of credibility
opened.[19] The older generation of intellectuals in France, said
Beauvoir, had not understood their epoch: 'all – or almost all – had
failed in the attempt, and the one we had admired the most, Alain,
had fallen into disgrace. It was our turn to carry the torch.'[20]

Second only to Bergson in his pervasive intellectual influence in
France in the first half of the century, and whatever the status of his
reputation after the 1940s, Alain set an example which nevertheless
served the following generation well in a number of respects. This
charismatic teacher was deeply committed to writing for the general public, thereby continuing the continental tradition of philosophers' close and accessible engagement with the issues of the day.
Alain's many years of writing on a wide range of subjects for the
newspaper *Dépêche de Rouen* offered a contemporary example of a
philosopher writing for a wide, non-specialist audience, an example
which Beauvoir was to follow from the 1940s onwards both in the
pages of her and Sartre's journal *Les Temps Modernes*, and in those of
many other magazines and newspapers, ranging from Camus's
Combat to the American *Esquire* and *McCall's*.

Among the lecturers important to Beauvoir, several other figures
must be mentioned. Of these, the Christian socialist, Robert Garric,
a literature lecturer at the Institut Sainte-Marie, first held Beauvoir
completely 'spellbound'.[21] Her enthusiasm was so great that she
joined Garric's movement, Les Équipes Sociales, dedicated to uplifting the working classes, and taught a night class for a time in the
working-class district of Belleville in Paris. Garric was a crucial
transitional figure for Beauvoir: he provided her with her first convincing experience of left-wing activism, while grounding his theories in the Roman Catholicism in which she had been raised. There
was, in her mind, no conflict between Catholic ideas of devotion
and duty and the ideas of a life of classless service proposed by
Garric.[22] Beauvoir explicitly links her nascent left-wing politics with
elements of her Catholic background (that is, with the notion of the

equality of souls). Although Garric was soon left behind by
Beauvoir as an intellectual beacon, it is clear that, with his respect
for equality and his valuing of all individuals, he provided Beauvoir
with some of the arguments she needed to make the transition from
the philosophy of Thomas Aquinas to that of the philosophical
mainstream. But Garric did more for Beauvoir than help her build a
bridge between theology and philosophy: he also served for her as
an example of an individual who lived for an idea and who had
chosen his own projects with an eye to the larger commonality and
its needs. And although Beauvoir, at the time she was taught by
Garric, was a firm individualist, some of the first seeds of what
would become her theory of the Social Other can be traced back to
Garric.[23]

If Beauvoir was caught up in something of a classic student
infatuation with Garric, her attitude to her most important woman
lecturer, Mlle Mercier – like Garric, part of the staff at the Institut
Sainte-Marie – was also one of fascination and respect.[24] It was
Mlle Mercier who first recognized Beauvoir's brilliance as an undergraduate; it was she who gave Beauvoir her first teaching as-
signment (part of her own school-leaving class at the Insitut
Sainte-Marie in psychology) and thus her first opportunity to earn
money; it was with her support that Beauvoir launched herself on
her philosophy course.[25] If anyone, it was not Sartre but this woman,
who was one of France's female philosophical pioneers who first
took Beauvoir under her wing. She was a teacher of the utmost
importance for Beauvoir. As well as studying logic and the history
of philosophy under Mercier, Beauvoir used her as a serious confi-
dante with whom to discuss the great questions of life. Mercier took
Beauvoir's loss of faith as natural (though she continued to discuss
God with her still theologically anxious student); she helped her
consider the role of women; she lent Beauvoir books, introducing
her for example to the work of Malraux. Further, she did Beauvoir
the great favour of measuring her work by the highest standards:
she let Beauvoir know that she considered her dissertation on
'Descartes and the Ontological Fallacy' only 'mediocre'.[26] With the
rumours of flirtations with her female students which followed her,
and stories of a fiancé who had been killed in World War I, Mlle
Mercier was also a shadowy example of the bisexuality Beauvoir
herself was to choose.

For all this, Beauvoir notes that, important as Mlle Mercier was to
her, this dedicated professional woman's life seemed incomplete in
a way that Garric's did not (and Beauvoir treats her two lecturers at

the Institut Sainte-Marie as a pair, much as she treats her friend
Zaza and cousin Jacques in mirrored ways in her autobiography).
Beauvoir located the difference in what she saw as Mercier's neglect
of life in favour of thought. Beauvoir wanted both. But whatever her
reservations about her mentor, Beauvoir was grateful to Mlle
Mercier for her example, her attention, and her concern. The relationship between student and teacher was so important that, at least
for a time, Beauvoir's parents' suspicions about her progressive
ideological alienation from them manifested itself largely through
exasperated questions about her lecturer.[27]

When she began her philosophical studies with Mlle Mercier,
Beauvoir possessed only the insufficient Aquinine tools given her
by Abbé Trécourt at Le Cours Désir. Nevertheless she gamely blun-
dered through her initial encounters with the systems of Descartes
and Spinoza, which alternately struck her as openings out to the
infinite and as preposterous jabbering which bore no relation to the
world. While on holiday at her paternal relatives' country house in
Meyrignac in 1926, immediately before beginning her formal undergraduate courses in philosophy, she felt her increasing alienation
from her parents, but took comfort in philosophical reading. The
study of Kant, the philosopher who most impressed her as a student, encouraged Beauvoir's passion for 'critical idealism', which
reinforced her loss of faith, while in 'Bergson's theories about "the
social ego and the personal ego"' she 'recognized' her 'own experience'. For all the sense of recognition of truth that Kant and Bergson
brought her, Beauvoir was chilled by the impersonality of their
philosophical writing, and felt lonely, sad and bored without the
comfort which, she says, literature afforded her.[28]

This alienating sadness of the young woman who had broken
from her background in fundamental principles but had not yet
found others to replace them was assuaged and exacerbated in the
next academic year by her reading of Kant, whom she took enormous pleasure in comprehending, and whose work would ultimately prove foundational for her own. Kant soon became for her
the watchword for philosophy and reason itself. But with a typical
reaction for a twentieth-century philosophy student, Beauvoir felt
that Kant also represented a dead end. His attempted synthesis of
rationalism and empiricism, and his scepticism regarding rationalist claims to access to metaphysical knowledge supported the
highly tentative position which Beauvoir was only beginning to
work out for herself. However, Kant's *Critique of Pure Reason*, while
impressive in its argumentation, also led her to a sort of despair. She

worried that philosophy had no point, that there was no way out of scepticism or of a confession of ultimate metaphysical ignorance. And while – in debate with her presumably bemused conventional relatives and acquaintances – she cited Kant as the ultimate authority on the impossibility of finding absolute foundations on which to build, and on scepticism with regard to religious truths, her own views remained in an inchoate state.[29]

Refining or even forming such views was, in fact, a secondary activity for Beauvoir as a student. Her immediate task was one of absorbing the major ideas in the history of philosophy and of building a body of knowledge in the subject on which she could (and would) draw later. Again, like most students, she was attracted to various philosophers because their interests coincided with her own. With her personally grounded metaphysical fear of and fascination with death,[30] Schopenhauer's pessimism galvanized her: she copied out pages of his work, along with those of the blood-and-soil French nationalist Maurice Barrès and the poetry of Mme de Noailles.[31] She lists Bergson, Plato, Schopenhauer, Leibniz and Hamelin as the philosophers she read when she achieved an initial measure of philosophical competence, and mentions her first reading of Nietzsche as especially enthusiastic. Nietzsche's is not usually a name which is linked with Beauvoir's but they shared central common ground. The link lies in Nietzsche's addressing of the question which would also be Beauvoir's, that is, what happens to values in a world in which the divine is no longer present. His attack on seriousness would also prove suggestive for Beauvoir, though the ways in which she treats these Nietzschean themes diverge from his positions as much as develop them.[32]

During her first year as a serious student of philosophy, Beauvoir began to place herself, tentatively, in terms of the tradition she was engaged in absorbing. Aristotle, Jacques Maritain (the neo-Thomistic and anti-Bergsonian contemporary philosopher), as well as Aquinas himself, in addition to philosophies which emphasized materialism or empiricism were rejected. Adopting a position of critical idealism very much in vogue in Paris in her day and central to the continental tradition in philosophy in general, Beauvoir recovered her excitement about philosophy as she became more fluent in its practice. In her memoirs, she stresses the range of her interests (all of which would display themselves in her mature writing, though sometimes in unexpected ways): 'the values of science, life, matter, time, art'.[33] And while, she says, she was still devoid of ideas of her own, she was starting to piece together a philosophical inheritance for herself. She knew now what she wanted to reject, even if what she wished to affirm was not yet in focus.

What did, however, fill her with instant and pleasurable excitement was the sheer outrageousness of contemporaray avant-garde writing. She became a devotee of the experimental magazines flourishing in Paris in the 1920s, and particularly took to surrealism's excess and destructiveness, which systematically and thoroughly delighted her. The pleasure offered by surrealism resided, for her, in its pure negativity, its impulse for annihilation in 'art, morals, language' and in its delight in 'derangement of the senses' and 'suicidal despair'.[34] Beauvoir read Louis Aragon and André Breton, ex-Dadaists who became the leading surrealist theorists, with particular rapture. Aside from the banal comment that, as a fully fledged member of her intellectual generation, Beauvoir was likely to be attracted to the most visible and flamboyant avant-garde movements of her day (young intellectuals' passion for annoying the conventionally minded should never be underestimated), there were elements in surrealist practice which Beauvoir would take for her own. While the excesses of surrealism tended, at times, to veer between the pathological, the credulous and the incomprehensible – automatic writing, cut-up poetry, the passion for found objects as art, the dreamy (sometimes nightmarish) blur of its fiction, drama, film and poetry are all hallmarks of surrealist practice – its theoretical basis was clear, and, for Beauvoir, both attractive and useful as part of her characteristically twentieth-century intellectual formation. Surrealism, the successor to Dada, whose nihilism was a direct response to World War I, attempted to pull back from the cultural abyss of violence, aggression and meaninglessness which Dada both attacked and reflected. The surrealists' reading of Freud (especially Breton's) was important here, and their interest in dreams as the link between consciousness and the unconscious, as well as in the potentialities in empirical objects, signalled a move away from the total irrationalism of Dada to a position where dualism of mind and body would be dissolved away in a new *rapprochement* of being.

All this thrilled Beauvoir in ways that the art of disquiet which preceded surrealism, and which was epitomized for her and her friends by Alain-Fournier's novel *Le Grand Meaulnes*, never could. In addition, and in a manner complementary to the philosopher Alain's much more conventional writing, surrealism insisted on the breaking down of boundaries of all kinds. In terms of its aesthetic practice this meant the dismantling of the boundaries between disciplines and genres as well as those between consciousness and the unconscious. This example was to be a productive one for Beauvoir, as it has been for twentieth-century art and thought in general. But equally compelling was the surrealist code of living dangerously, a principle Beauvoir put into immediate practice with adventures in the rough bars and seedier streets of Paris in the late 1920s. They initiated a taste for physical independence and daring which would remain a constant in her life and help her to overcome the limitations which her position as a woman of her class had conventionally imposed. Finally, surrealism, with its revolutionary edge, fed into Beauvoir's evolving leftist politics and provided another counterweight to her family's reactionary views.[35]

Surrealism's sheer exuberance coupled with its abstruse and abstract theory also accorded well with Beauvoir's intensifying self-evaluation in 1927. Working hard and sailing through her exams in general philosophy (with a pass list that year that had the three philosophers Simone Weil, Simone de Beauvoir and Maurice Merleau-Ponty at the top, in that order) and in Greek, she was affirmed in the sense of superiority which formed one of the enduring aspects of her character – while still searching for the abstract and absolute principle which would secure answers to her metaphysical questions. Beauvoir was well aware of the contradiction between her continuing, and indeed growing, ambition to write in a detailed and personal way which would allow her to 'tell all' about her experience, and the continuously more abstract nature of her thought fostered by her philosophical development. She is wry, too, in retrospect, about her youthful embracing of extreme scepticism regarding all human projects while at the same time working overtime to secure the educational qualifications which would guarantee her a respectable post in the ordered and hierarchical world of French education.

But if Beauvoir worked hard for the post she eventually secured, she also cultivated higher ambitions. Her ambition tended to alternate with complete despair regarding her capabilities and regarding the purpose of the intellectual life in general. Tellingly, she says she 'wanted to construct a system of thought, a work of art',[36] making no distinction between the two. Vacillating between extraordinary confidence and equally low self-esteem, her new (and lifelong) friend Merleau-Ponty helped her to draw back from what she called 'the abyss, the void' of her 'metaphysical anxieties'.[37] While such intensity of self-doubt is not uncommon in the most gifted students, she found a great deal of reassurance in Merleau-Ponty, who helped her overcome her anxieties as she moved from her undergraduate work into the postgraduate studies necessary for her teaching diploma and the *agrégation*.

Meanwhile, though beset by doubts, Beauvoir's educational experience deepened. She went through a period of reading Plotinus and mystical psychology, and attended peculiar parades of the mad which her lecturer, Georges Dumas, organized to illustrate how the deranged enacted his theories. All this fitted in well with Beauvoir's rather morbid preoccupations, and she toyed with the possibility of a mysticism that would reach beyond the abstractions of philosophy, which she temporarily regarded as a frustrating 'desert'.[38] It was in this general context that Beauvoir first attended Jean Baruzi's lectures. Baruzi's *Saint Jean de la Croix et le problème de l'éxperience mystique*, published in 1924, opened the writing of the sixteenth-century Thomistic mystic and associate of Teresa of Avila, St John of the Cross, to serious modern analysis. Baruzi was also a Leibniz specialist, and produced two books on the subject. He himself cultivated a histrionic hypersensitivity and presented an intriguing spectacle as a lecturer. His lectures failed to attract the most elite corps of students, but they drew strikingly eccentric avant-garde writers committed to irrationalism and tempted by the mystic. It is fascinating that Beauvoir, whose mature thought is characterized by its attention to ordinary lived experience, should have passed through a phase of attraction for this kind of mystic eccentricity. Yet her irrationalist interests in 1927 and 1928 form a coherent pattern with her passion for surrealism and mysticism. Beauvoir's concurrent enthusiasm for psychopathology and for Nietzsche signal a continuing desire to go beyond or to sidestep reason without falling back into the confines of organized religion.

Baruzi's formal contribution to Beauvoir's education (aside from leading her to read John of the Cross) was his supervision of her dissertation on the personality, a huge project in which Beauvoir says she 'displayed the sum total of my knowledge and my ignorance'.[39] Baruzi praised Beauvoir's dissertation extravagantly: he hoped it might be the basis of significant further work. Beauvoir, understandably, was more than ever convinced of her superiority. And, again understandably, given the intellectual diet on which she was feeding (and, it must be added, the years of overwork to which she subjected herself), Beauvoir believed that she herself was becoming an initiate, cultivating states of mind which transcended the contingent, attaining 'the Unknown'.[40] This flirtation with mysticism stopped abruptly after Beauvoir spoke of it to Merleau-Ponty and Mlle Mercier, and noted their embarrassed reactions. For Beauvoir that was the end of the experiment not only with mysticism but irrationalism, though she would return to the subject in illuminating ways in *The Second Sex*.

If Baruzi ultimately was seen as an eccentric quibbler in Beauvoir's eyes, she seems to have retained at least a student's respect for Professor Léon Brunschvicg, who, according to Sartre, 'totally dominated French philosophical thought' in the late 1920s. He was certainly the dominant force in philosophy for the students both at the Sorbonne and the École Normale Supérieure, and as such, and as the academic in charge of the Diplôme d'Études Supérieures, had the guidance of a generation of academic French philosophers and philosophy teachers in his hands.[41] The year 1927 had seen the publication of one of Brunschvicg's most significant works, *Le Progrès de la conscience dans la philosophie occidentale*, which, like his writing in general, stresses the connection between science, mathematics and philosophy. Beauvoir consulted Brunschvicg about her desire simultaneously to complete her diploma and study for the *agrégation*. He encouraged her to do so, and took her on as his student, suggesting the thesis topic of 'The Concept in Leibniz' for her diploma, to which she agreed.[42]

The scientific and mathematical connection with philosophy needs to be stressed here, especially since Beauvoir's interest in science is little noted, although it dominates large sections of her later writing, most notably in *The Second Sex* and *Old Age*. The subject of her thesis, Leibniz, was philosophically important for his anticipation of symbolic logic (and, simultaneously with Newton, he invented the infinitesimal calculus), and for his significance as a thinker riding the line between thoroughgoing rationalism and the empiricism of the modern period, as well as for his rather strange metaphysics governed by his theory of the monad. As well as working with Brunschvicg on her thesis topic, Beauvoir attended Brunschvicg's lectures on the history of scientific thought and was drawn to his neo-Kantian idealism. It was through discussions of Hume and Kant, and of Brunschvicg's lectures, which they both attended, that Beauvoir struck up her acquaintance with her fellow student, René Maheu. This relationship, which became intimate, led directly to her meeting Maheu's friend, Sartre. He had also studied under Brunschvicg, attending his seminar on Nietzsche in 1927–8, before his first failure of the *agrégation*. It was in this seminar, said Sartre's friend Raymond Aron, that Sartre first began to develop his notions of contingency.[43] Whatever the case, Sartre in his youth construed Brunschvicg as the enemy against whom he needed to define and reposition himself while at the same time taking account of his ideas. Beauvoir, with no great personal investment in her lecturer, simply put Brunschvicg to use.

In many ways, Brunschvicg was an ideal supervisor for Beauvoir. In addition to his unparalleled position of influence, he was sympathetic to women's education, and, further, was married to Cécile Brunschvicg, one of France's leading feminists. Both Brunschvicgs were heavily involved in the French campaign for women's suffrage. Beauvoir later denied any knowledge of Brunschvicg's political commitment to the cause of women, saying indeed that she 'might have been kinder to him had I known this'.[44] As when discussing other matters with interviewers, Beauvoir's response may be unreliable.[45] In the early 1930s, when she was avoiding securing her first teaching post, a cousin recommended she consult Mme Le Verier, a close associate of the feminist Louise Weiss, for advice about a career in journalism. The two women edited *L'Europe Nouvelle*, a radical magazine espousing the causes of feminism, pacifism, freedom and equality. Weiss worked closely with Cécile Brunschvicg, who was also associated with the magazine. They were particularly good at organizing attention-getting publicity for women's suffrage and for pacifist ideas. For example, they chained themselves to railings for the cause, and organized a Christmas demonstration against war-toys by young feminists in 1930. Beauvoir was not enthusiastic about such activism at this point in her life, and since she had no discernible ideas to contribute to the magazine, she was advised to stick to teaching, but she did attend a *L'Europe Nouvelle* party, at which she felt both shabby and intimidated.[46] In all this Cécile Brunschvicg was such a public and visible figure that it is more than unlikely that Beauvoir never knew of the connection between her proposed journalistic colleague and her professor.

Whatever she knew or did not know about Brunschvicg's politics, and whatever her own political views were at that point, Beauvoir worked well under his supervision. In the late 1920s, she applied herself to her Leibniz dissertation with characteristic energy. She began reading for it in the summer of 1928 and, late in life, she recalled that the thesis she eventually produced was an 'ambitious undertaking, very long and detailed'.[47] Leibniz is a notoriously difficult thinker, but Beauvoir's interest in mathematics and science, along with her training in metaphysics, afforded her the tools to approach his thought seriously. She took pleasure in explaining his ideas to friends, and it is significant that it was while she was at work on Leibniz under the supervision of Brunschvicg that she studied Einstein's then quite new theory of relativity with absorbed interest.[48] Again, what needs to be stressed here is the attraction for Beauvoir of science, history of science and philosophy of science, in which she was particularly well grounded.

By the time she was writing about Leibniz, Beauvoir had left behind her fascination with Mlle Mercier; her enthusiasm for Garric had been lost long before. When she did her official teaching practice at the Lycée Janson de Sailly (a boys' lycée) along with Merleau-Ponty and Claude Lévi-Strauss, she was almost ready to stand on her own philosophical feet. Compliments of her fellow students mattered most to her when she gave a lecture on Plato.[49] As she worked on yet another dissertation, this time on Hume and Kant, under the direction of the Hume specialist Laporte, she felt she had taken what she could from her lecturers. Brunschvicg now seemed repetitious. Laporte invited her to his flat to discuss her work (Beauvoir records his comments on it: ' "Great qualities; but very antipathetic. Style obscure; a false profundity: when one thinks of what one has to say in philosophy!" '),[50] and tore apart Brunschvicg, the Ancients, Spinoza and Kant, leaving only Hume intact, while Beauvoir tried to defend her preference for Kant as well as the importance of philosophy itself. When she insisted on the need to reject total scepticism (her views on this were firm from an early age despite her previous flirtations with nihilism), Laporte let her go politely but with some distaste. She thought his ideas distressing and linked him with the world-weary excesses of Baruzi. It was time for her to graduate.

Interestingly, Beauvoir recalls her judgements of her fellow students as based almost exclusively on her view of their capabilities as philosophers. Most of them were still Christians, and this made for difficulties. When Beauvoir was strongly attracted to Maheu, she nevertheless took the trouble to analyse his (rather inadequate) philosophical skills in her diary; she had written a dissertation for Baruzi on the personality, of which she was proud, and she gave it to Maheu to read (he criticized it for its romanticism and Catholic residue, and Beauvoir welcomed this advice).[51]

It is in this context of almost complete submersion in the process of finding her own philosophical orientation that Beauvoir's first encounters with Sartre need to be placed. After finishing the draft of her thesis during the spring of her final year as a student, she extended her research on Kant and felt more certain than ever of her success in her studies. She saw the death of her paternal grandfather as another sign of the severance of her ties with her family and her childhood: Maheu fortuitously rechristened her with a nickname, just in time for her life as an independent adult. From now on Beauvoir would be 'Castor' (French for 'beaver') to her friends, an affectionate multilingual play on her surname which Maheu said caught both her sociability and her 'constructive bent'.[52]

Both comments were apt. Her purposefulness continued to bring rewards as she successfully sailed through oral examinations and through her final written exams, which opened, presciently, with a question on 'liberty and contingency', topics which would be hers for life. In the time before the oral examinations for the *agrégation* Beauvoir frightened her former mentor, Mlle Mercier, with her calm confidence. And it was with this sense of complete ease with her subject that Beauvoir was invited to help Sartre, Nizan and Maheu study Leibniz in preparation for their final hurdle as students. These cramming sessions seem to have consisted of a typical student combination of intense work and incipient, jokey hysteria. After a day, Leibniz was judged dull, so the study group concentrated on Sartre's accounts of Rousseau instead. They shared jokes about Descartes, and Nizan drew cartoons of Leibniz and Spinoza. The foursome soon split when Maheu found he had failed the written part of the exams while the others had passed, and Beauvoir spent her first significant period of time with Sartre going together to the Sorbonne to sit their oral examinations and listen to those of their fellow students.[53] From the first, theirs was a relationship grounded in, drenched in philosophy.

Beauvoir regarded Sartre, however, not so much as an individual as a member of a group of contemporary philosophy students as she reappraised her sense of herself on the completion of her studies. Finally moving among her rare intellectual equals, Beauvoir felt that her accelerated education left her less advanced and culturally grounded than Nizan, Aron, Sartre and Georges Politzer, a leftist *normalien* who was also to remain part of the Beauvoir/Sartre circle. (Beauvoir was also, simply, younger than these male friends.) But although Beauvoir also judged herself as lacking in further plans when compared with the men of her philosophical generation, she regarded her future optimistically, even if its shape was unclear.[54] In 1929, however, Beauvoir was exhausted by the prodigious, if exhilarating effort her education had demanded.

Two years would pass before Beauvoir took her first full-time teaching post in 1931, and she spent the intervening time not only firmly establishing the final aspects of her independence from her family (she rented her own room; claimed sexual and intellectual freedom in her relationship with Sartre; tried to write fiction; earned her living with part-time private tutoring), but also consolidating and refining the philosophical knowledge that she had absorbed so quickly at the Sorbonne. Though time simply to mature was something she badly needed (and wisely took), Beauvoir had no intention of falling into the pattern of many early high achievers: a prodigious beginning followed by subsidence into the ordinary. Beauvoir read voraciously and worked out the next stages of her apprenticeship as a writer. At this point Sartre was as much a help to Beauvoir as she to him. Together they comprised a two-member philosophical debating society, and the position they held to most firmly in their first years together was later described by Beauvoir as 'Kantian optimism'. Wedded to the idea of 'radical freedom' and convincing themselves that 'ought' does indeed imply 'can', they exhorted each other to write, to think, to succeed. Buoyed up by the Cartesian rationalism they found in Alain, they defined themselves as free from family and political impediments, creatures who would be judged by reason alone. Their joint rejection of Marx and Freud (of whose work they were almost totally ignorant) conferred the compensatory benefit of freeing each of them to think out questions of psychology and society in strikingly original ways.[55]

Beauvoir's position as a woman, however, meant that despite her sharing notions of voluntarism and freedom with the young Sartre, she was always differently located than he, and was aware of it. She notes that there was a 'marked difference' between their positions in that she had already broken the fundamental mould of what it meant to be a woman in her culture through her education and her concomitant capacity for self-sufficiency. Sartre's position was radically other. He merely fitted the set male pattern of education followed by career. Where she was a marvel, he was only a typical young adult male of his class and intellectual propensities, a role he detested and feared, while Beauvoir still rejoiced in overriding her excessively limiting bourgeois female destiny. This difference was to be crucial in the divergence of Beauvoir's philosophy from Sartre's. She was never in a position *not* to know the pressure society brought to bear on each of its members, as well as being convinced that such pressures could be resisted and overcome.

If both she and Sartre felt themselves as lovers, comrades and colleagues to be marked with 'the identical sign upon our brows', as
Beauvoir put it,[56] nevertheless the experience of freedom which they
both wished to embrace and to which they were determined to bear
witness was, from the first, radically different.

Their main divergence, despite their shared Kantian optimism,
was located in their differing views about the social, an area directly
linked to Beauvoir's female gender position and her self-conscious
rejection of many aspects of her class position. Her education did
not provide her with enough philosophical tools for her revisionary
project. Beauvoir was very much a product of the French academic
system of her time. She received, in effect, a nineteenth-century
education in philosophy, which she supplemented on her own. As
has been mentioned, she knew almost nothing of either Marx or
Freud. Brunschvicg treated Marx with disdain.[57] In this he was
typical: Freud's belated impact on French intellectual life is well
known (and one reason for its curious tangential position vis-à-vis
American, German and British Freudianism). Hegel was similarly
marginalized by Beauvoir's professors, and she completed her studies at the Sorbonne too early to be taught by Alexandre Kojève,
whose lectures on Hegel from 1933 to 1939 profoundly affected the
group of intellectuals who attended them. This group included
Georges Bataille, André Breton, Jacques Lacan and Beauvoir's
friends Aron, Merleau-Ponty and the novelist Raymond Queneau,
who discussed his Kojèvian version of Hegelianism with Beauvoir
immediately after the war.[58]

Again, the peculiarity of Beauvoir's position must be stressed.
She had been a twentieth-century student (and teacher) of psychology without Freud, and a student of social philosophy unexposed
to Marx and Hegel. Well grounded in the rationalist tradition and
in Kantian synthetic idealism, with a strong theological underlay
and a knowledge of Nietzschean irrationalism, Beauvoir followed
the completion of her formal studies with philosophical reading
which filled the gaps necessary for her to take her place within the
phenomenological line. And although, at this point, her admiration
for Kant was the most pronounced of her philosophical affiliations,
it needs to be noted that Beauvoir, even as a novice and unlike many
students, did not feel herself to be the advocate of any one position,
or the disciple of any one philosopher.[59] Despite claims to the contrary, this independence of mind was to continue throughout her
relationship with Sartre, with whom Beauvoir productively dis-
agreed on points of central philosophical importance.

With a great respect for Virginia Woolf's fiction and for Woolf's views on language, and with her continuing pronounced taste for abstraction in poetry and art, and surrealism in film, Beauvoir embarked on a period of completing her 'cultural education'.[60] She read Marx and Engels for the first time. They had little impact. Neither she nor Sartre could see the point of Heidegger's ideas when *What is Metaphysics?* was first translated into French.[61] Kierkegaard did not strike Beauvoir as important and Hegel remained almost unknown. Interestingly, the existential and phenomenological tradition as a whole was still closed to her, as it was to Sartre, who had first learned of it through correcting the proofs of a French translation of Karl Jaspers's *Psychopathology* with Nizan in 1927. Her friends Fernando Gerassi and Raymond Aron introduced Beauvoir to Husserl's ideas in the early 1930s, but she did not read the German phenomenologist until 1934. Her response was enthusiastic.[62] She also was intrigued by, if somewhat dubious about, Sartre's interest in Heidegger in the mid-1930s.

Throughout the 1930s Beauvoir developed the major outlines of her own philosophical principles. A great corroborating pleasure came much later for her, in 1940, when she read Hegel seriously. Though she found his notoriously opaque *Phenomenology of Mind* difficult, she also discovered significant areas of overlap with her own thought and writing, and used an epigraph from Hegel ('Each consciousness seeks the death of the other') for her first published novel, *She Came to Stay*.[63] As Hegel became clearer to her, so portions of Heidegger's work seemed valuable. Kierkegaard, too, came into better focus, and she read him with intense interest. And it was, finally, alongside Hegel and Kierkegaard that she located herself as a philosopher, saying that she felt in accord with their philosophies and could adhere to them 'without reservation'.[64] It was the first time, she noted, that she could make such a judgement of other philosophers' work. With a philosophical way into history which allowed her to address her original project of devising a philosophy which merged explicitly with her own experience, Beauvoir completed her philosophical education. She had finished her apprenticeship both as a philosopher and as a writer. What she needed now was to find her way into print.

2

Writing for her Life

Before examining the most substantial, influential and characteristic elements in Beauvoir's philosophy, surveying the shape of Beauvoir's publishing career is highly illuminating. Most importantly it must be noted that the majority of her key ideas are present in her earliest published fiction and essays. In addition, Beauvoir first broke into print as a writer who was improbably impressive both in terms of her originality of method and in the sure-handed deployment of it. This is not so surprising, however, after recalling that Beauvoir's apprenticeship lasted for a decade. As she worked throughout the 1930s to refine her philosophical position, so too she honed the fictional method through which it reached her readers. When her skill in handling her literary-philosophical method crossed the threshold of her own high standards, and she had written the first book which satisfied her, Beauvoir, the aspirant female writer, faced the common dilemma of almost all new novelists – how to get into print.

The precise form this classic problem took in Beauvoir's case is central when considering the directions she took her writing. Further, understanding the detailed circumstances surrounding the first formal rejections of Beauvoir's writing is linked to understanding of her refusal of classification as a philosopher. In the introduction we considered the highly idiosyncratic and double-edged definition Beauvoir employed when discussing herself as a philosopher. Her adamant and consistent appeal to a definition which at first glance excludes her from the ranks of philosophers, but which in another reading very much includes her, looks like a typical, self-protective instance of Beauvoirian mystification. It makes most sense when this ambiguous self-definition is connected to Beauvoir's first forays into the publishing marketplace as well as to her already noted statement that 'the female condition does not dispose one to this kind of obstinacy,' that is, to the problems encountered in enacting the 'concerted delirium' of philosophical systems-building.

For it is wrong ever to underestimate Beauvoir's shrewd understanding of her own place in the intellectual market. She was always a woman with her living to make, and her first attempts to break into publication carried lessons she never forgot. In *Memoirs of a Dutiful Daughter* and *The Prime of Life* she repeatedly underscores her early commitment to a writer's life – which, indeed, had been hers for over fifteen years by the time she began writing her memoirs in the mid-1950s. These volumes of autobiography appeared in 1958 and 1960. This was the highly successful Beauvoir of the 1950s, who had published *The Second Sex*, *The Ethics of Ambiguity*, three novels, a great deal of journalism and a series of philosophical essays as well as a moderately successful play in the 1940s. She had won the Prix Goncourt in 1954 for the novel *The Mandarins*, and had been at the centre of the international existentialist craze for over a decade. This Beauvoir was situated very differently from the thirty-year-old secondary-school teacher, desperate to break into print, she had been when her initial attempts to publish had abjectly failed in 1937 and 1938.

The writing in question was her first serious attempt at fiction (though she had written numerous abandoned apprentice pieces before this time), a collection of short stories later entitled *When Things of the Spirit Come First*, which did not appear until forty years later, in 1979. In the mid-1930s, during the two years she worked on the stories, Beauvoir said she 'was sustained by the hope that a publisher would accept them'.[1] Sartre had a book on psychology and a long philosophical essay published in 1936 and 1937; his philosophical novel *Nausea* had been accepted by Gallimard and was soon to appear to immediate acclaim. The couple were hungry for success for their writing, success which would lift them out of lives as schoolteachers which now bored Beauvoir, and which looked to her too enclosed. Those 'past nine years began to look rather threadbare', she explained. She wanted, she said, 'something to happen to me from the outside, as it were, something new and different'.

In *The Prime of Life* Beauvoir treats the rejection of her volume of stories by two publishers offhandedly. The book, she said, 'was defective', her 'didactic and satirical aims were laboured far too heavily'.[2] Beauvoir's autobiography blurs the disappointment which the rejection of *Things of the Spirit* caused. She had been so certain of publication that she told her family and friends of the imminent appearance of the book.[3] But Beauvoir's rather anodyne account concerning the stories' rejection in *The Prime of Life* takes on quite a different colour when supplemented by the comment she made to her biographer, Deirdre Bair:

> 'Sartre told me that [Brice Parain (the editor at Gallimard) said] it really had nothing to do with me or the quality of my writing, but that the house of Gallimard did not understand books written by women which were about the lives of women of my generation and background; that modern France and French publishing were not yet ready to deal with what women thought and felt and wanted; that to publish such a book would brand them a subversive publishing house and they couldn't risk offending all sorts of patrons and critics . . . and he told me not to say anything negative about Gallimard, because they were so powerful and he needed them and perhaps with my next novel I would, too. So I kept my mouth shut and swallowed the hurt and told everyone the book was poorly written and because it dealt with silly girls it would probably not have sold anyway.'[4]

Anyone who has received their first rejections after venturing their writing in the marketplace can imagine Beauvoir's reactions. And criticism made in such vulnerable circumstances tends to influence its recipient in ways that no later critique, made after some degree of success, can ever do. Sartre's mercenary, but realistic warnings presented an additional, difficult factor for Beauvoir. His pleas were also prescient. Beauvoir did indeed, in the end, need Gallimard, who published most of her books, including *The Second Sex*, Beauvoir's most subversive treatise on the condition of women. In the 1930s, however, despite a bout of depression, Beauvoir let Sartre take her stories to another publisher, Grasset. The book was turned down again: she then refused to submit it elsewhere, despite Sartre's continued encouragement. Just before the English translation of the collection appeared in 1982, looking back on her initial defeat, Beauvoir admitted just how hard these early failures hit her:

> 'Two rejections were enough insult, enough humiliation. I was so naive then! If I had only known how many great writers are hurt by repeated rejection of their work, then I might have had the courage to try again with another publisher, but at the time I only believed that my work was inferior, undeserving of public attention. I saw myself as a failure and for a long time viewed myself as unworthy.'[5]

If the market could not accept what one of the publishers' readers called her 'description of postwar young women influenced by the intellectual currents of the day' in stories laced through with 'intelligence' and 'the ability both to observe and to analyse' and which gave accounts of 'certain contemporary milieus' which were 'extremely accurate',[6] there clearly would be no place for a woman to claim a place among the handful of thinkers over the centuries who dedicated their lives to the 'concerted delirium' of constructing philosophical systems. The ambitious writerly neophyte who was Beauvoir at the end of the 1930s listened carefully to the voice of the market. She would tell her stories of intelligent women in the particular intellectual milieus she knew best, just as she would present her philosophical position in a series of publications which had their influence without calling much attention to their intellectual classification. But from now on she would give the market what it wanted as well. The door to recognized success in philosophy, even if it had been the one against which she most wanted to push, must have looked absolutely closed to this humiliated schoolteacher.

If this young woman, 'infused with philosophy', had good reason to believe that the market did not want what she had to give in terms of textual treatment of either women or philosophy, she nevertheless was outstandingly successful in finding means of writing her way into the market that allowed her simultaneously to exercise her philosophical drive and to report on the condition not only of women, but of the elderly, of the young, and of the racially and the colonially oppressed. And she slipped though the previously closed doors remarkably quickly. *She Came to Stay*, the novel she was writing when the rejections for *Things of the Spirit* were received, is structured by a profoundly original treatment of the problem of the Other, finding a path out of the impasse of Hegel's master/slave dialectic on to the open ground of situated existential reciprocity. At the same time it offered exactly the kind of commentary on the problems faced by twentieth-century intellectual women which had so disturbed Gallimard in Beauvoir's first manuscript. The philosophical content of *She Came to Stay* is handled so deftly that this particular aspect of the novel has still not been fully analysed. And Beauvoir's deftness was a precondition for publication. As with *Things of the Spirit*, Gallimard's preliminary opinion on the first chapters of the novel was to reject them. In the end, this philosophical novel, which Gallimard did publish in 1943, marked Beauvoir's entry into the market. The book was received as the kind of sex, scandal and confessional composition with which the market rarely has problems. Beauvoir noted all this with the real pleasure of any newly published writer, but with her rough lessons in what the market would bear very much in mind.

All this is not to say that Beauvoir's work is particularly philosophically muted; or that she worked so stealthily to disguise her literary-philosophical method that it had no effect on the world and remained, as it were, a guilty secret of her texts, only to be discovered nearly a decade after her death. Rather, Beauvoir skilfully deployed various strategies to subsume her philosophical output in the other categories (the essay, fiction, autobiography), moving fluidly across their boundaries in much of her writing. When this was impossible, she used the tactic of emphasizing her philosophical derivativeness (and no one can venture on to philosophical terrain without an intellectual genealogy of substance, such as Beauvoir possessed) rather than her originality.

Beauvoir's publishing history demonstrates her versatility. In each decade of her writing career, Beauvoir slides easily from one genre to another, with shared elements in her work linking all of her texts as parts of the same enterprise. The variousness of Beauvoir's writing is fascinating; the constant underlying its diversity is the coherence of her philosophical principles.

Beauvoir's suppleness as a writer was evident from the first. If it had been tricky for Beauvoir to shape her writing in such a way as to secure her first publishing contract for *She Came to Stay*, there was, seemingly, no stopping her once she began publishing. The 1940s saw not only the publication of her first novel, but of her second and third: *The Blood of Others* in 1945 and *All Men Are Mortal* in 1946. Both novels address questions of mortality and the ethics of intersubjectivity. While she produced her fiction, Beauvoir also wrote in other modes. The year 1943 saw the composition of her first published traditional philosophical essay on ethics, *Pyrrhus et Cinéas*. In 1944, Beauvoir began a lifelong commitment to journalism. She wrote articles describing the Liberation of Paris for Camus's paper *Combat* (these were published under Sartre's name), and helped set up the editorial board for *Les Temps Modernes*, the journal of the Beauvoir/Sartre circle, with which she was involved until her death in 1986. Beauvoir also composed her only play, *Les Bouches inutiles*, in 1944. Although the play had a moderate run in performance, it was not a great success, and drama thereafter remained one form Beauvoir did not attempt again.

The late 1940s saw Beauvoir writing, as it were, with many hands.

Simultaneously she worked on her most formal philosophical book, *The Ethics of Ambiguity*, which was published in 1947; on the social and philosophical essays for *Les Temps Modernes*, which were collected in *L'Existentialisme et la sagesse des nations* in 1948; on her account of her impressions of America, which appeared as *America Day by Day* in 1948; and on her feminist classic, *The Second Sex*, which appeared in 1948 and 1949. All these works are closely related, held together across the boundaries of fiction, formal philosophy, travel writing, drama and journalism by the philosophical ideas which inform them.

Transgression, clearly, was Beauvoir's most characteristic mode, whether in her personal life or in her writing (which, by the 1950s, left her financially secure). Beauvoir enjoyed breaking rules, and her persistent violating of genre boundaries in her writing accords well with her personal habits and predilections. In textual terms, the 1950s were as characteristic of this transgressive impulse as the 1940s. Beauvoir's Prix Goncourt-winning novel, *The Mandarins*, came out in 1954. One of the most impressive novels of ideas of the century, this work signalled a pause in Beauvoir's writing of fiction as she concentrated on other forms. A volume of essays, *Privilèges*, which must be seen as a companion to *L'Existentialisme et la sagesse des nations* of 1948, appeared in 1955, followed in 1957 by what is indisputably her worst book, *The Long March*, which gives an account of her official visit to China.

At the same time, Beauvoir undertook the composition of her autobiography. The first volume, *Memoirs of a Dutiful Daughter*, was published in 1958; the second, *The Prime of Life*, came out in 1960; the third, *Force of Circumstance*, in 1963; while the fourth and final volume, *All Said and Done*, did not appear until 1972. During the composition of the first three volumes, Beauvoir's attention was focused on Algeria's war of independence from France. The conflict sickened Beauvoir, who strongly backed the anticolonialism of the Algerians. Her support for the campaign against French atrocities in the war crystallized in her joint authorship, with Gisèle Halimi, of *Djamila Boupacha* (1962), a book which documents the case of a young Algerian woman who was tortured. The account is philosophically informed by Beauvoir's ethics of support for women, and for the politically oppressed in general.

In the 1960s Beauvoir's writing ranged over the genres of memoir, fiction and sociology. Her meditation on the loss of her mother in *A Very Easy Death* (1964) addressed questions of mortality and the fragility of the body, and of the intersubjective relations between her and her mother both as individuals and as historically located instances of the roles of women. In her fiction, *Les Belles Images* of 1966 and *The Woman Destroyed* of 1968 both represent aspects of Beauvoir's ethical dissection of the place of women in an increasingly consumerist culture. The decade ended with Beauvoir finishing *Old Age*, which, following *The Second Sex*, must be seen as her second great theoretical work of applied ethics. *Old Age* appeared in 1970. Beauvoir now entered her own old age and her writerly production slowed. She shifted her attention to other kinds of activities, such as the feminist activism which increasingly dominated her attention in the last decade of her life, and to participating in interviews and documentary films about her and her circle.

After *Old Age*, Beauvoir's major publications consisted of her account of Sartre's death (he died in 1980) and her transcriptions of long interviews with him which made up *Adieux: A Farewell to Sartre* (1981), and her edition of his letters published as *Lettres au Castor et à quelques autres* in 1983. Her last published fiction was *When Things of the Spirit Come First* (1979), the collection of short stories which she wrote in the 1930s and which had attracted such discouraging responses from then hostile publishers. There is a wonderful irony in the fact that these philosophically minded stories of women which were judged to be too intelligent, too advanced, indeed altogether too frightening for the French public of the 1930s for any quality publisher to risk publishing them, should surface as Beauvoir's last published text.[7]

Beauvoir died in 1986, greatly mourned not only by her intimate friends but by the women throughout the world to whom she had shown such formidable intellectual generosity throughout her public career, and particularly in her last decade. Without doubt, Beauvoir left an important intellectual legacy. She continues to attract attention as a novelist whose fiction is still in print, as the writer of some of the most famous memoirs of the century, and as a foundational feminist thinker around whose ideas subsequent feminist debates have revolved, whether in agreement or contestation. For all this, Beauvoir's reputation as a philosopher remains insecure, largely because it has still not been adequately addressed. However, her philosophical influence – through the impact made by her ideas on the work of her colleagues, Sartre and Maurice Merleau-Ponty – has been enormous. And, as the next chapters will show, and despite her achievements in other fields, her philosophy is one of Beauvoir's most important legacies.

3

Literature and Philosophy

This and the following three chapters address the key features of Beauvoir's philosophical practice. Beauvoir's metaphysics, her ontology and her ethics are all in place at the beginning of her publishing career and feature tellingly in both her fiction and her non-fiction throughout the 1940s. Our concern here is to provide a map of her ideas, drawing on the early novels *She Came to Stay* (1943), *The Blood of Others* (1945) and *All Men Are Mortal* (1946), as well as her essays, before moving on to her two books on ethics, *Pyrrhus et Cinéas* (1944) and *The Ethics of Ambiguity* (1948). These chapters are particularly concerned to investigate Beauvoir's philosophical method, which has to be understood to comprehend both her formal philosophical writing and her fiction. The second, related item concerns the use which Beauvoir consistently made of her own experience in the formulation of her metaphysics. More overtly than most philosophers, Beauvoir treated her personal metaphysical questions and experiences as the basis on which her thought was built and against which it must be tested. She began to accumulate these experiences in childhood, carrying them into adulthood, and then directly into her philosophical analysis of conscious and non-conscious being. In an influential and original way, Beauvoir is a philosopher of experience. All of Beauvoir's thought rests on a first principle which rejects philosophical universalism, and this chapter explores precisely what this means.

'A New Dimension of Investigation'

In 1946, when Beauvoir published her essay 'Littérature et métaphysique' in *Les Temps Modernes*, she had been using fiction as a method for presenting and, more crucially, for inventing philosophy for a decade. Although her earliest serious works, *When Things of the Spirit Come First* and the first two (later discarded) chapters of *She Came to Stay*, would have to wait until the 1970s to find their way into print, by the end of 1946 *She Came to Stay*, *The Blood of Others* and *All Men Are Mortal* had all been successfully published. Her play, *Les Bouches inutiles*, had been performed, and, in addition, Beauvoir had a good deal of experience as a journalist behind her. When she wrote 'Littérature et métaphysique' the efficacy of her technique of treating fiction as a philosophical form could not have been even remotely in doubt in her own mind. Beauvoir had already seen many of the concepts and theories developed in her fiction taken up and utilized by other philosophers. In 1946, in 'Littérature et métaphysique', Beauvoir explains how such success is possible; shows why the metaphysical novel is a valuable addition to philosophy's toolbox; disarms the traditionalist opposition; and, perhaps most of all, reminds readers of the primary subject matter and mission of her early fiction.

Beauvoir was preceded in these purposes by her friend and associate Merleau-Ponty, whose essay 'Metaphysics and the Novel', published in 1945, explained the importance of *She Came to Stay* as a philosophical text. Taken together, Merleau-Ponty's essay on his friend's method and Beauvoir's gracious corrective and expansive response to it provide a lucid guide both to her literary-philosophical method and to the reception of her work by those who knew her well and understood the import of her writing.[1]

Merleau-Ponty begins his essay by noting that since the end of the nineteenth century the boundaries between literature and philosophy had dissolved: 'hybrid modes of expression' had developed in response to the opening up of 'a new dimension of investigation', one of which would grow into French existentialism.[2] This new dimension grew from the apprehension that all intellectual works are 'concerned with establishing a certain attitude toward the world, of which literature and philosophy . . . are just different expressions'.[3] Beauvoir not only accepts Merleau-Ponty's remarks on this matter (and she could scarcely do otherwise, given that her method embodies just these principles) but largely uses her own essay to expand on Merleau-Ponty's thesis.

In 'Littérature et métaphysique' Beauvoir treats 'metaphysics' and 'philosophy' almost synonymously. She begins her exposition by dividing philosophy and philosophers roughly into two camps. The first, which includes Aristotle, Leibniz, Spinoza and Kant, holds that philosophical truth exists only in a 'timeless and objective' sense, and thereby regards 'as negligible the subjectivity and historicity of experience'.[4] In denying the philosophical relevance of the individual and the concrete, this school implicitly presumes that philosophers are capable of taking a universal rather than merely an individual point of view towards the metaphysical reality they seek to explain. Beauvoir, however, as Eleanore Holveck notes, 'argues that philosophers pretend to explain all things universally, but in fact these "universals" are based in the consciousness of some individual thinker who claims knowledge of the universal, a claim that must be justified.'[5] Beauvoir regards this universalist presumption as largely delusory, egomaniacal and only even apparently tenable when claimed from a position of masculine privilege.[6] Earlier, in *Pyrrhus et Cinéas*, she had argued that personal arrogance was the sole foundation of Hegel's declaration that individuality is only a moment of a universal future: 'Man cannot escape from his own presence or from the singular world that his presence reveals around him; even his effort to uproot himself from the earth makes him dig a hole for himself. Spinozism defines Spinoza, and Hegelianism Hegel.'[7]

Against these universalist delusions, Beauvoir juxtaposes the orientation of thinkers who, like herself, insist on the philosophical relevance of individual human experience. She believes (and this is where her anti-universalist principles accord with and feed into the thought of the philosophical postmodernists) that a fundamental characteristic of human reality is that no one, including all of history's great male philosophers, can take a universal or God-like point of view, whatever they may claim to the contrary. This point is essential for Beauvoir and she stated her position on it clearly in *Pyrrhus et Cinéas* in 1944. Beauvoir's attitude towards the universalist standpoint of most traditional philosophy is one of intellectual and moral contempt, a contempt she announced vehemently:

> The universal mind is without voice, and every man who claims to speak in its name only gives to it his own voice. How can he claim the point of view of the universal, since he *is* not the universal? One cannot know a point of view other than one's own.[8]

Beauvoir's own position with regard to the universalist philosophical perspective was, in fact, settled in the 1930s, a fact that her fiction of that decade demonstrates and which Merleau-Ponty shows he understands well in his essay on her work. For Beauvoir, truth, including metaphysical truth, is always relative to a knowing subject. She believed, as she noted succinctly in her preface to *America Day by Day* in 1948: 'concrete experience envelops at once the subject and object.'[9] Margaret Simons, one of the most sensitive readers of Beauvoir's philosophy, remarks that Beauvoir always took the view that any 'attempt to describe reality without reference to the experiencing subject' was 'as distorting as trying to describe the subject without reference to the context of circumstances'.[10] But if, for Beauvoir, no member of the human race is granted a detached Archimedean point of view of their fellow (and inferior) human beings, if pure thought and the contemplation of equally pure existence are impossible, and if, in addition, the pretence of being able to do so is abandoned, then strong methodological implications follow for philosophy.

Merleau-Ponty understood (and accepted) Beauvoir's anti-universalist arguments. Further, he understood the techniques she employed in her fiction as ways of practising the new philosophical methodology demanded by acceptance of her argument. Merleau-Ponty's analysis of the impulse behind Beauvoir's success at using fiction as a philosophical medium matches her own. He distinguishes between two kinds of metaphysics. 'Classical metaphysics', he writes, 'could pass for a speciality with which literature had nothing to do because metaphysics operated on the basis of uncontested rationalism, convinced it could make the world and human life understood by an arrangement of concepts.'[11] Furthermore, even philosophers who begin on the experiential level end by explaining the world on the basis of abstractions. 'Everything changes', however,

> when a phenomenological or existential philosophy assigns itself the task, not of explaining the world or of discovering its 'conditions of possibility', but rather of formulating an experience of the world, a contact with the world which precedes all thought *about* the world. After this, whatever is metaphysical in man cannot be credited to something outside his empirical being – to God, to Consciousness. Man is metaphysical in his very being, in his loves, in his hates, in his individual and collective history.[12]

'From now on,' concludes Merleau-Ponty, 'the tasks of literature and philosophy can no longer be separated.'

Beauvoir's 'Littérature et métaphysique' outlines a philosophical method that inverts the universalist presumption. If the world can be viewed only from a particular point of view, then the philosophical enterprise must begin with particular and concrete descriptions of subjects' relations with the world and with other consciousnesses. Beauvoir's chosen philosophical domain is what she calls 'the metaphysical dimension' of human reality, that is, 'one's presence in the world, for example, one's abandonment in the world, one's freedom, the opacity of things, the resistance of foreign consciousnesses'. 'To make' philosophy, she says, is 'to be' philosophical in the sense of sensitizing oneself to these individual metaphysical experiences and then describing them.[13] If these particular statements are recognized by others as true for them, they can then be used to construct general statements about 'the essence at the heart of existence'.[14]

Beauvoir 'was able', argues Eleanore Holveck, 'to ground her abstract philosophical positions in the real world of lived experience, a lived experience she created imaginatively in ordinary language that was more concrete, more rich than any abstract philosophical language.'[15] With Beauvoir's rejection of apriorism and of a universal point of view, a good philosophical argument becomes, for Beauvoir, a description of a particular individual's metaphysical relations with the world which the reader recognizes as characterizing his or her own experience. Beauvoir identifies fiction as a medium especially well suited to this end and she takes care to explain what she means by this in 'Littérature et métaphysique'. Although she notes that philosophers may use the essay to give 'to the reader an intellectual reconstruction of their experience, it is this experience itself, such as it presents itself before any elucidation, that the novelist claims to reproduce on an imaginary plane.'[16] Beauvoir continues:

> In the real world the sense of an object is not a concept knowable by pure understanding: it is the object in that it unveils itself to us in the global relation that we maintain with it and in that it is action, emotion, sentiment; one asks of the novelists to evoke this presence of flesh and bone whose complexity, singular and infinitely rich, overflows all subjective interpretation.[17]

In her essay, Beauvoir is particularly anxious to guard against what she sees as philosophy's traditional authoritarianism and mystification, whereby 'the theoretician'[18] presents certain concepts as articles of faith to his supine readers. She identifies a constituency of readers who are out of sympathy with this tradition of the philosophical messiah, who 'want to guard the freedom of their thought', who 'find repugnant this intellectual docility' demanded of them.[19] This kind of reader, says Beauvoir, is only willing to accept others' propositions after

a movement of his whole being before forming judgements that he pulls
from himself without someone having had the presumption of dictating
them to him. It is this which is the value of a good novel. It is capable
of inducing imaginary experiences as complete, as disquieting as lived
experiences. The reader interrogates, doubts, he takes sides and this hesitant elaboration of his thought is for him an enrichment that no doctrinal
teaching could replace.[20]

Novels which appeal to a reader's liberty in this way are also
intended to serve as a valuable form of philosophical research. But
the writing of fiction, Beauvoir argues, requires a form of reciprocity
from the philosopher-novelist. It

> demands that the novelist himself participates in this research to which he
> admits his reader: if he foresees in advance the conclusions which the
> reader must reach, if he indiscreetly places pressure on him to give up his
> adherence to pre-established theses, if he grants him only one degree of
> freedom, then the novelistic work is only an incongruous mystification; the
> novel takes on value and dignity only if it constitutes for the author as for
> the reader a living discovery.[21]

It is notable that Beauvoir calls up the prestigious word 'research'
to focus her ideas in this matter, which is crucially one of ethics. The
ethical principle which Beauvoir demands of philosopher-novelists,
namely that the results of their research should not be predetermined, is indeed cognate with the professional codes of the laboratory scientist. By linking the codes of experimental science and
those of the philosopher-novelist, Beauvoir underscores both the
precision of her demand and its intellectual and social value.

Beauvoir considers her analogy between philosophical fiction
and experimental science so apt that she pursues it further. The
validity of a scientific law is based on the series of experiments
which have established it and which it summarizes. Beauvoir insists
that, in a similar manner, the collection of singular experiences
examined by the philosopher-novelist and/or essayist is the only
legitimate foundation for metaphysical truth. Moreover, just as the
ethically rigorous sciences continue to confront established laws
with new and more sophisticated empirical data, so too the philosopher must continue to appraise her general philosophical propositions against the results of fresh applications to concrete existence.
The novel, because of its grounding in the concrete, facilitates this
movement beyond the traditional dogmatic (and unacceptable)
abstraction of philosophy and philosophers. But the literary-
philosophical method, warns Beauvoir, only works if the author
remains willing to reflect on the problems and unforeseen develop-

ments which the philosophical novel, like the scientific experiment, may throw up.

If 'Littérature et métaphysique' must be seen as a clear statement of Beauvoir's literary-philosophical method, it must also be treated as Beauvoir's formal declaration that *she* was the original source of all the philosophical content of her novels. As we have noted above, Beauvoir views a novel as merely a 'mystification' if it employs 'pre-established theses', if it does not constitute for the author 'a living discovery'. Her essay keeps returning to this theme. A novel's philosophical content, she insists, must not predate the novel itself, but instead must be the result of the philosophical research of which the novel consists. This is the basic requirement for what she calls an 'honestly written' metaphysical novel.[22] Given that the title of Beauvoir's essay alludes directly to Merleau-Ponty's 'Metaphysics and the Novel', which hails her *She Came to Stay* as a philosophical text, it is, by implication, to her own novel that her essay points as an example of one honestly written.

The methodology which Beauvoir outlined in 'Littérature et métaphysique' was already, as Merleau-Ponty intimated, part of a larger modern tradition. That tradition is, of course, existentialism, and it is in this philosophical lineage that Beauvoir's philosophy must be placed. As Mary Warnock explains in her classic introduction to that lineage: 'The methodology of Existentialism . . . consists in a perfectly deliberate and intentional use of the *concrete* as a way of approaching the abstract, the *particular* as a way of approaching the general.'[23] Warnock continues:

> The existential philosopher, then, must above all *describe* the world in such a way that its meanings emerge. He cannot, obviously, describe the world as a whole. He must take examples in as much detail as he can, and from these examples his intuition of significance will become clear. It is plain how close such a method is to the methods of the novelist, the short-story writer . . .[24]

Indeed, Beauvoir was not the first existentialist philosopher to use dramatic narrative devices to describe and analyse metaphysical experience. Kierkegaard's *Fear and Trembling* (1843), with its examination of the problem of self and conscience through the story of Abraham and Isaac, stands as a famous case in point. (Nor does existentialism and phenomenology include more than a small part of the range of philosophy's narrative tradition. At one extreme of philosophical importance stand Plato's dialogues, and at the other – what is probably the largest-selling philosophy book of all time –

Jostein Gaarder's recent *Sophie's World*. In between are productions like the fables of the Enlightenment philosophers, Nietzsche's fantastic parables and aphorisms, and Hume's dialogues.) But existentialism employs these philosophically unusual narrative forms (as well as more traditional ones) not only because of its commitment to describing the world, but also because it attaches importance to the individual in the world. And this is especially so for Beauvoir's existentialism, with its insistence on the untenability of universal descriptions and its rejection of the possibility of thought about abstract existence. In lieu of the impersonality traditional to speculative metaphysics, Beauvoir calls for the establishment of a new philosophical form which moves easily between the essay and fiction, a symbiotic relationship which she sees as similar to that in science between theory and experiment.[25]

Under the aegis of this literary-philosophical method, on which Beauvoir elaborated further in a pair of essays in the 1960s ('Que peut la littérature?' (1965) and 'Mon expérience d'écrivain' (1966)), general philosophical statements must be made on the basis of particular and concrete statements which are openly grounded in individual points of view. In response to these statements, readers, acting as peers, confirm or reject the philosopher's propositions on the basis of their own experience. In this manner, analogous to the procedures of science, Beauvoir's philosophical research programme aims to identify an invariant structure of conscious being, or, in other words, appeal to and find confirmation for what she calls 'the essence at the heart of human existence'.[26] Beauvoir's operative presumption here is that humankind shares a core metaphysical reality as much as it shares a biological one.

All Men Are Mortal

Beauvoir deployed her literary-philosophical method in all her fiction, but nowhere so saliently as in *All Men Are Mortal*. Published the same year (1946) as 'Littérature et métaphysique', this novel explores a number of philosophical questions, but most especially the issue of individual versus universal points of view and the part mortality plays in the human being's metaphysical reality. *All Men Are Mortal*, which, like Virginia Woolf's *Orlando*, is a fiction concerned with the unnatural persistence of an individual who lives through many centuries, is not only the most transparently unconventional of Beauvoir's fiction, it is also, quite literally, a lengthy exercise in experimental metaphysics. Its debt to the procedures of empirical science is self-evident: by featuring a character whose biology differs in one fundamental respect from that of 'men', Beauvoir isolates the part mortality plays in defining humankind's metaphysical outlook.

All Men Are Mortal is divided into seven sections. The first and the last focus on an ambitious young actress, Régina, who suffers constant regret at the thought of her finitude, and who seeks compensation through fame. During an engagement at a provincial theatre, she observes a man in her hotel's garden, sitting from dawn to late at night 'as immobile as a Hindu ascetic'.[27] Attracted by his self-sufficiency and by what she wrongly interprets as his immunity to boredom, Régina asks him to teach her his secret. His name is Raymond Fosca, and he claims that he is immortal due to a potion he drank in young middle-age in the early fourteenth century. Not unreasonably, Régina is incredulous. So Fosca provides a demonstration: he slashes his throat. A bloody spectacle results, but one from which Fosca emerges none the worse within minutes. Régina then drags her discovery back to Paris, where he tells her the story of his six centuries of existence.

Beauvoir carefully fills the five books of Fosca's autobiography, which are bracketed by Régina's prologue and epilogue, with rich historical detail. Book 1 covers two centuries of Fosca's life as a powerful count in medieval Italy; Book 2, three decades as personal adviser to Charles V of the sixteenth-century Habsburg empire; Book 3, a few years as a vagabond in the interior of North America in the 1650s; Book 4, several decades as a wealthy scientist in eighteenth-century Paris; and Book 5, as a witness to the events leading up to and including the 1848 Revolution in Paris. This fantasy of a 'human life' stretching over six centuries, unencumbered by fear of death, is charming and intriguing. But Fosca's immortality, far from being merely a novelist's fancy, serves Beauvoir as an analytical device for exploring three aspects of the human condition: the illusory nature of the universal point of view; how the pursuit of this illusion destroys individual freedom; and how mortality is essential to human meaning and value.

Fosca successfully plots to become ruler of his native Carmona, a fourteenth-century city-state. He aspires to lead Carmona to what he foresees as its prosperous and glorious destiny, but the same Machiavellian realities by which he came to power soon overtake his hopes. He feels himself surrounded by would-be assassins, a danger which reminds him not only of his mortality but also of the shortness of his natural lifespan relative to the unboundedness of his autocratic dreams. His political goals – the security and expansion of his principality – are realizable only in the longer term. So when an elderly beggar offers him a 'cure', an 'elixir of immortality' whose powers are first demonstrated on a mouse, Fosca partakes.

Fosca's immortality begins with optimism and high purpose. He wants to improve the condition of his people, but his point of view on the world, even without immortality, is wider and more elevated than that of the individuals he rules. It is the ruler's inclination to the illusion of universality that recommends Fosca to Beauvoir as the subject for her experiment. Even before gaining immortality, Fosca thinks in terms of 'purposes' which, although rationalized in the name of serving his individual subjects, in practice show them scant regard. Immortality allows him to project his purposes through time without limit. But in doing so his sense of the value and significance of mortal lives progressively weakens. Fosca's outlook from eternity is far removed from the primary concerns of individual mortals' lives, so far so that he no longer finds in his subjects a rationale for his goals. Nihilism is not far away. 'What purpose did Carmona serve?' Fosca asks himself. 'What purpose did the sky serve, and the flowers of the meadows?'[28] Exiled from the perspectives of mortal beings, Fosca is overtaken by nihilism even when he thinks of his beloved son. Nor is it only mortal life that loses its value for him. He also increasingly experiences disenchantment and weariness with his own existence. With all purpose gone, life for Fosca tends towards a series of empty gestures. Boredom overtakes him not only when awake but also in his dreams. Courage, by definition, is beyond him. So too is generosity, since, having unlimited life, he can never really sacrifice anything. He finds it difficult to project himself towards the future, which, because it is infinite, seems to repeat itself. In eternity, he discovers, time is directionless and turns in on itself.

Fosca responds to his disillusionment by pursuing still greater degrees of universality. Whereas he previously believed he held Carmona's destiny in his hands, he now – early in the sixteenth century – sees Carmona's destiny as dependent on world events. Nothing, he concludes, can really be accomplished unless a single man rules the whole world. For this reason, Fosca leaves Carmona to offer his services to the Holy Roman Empire, and eventually to its emperor, Charles V.

Seen through Fosca's 'new eyes', Carmona appears as 'only a minuscule particle in that vast conglomeration, the Holy Roman

Empire'. Entering zealously into the universalist spirit of his new employer, Fosca pursues the notion of the universal in all its dimensions. He dreams of *universal reason*, of the day 'when man would completely unravel the secrets of nature and by so doing dominate her . . . Nothing will be left to the capriciousness of men or the hazards of fate. Reason will govern the earth.' He dreams of *universal political power*, of the day when he or someone will 'take this world that's split up into little bits, and make it a single, unified world again, like the day it left His hands'. He dreams of *universal will*, of sailing to the new world where he will 'mold those virgin lands exactly the way I want'. And he dreams of *universal truth and happiness*, of a world where 'Everyone was rich, strong and handsome; everyone was happy. "I'll create a paradise on earth."' Fosca's intoxication with the idea of the universal becomes so complete that, as he later admits, its 'voice deafened me to all other sounds'.[29]

When confronted first with the individualist teaching of Martin Luther and then with the man himself, Fosca is dismayed. 'I wanted', recalls Fosca, 'to gather the universe in my hand and *he* declared that he was a universe in himself.'[30] From Fosca's universalist heights the significance of individual human life recedes to vanishing point. His metaphysical transformation – notwithstanding his continuing high purpose of improving the human lot – brings him to think that a human life is as insignificant as a gnat's. Fosca shares Hegel's belief that individuality is only a moment of a universal future. In his eyes, human lives compare unfavourably to roads, cities and canals, which persist through many generations. He even thinks ill of Charles V because he does not appreciate how brief and unimportant a human life is. Nor are these merely abstract sentiments for Fosca. For example, travelling through Germany after the emperor's troops suppressed a peasants' revolt, Fosca considers the devastation from his universalist viewpoint. He looks indifferently at the aftermath of fires and massacres. '*After all, what does it matter?*' he thinks. The dead were dead and the living were living. To Fosca 'the world was just as full as ever, the same sun was shining in the same sky. There was no one to feel sorry for, nothing to regret.'[31]

Nevertheless, Fosca's enchantment with immortality and his hope of creating a human paradise are already waning when, as Charles's envoy, he sails for the New World in 1550, intent on surveying the 'accomplishments' of the Spanish conquistadores. Fosca's voyage becomes one of metaphysical discovery. It leads him through a series of experiences which decisively disabuse him of his universalist illusions. Crossing the ocean, he thinks:

> I had dreamed of holding the world in my hands – the world, a smooth, round sphere. But now, as we sailed day after day over the blue waters, I often asked myself, 'What, after all, *is* the world? *Where* is it?'[32]

Whereas on Fosca's map the Bahamas were 'nothing but a semicircle of insignificant spots', sailing slowly past them he is enchanted by their birds and flowers. Being confined to a ship for weeks on end restores Fosca's sensitivity to the concrete and singular realities which his embodied presence reveals around him. Space for him loses its geographer's universality and becomes instead essentially relative and personalized. His body, engaged in the project of sailing, acts as a shifting reference point or pole around which physical space is organized. The centre of Fosca's perspectives, the primary place from which distance is measured and the position from which subspaces and their contents are now organized is his psychophysical body. It is this configuration of oriented spaces which Beauvoir, beginning with her earliest fiction, presents as the subject's broad sensory field, rather than the homogeneous, idealized, universal space assumed by rationalism and empiricism.

Fosca's voyage has transported him from the universalist to the existential level. He has regained contact with the concrete and the particular. His changed metaphysical relations with the world make it impossible for him to dismiss as insignificant the desolation which the Europeans, in the name of his and Charles's totalitarian dream, have wrought on Inca civilization. Sickened by the sight of the human suffering in the silver mines, Fosca concludes that the pursuit of the universal has destroyed a world.

Returning to Europe, Fosca tells Charles that he, Fosca, was wrong. ' "I wanted to make you ruler of the Universe. But there isn't any Universe." ' The 'Universe', explains Fosca, is only a word which serves the purpose of rationalizing the misdeeds of the egomaniacal. 'The Universe is somewhere – always somewhere else, of course, but somewhere. And it's *nowhere*. There are only men, men forever divided.' Fosca also now understands that human beings do not want to be part of a 'paradise' in which everything is perfectly ordered, where everything has its place. Instead they have to be free to change what is, to rebel against the status quo, because otherwise they would not be human. What they value is what they do and create for themselves.[33]

In Book 3, Fosca's days of seeing the world from a ruler's point of view are long past. It is the mid-seventeenth century and Fosca is now nearly four centuries old. For a hundred years he has toured the planet, and for the past four he has wandered alone on foot without a compass in the interior of North America. Deprived of his universalist illusions, but not of his immortality, Fosca finds it impossible to establish value, meaning and purpose in his life. He has learned to dissociate the individual from the universal, but the 'why' of human endeavour escapes him. He finds existence flat and tasteless, until he encounters a lost explorer. This stranger's plight confronts him with the value which mortality confers on human life, and, by association, on his own. Faced with the explorer's near starvation, Fosca's aimless wandering comes to an end as he undertakes a rescue mission for food. By helping the explorer with his problem of mortality, Fosca feels his own life beginning to take form again. When, in the end, the explorer kills himself, Fosca is forlorn and envious.

In Book 4, Fosca's confirmed disillusionment with universalism acts as a foil to the eighteenth century's exaggerated optimism, especially regarding the capabilities of scientific knowledge. Fosca is now a scientist, apparently one of considerable distinction, but he does not share in his contemporaries' belief in the benefits and nature of scientific progress. In fact, science's claims to universal knowledge leave him cold. And on this epistemological point Fosca very much speaks for Beauvoir's views, which today are central for postmodernism, but which were unspeakably heretical half a century ago. The novel's argument about the nature of knowledge develops as a special case of Beauvoir's more general one about individual versus universal points of view. Fosca, the scientist, no longer believes that he will ever see beneath 'the crusty surface of the apparent world'. He now realizes that even when he looks through microscopes and telescopes it is still only with *his eyes* that he sees, and that invariably the things he sees are situated among other things. The tangible objects of the scientific laboratory exist only through the scientist's senses, which in turn always function in frames of spatial, historical and cultural reference. Even if, thinks Fosca,

> we were to fly to the moon, or go down to the bottom of oceans, we would still be men in the heart of a human world. As for those mysterious realities which revealed themselves to our senses – forces, planets, molecules, waves – they were hidden by words and protected by the yawning gap of our ignorance. Never would nature deliver up to us her secrets; she had no secrets. We were the ones who invented questions and then formulated the

answers to them; in the bottoms of our retorts we would never discover anything but our own thoughts, thoughts that might in the course of centuries multiply, become more complex, be formed into vaster and more subtle systems. But never would these thoughts be capable of tearing me from myself. I put my eye to the microscope; everything would always pass through my eyes, through my thoughts. Never would anything be *something else*, never would I be someone else.[34]

The fifth and final section of Fosca's narrative shows him reconciled to a limited optimism for the possibilities of human action. Whereas as a ruler he acted *for* others and for unlimited goals (paradise), he now acts *with* others for achievable and historically situated results. His great-grandson, a prime mover in the revolutionary activities in Paris in the 1840s, expresses Beauvoir's own belief, with which Fosca now finds himself in sympathy: 'Paradise for us is simply the moment when the dreams we dream today are finally realized. We're well aware that after that other men will have new needs, new desires, will make new demands.'[35] In other words, just as the pronouncements of philosophers emanate from particular vantage points, desires emanate not from the desirability of a universal scheme, but rather from individual human beings situated in time and place. The world, insists Beauvoir, discussing *All Men Are Mortal* in *Force of Circumstance*, 'resolves into individual liberties'.[36] This ethos grounds political ambitions in the limited points of view of individual mortals and formulates goals in concrete terms. For example, the primary goals of Fosca's great-grandson are child labour laws, a ten-hour maximum working day, democratic government and a free press.

'A limited future, a limited life: that's man's lot.'[37] But not Fosca's. And in the course of his centuries of existence he has come to see that it is the finite nature of individual lives that gives them value. For a mortal, today is part of their limited and contingent life; for Fosca it is part of eternity from which there is no escape. Lacking mortality he is left with nothing personal to hope for. He belongs to no age and to no place; his life is boundless and therefore without shape, without risk, without meaning, without value. For Fosca, notes Beauvoir, again in *Force of Circumstance*, there cannot exist, except vicariously, 'any of the living values instituted by human finitude'.[38] He is excluded from the human lot, a fact that weighs on him more heavily than ever when after the successful storming of the Bastille a banner is hung from the balcony: LONG LIVE THE REPUBLIC. The wild jubilation around him aggravates his alienation. He cannot, by definition, risk his life for the cause of human liberty.

There was never, he reflects, a flame in his heart or tears in his eyes.[39] In despair, Fosca retreats to a forest where he goes to sleep – for sixty years – only to emerge to tell his tale.

In its attention to the historical locatedness of its protagonist, to the formative inescapability of experience as the grounding for more general principles, and to the impact of mortality on the constitution of the human, Beauvoir's *All Men Are Mortal* serves as an excellent example of her literary-philosophical method in play. 'The new dimension of investigation' within which this text operates informs every facet of the narrative, and richly illustrates the extraordinary range which Beauvoir's literary-philosophical method opened to her.

4

Narrative Selves

Beauvoir's literary-philosophical method gave her a flexible tool which allowed a free and fluid symbiotic exchange between her personal experience and her philosophical research, and avoided what she saw as the untenable abstraction of universalist philosophical practice. The previous chapter explained Beauvoir's anti-universalist principles, showed their logical relation to her innovative method, and considered an extended application of those principles and method to the pretence of universalism in human affairs. This chapter concentrates on Beauvoir's theories of consciousness and self, theories which underpin her later works in applied ethics, especially *The Second Sex*. Appreciation of Beauvoir's contribution to these issues requires an understanding of the context of philosophical traditions and controversies in which she was working.

The Philosophical Background of Existentialism

It is impossible to understand Beauvoir's philosophical quest or that of other existentialists without considering Kant's transcendentalism. Beauvoir's enthusiasm for Kant's ideas and yet her profound distrust of them has been mentioned as a productive turning point in her philosophical training. To understand how Beauvoir addressed the problems Kant's work posed for her, some idea of his philosophy's impact is needed. Kant's *Critique of Pure Reason* (1781) prompted a dramatic shift in Western philosophical thought by changing how it regards the human mind. His philosophy effected this change by finding a middle ground between two philosophical extremes. Against Leibniz's rationalist view that reason is an in-built system of knowledge guaranteed by God, Kant held that a mind without sensory input is a mind without contents, without anything to think about. And against the empiricist view of Locke and Hume that the mind is a passive receptor of sense-data out of which it forms ideas, Kant argued that the human mind possesses certain innate ideas which impose order on the natural world. This rather spectacular claim that it is human beings who give form to the world has been at or near philosophy's centre ever since.

Kant held that the innate concepts by which individuals organize and process their sensory input are the same for all human beings. This presumed core of universal ideas is known variously as the 'transcendental ego', the 'transcendental self', and the 'universal subject' or 'universal self'. Through a method which he called the Transcendental Analytic, which exemplifies the kind of methodological approach to which Beauvoir was so opposed, Kant claimed to have identified, by pure thought, the constituent concepts of *the* transcendental self, the 'pure cognition of the understanding' by which we all perceive and conceive of the experiential world and which are necessary conditions for any experience.[1] Kant's interest in 'experience', however, was highly circumscribed. Like most philosophers in the centuries immediately before and after him, he limited his interest in the main to questions about the foundations of knowledge.

Early in the twentieth century, Edmund Husserl successfully relaunched the Kantian programme under the banner of 'phenomenology'.[2] In place of the Transcendental Analytic, phenomenology offered itself as a new and 'scientific' method for discovering the body of indubitable truths which constitute the transcendental ego or universal self. Phenomenology's basic assumption is the Kantian one that human consciousness contributes the structures of the world as it is experienced. Husserl proposed to reveal these universal structures through the not overly precise technique called the phenomenological reduction, a process of bracketing whereby the philosopher suspends the presuppositions through which he or she normally perceives objects. Phenomenologists believe that purifying perception in this way strips the universal structures of human consciousness bare, that is, allows access to the transcendental ego.

This tradition of the universal self and of rarefied methods for its discovery, together with philosophy's centuries-old preoccupation with knowledge, offered an increasingly tempting and vulnerable heritage against which young, irreverent and original twentieth-century philosophers could rebel. Søren Kierkegaard (1813–1855) sowed the seeds of this rebellion in the nineteenth century. This Danish philosopher, although concerned primarily with the failure of absolute or pure reason to provide a satisfactory basis for religious faith, raised most of the questions and invoked the distinctive philosophical sensibility that were to become the hallmarks of twentieth-century existentialism. On one hand, Kierkegaard emphasized human freedom and thus humanity's transcendent nature. On the other, he called attention to the contingency of human existence, how humans are thrown into the world with an unknown future, and how they seek refuge by 'following the crowd'. 'Where am I? Who am I? Who is it that has lured me into the world and now leaves me there? Why was I not consulted? . . . How did I obtain an interest in this big enterprise they call reality? Why should I have an interest in it?'[3]

Despite belonging to an age dominated by abstract thinking (and, he believed, a decadent age), Kierkegaard rejected the idea of the universal self, insisting instead that philosophy must consider individual human beings within the living context of a given world. In opposition to pure thought he called for existential thought, which demanded focusing on the actual and the particular, taking the point of view of individual common experience and recognizing that truth is truth for a subject. Kierkegaard emphasized concern for human freedom, will and the need for perpetual choice, especially moral choice.

Beauvoir never shared Kierkegaard's interest in the problem of religious belief. Instead, she focused on a set of philosophical problems centred on human consciousness: its relations with the body, with its own past, present and future, with the world and, especially, with other consciousnesses. These concerns about the nature of human identity, both individual and collective, inform a highly coherent and unusual research programme which she began in the late 1920s while still a student, and which grew over the next two decades into the theory of social relations that underpins *The Second Sex*, *Old Age* and her mature fiction. Her success in this pursuit owes much to her early discovery of an original point of departure. The student thesis she wrote in 1928, comparing the theories of Hume and Kant, appears to have been a determining factor in this development, since her approach to the notion of self exploits an unoccupied middle ground between the extreme positions of these two eighteenth-century philosophers.[4]

In *A Treatise of Human Nature* (1740), Hume, with whom Beauvoir shares a distaste for the pretence of a universal point of view, relates his personal attempts to identify, from within, his own self.

> For my part, when I enter most intimately into what I call *myself*, I always stumble on some particular perception or other, of heat or cold, light or shade, love or hatred, pain or pleasure. I never can catch *myself* at any time without a perception, and never can observe any thing but the perception.[5]

Hume then ventures the argument that the same holds for 'the rest of mankind, that they are nothing but a bundle or collection of different perceptions'. In support he offers a famous analogy: 'The mind is a kind of theatre, where several perceptions successively make their appearance; pass, re-pass, glide away, and mingle in an infinite variety of postures and situations.'[6]

However, in the appendix to his treatise, Hume exposes the short-comings of his own arguments. In a paradigm of intellectual integrity, he says that he can find no principles 'that unite our successive perceptions in our thought or consciousness' and that thereby generate a lived sense of self. In the shadow of his own failure he poses a challenge to future philosophers.

> For my part, I must plead the privilege of a sceptic, and confess, that this difficulty is too hard for my understanding. I pretend not, however, to pronounce it absolutely insuperable. Others, perhaps, or myself upon more mature reflection, may discover some hypothesis, that will reconcile those contradictions.[7]

Kant sidestepped Hume's contradictions by introducing the idea of the transcendental self, a depersonalized vestige of the 'soul' of Christian theology. Kant maintained that it is from this putative universal self that the unity of one's individual self is 'deduced'.[8] But, of course, Kant's universalist concept does not refer to the individual or empirical self of everyday life for which Hume lacked a principle for uniting 'successive perceptions', and it was on this abiding philosophical/psychological problem that Beauvoir focused her early research. Before examining her solution, a key piece of the puzzle which was not available to Hume must be noted.

Consciousness as a Relation

Beauvoir believed that 'children who are not yet anchored firmly in their little corner of the universe' are especially sensitive to existence's metaphysical dimension.[9] Although this is a standard Romantic claim, it is clear that Beauvoir based this belief on her own childhood experiences. The first volume of her autobiography, *Memoirs of a Dutiful Daughter*, features numerous accounts of her attempts, beginning at the age of seven, to understand the fundamental nature of her and the world's existence. Not only did she have metaphysical experiences, she also kept track of them from one age to the next, reflecting on and adding to her personal record of such occurrences as she matured. By the time she was seventeen, Beauvoir possessed a set of philosophical questions which were not only profound but also integral to her personal development and identity.

Of all the philosophically formative experiences of her childhood, Beauvoir seems to regard one as the most important, describing it in *Memoirs of a Dutiful Daughter*, in the unpublished chapters of *She Came to Stay* and in *She Came to Stay* itself, and referring to it in several other places.[10] It was, at age seven, the first of her metaphysical epiphanies. Significantly, its description served as the opening scene of the original first chapter of *She Came to Stay*. The small child, Françoise, is at her grandparents' house in the country. Her family has gathered in the garden, when Françoise ventures alone into the empty house.

> Her old jacket was hanging over the back of a chair . . . It was old and worn but it could not complain as Françoise complained when she had hurt herself; it could not say to itself: 'I'm an old worn jacket.' It was strange; Françoise tried to imagine what it would be like supposing she couldn't say: 'I'm Françoise, I'm six years old, and I'm in Grandma's house,' if she could say absolutely nothing: she closed her eyes. It was as if she did not exist at all; and yet other people would be coming here, and would see her, and would speak about her. She opened her eyes again; she could see the jacket, it existed, yet it was not aware of it.[11]

As an adult, Beauvoir repeatedly emphasized her childhood insight into the existential difference between herself and a jacket because it relates significantly to ontology, that branch of philosophy concerned with being, especially with being's possible and primary categories. The ontology implicit in the child's metaphysical encounter differs profoundly from the Cartesian ontology of mind (or consciousness) and body which is central to the French philosophical tradition. The child, rather than identifying mind and body as the two primary categories of being, identified two kinds of body, one which, like herself, is related to the rest of being by mind or consciousness, and the other, like the jacket, which is not. This ontology identifies *consciousness* not as a form of being, but rather as a relation which one category of being has with the world.

Another metaphysical problem, that of the nature of self, loomed large in Beauvoir's childhood. Her memoirs reveal that as a child Beauvoir was keenly aware, often painfully so, of a subject/object split in human reality. In contrast to the 'solid as a block of marble' presence which her best friend Zaza presented to her, she found within herself only an 'interior void'. In consequence, says Beauvoir, 'I couldn't help seeing myself through the eyes of others – my mother, Zaza, my school-friends, my teachers even – and through the eyes of the girl I once had been.'[12] Thus, in contrast to the unity of self assumed by philosophers, Beauvoir found herself threatened with fragmentation into a horde of selves. Her journals from 1927, when she was a university student, show that Beauvoir continued to be interested in this philosophical problem. Like Hume, she examined her own experience and, far from finding evidence of an inner self, found only a 'void'.[13]

Beauvoir says that when as a teenager she began studying philosophy, 'I found the problems that had intrigued me in childhood treated in books by serious gentlemen.'[14] But until her mid-twenties Beauvoir was unable to integrate her radical ontological categories and her notion of an interior void with a philosophical tradition. Her reading of Edmund Husserl in 1934 decisively changed this. It introduced her to a philosophical principle which allowed her to reconcile her own ideas with a much wider research programme. The *principle of intentionality*, which originated with *Psychology from an Empirical Standpoint* (1874), by the Austrian philosopher/psychologist Franz Brentano was put to striking use by Husserl. Brentano's principle departs radically, but simply, from traditional ways of thinking about the mind and consciousness. It states that consciousness is always consciousness *of* something. Whereas it is traditional to think of consciousness as a kind of receptacle for perceptions and images, Brentano holds that consciousness is a *relation* which human beings have to objects, both real and imagined. According to this relational view, it follows that when consciousness attempts to suspend its reaching towards the world of objects, towards being, it falls back towards nothingness or the void which the child and the teenage Beauvoir experienced. Every moment of consciousness has something (the intended object: a human face, a memory of a human face, a blank wall, a musical tone, a cold wind, a concept, a number or its own nothingness) *of* which it is conscious.

The principle of intentionality accommodated Beauvoir's commitment to the individual point of view. It also pertained tangentially to two of the metaphysical conundrums which she carried forward from childhood, but with regard to which, as we have seen, she arrived at views that clashed with prevailing orthodoxy. There was her relational view of consciousness as manifested in her early metaphysical encounter with her old jacket, and there was her Humean failure to find anything resembling a self residing in her consciousness. With regard to her first deviation, the relevance of Brentano's principle was manifest and immediate: like her own principles, it recognized consciousness as a relation. Moreover, it suggested a useful revision of Beauvoir's initial ontological categories. Brentano's inclusion of immaterial objects, as well as material ones, as the objects of consciousness formed a primary ontological category, *non-conscious being* (also called *being-in-itself*), which, when set opposite her category of *conscious being*, provided her with an ontological framework that was, with the notable exception of interpersonal and social relations, inclusive.

Because these categories of being – and non-being – underlie Beauvoir's subsequent thought, and also because commentators have often conflated her categories with those of Descartes, reiterating her basic ontology is useful. Beauvoir's earliest fiction identifies consciousness as a relation (rather than as a kind of being) which some objects have to the world, and shows that *from the point of view of an individual consciousness* this relation neatly divides the world into two primary categories of being. The most elementary, non-conscious being or being-in-itself, includes anything which can be made an object of consciousness. This is a much wider category than material objects, embracing not only the meanings of words, as well as concepts generally, but also memories, including moments of consciousness reflected upon. Beauvoir's other primary category of being, conscious being, is synonymous with human being. It is an assemblage of non-conscious being, especially a body and a past, which possesses consciousness as a unit.

The principle of intentionality's inclusion of non-material objects brought Beauvoir's concerns with self and with consciousness into close juxtaposition. Brentano's relational view of consciousness, unlike the traditional view which treated it as a separate region of being, explained the futility of looking inwards for the self or ego and, in addition, predicted the void or nothingness that Beauvoir found within herself. This principle also implied that the self – or selves – was, like everything else in the world, merely an object *of* consciousness. On this basis, Beauvoir founded her own research into the nature of self. Finally, all this provided Beauvoir with another important idea. Her discovery that her own intuitive judgements, reached independently at a tender age, were consistent with a new but recognized school of thought, could only have given her philosophical heart.

Brentano's principle of intentionality contains a further innovative dimension. It maintains that it is the objects themselves – not mental images of them, as when Hume speaks of observing his perceptions – which figure in acts of consciousness. Philosophy's empirical tradition, as well as the Cartesian branch of the continental tradition, tends to regard consciousness as an indirect and passive experience of the world, as in Hume's theatre analogy. This school holds that when one looks at Jane, Jane is not the actual object of consciousness, but rather a likeness or picture of Jane which appears *in* one's consciousness. Perception, in other words, is only indirectly of things in the world. Against this 'internalist' view, the doctrine of intentionality posits consciousness as a direct, active and continuous relationship of engagement of the individual human being with the world. Instead of an internal slideshow, the world is experienced as external to consciousness and as something through which consciousness moves and into which consciousness intervenes. Blue and red, for example, are not sensations, rather they are what is sensed. These colours are properties of the objects which consciousness intends, rather than elements of consciousness.

The principle of intentionality became the keystone of Husserl's phenomenology, and, more generally, of what Beauvoir called 'the phenomenological attitude'. An abiding characteristic of Beauvoir's work is that it seeks to establish positions in the exposed but fruitful grounds between the polarized doctrines which tend to define the philosophical landscape. In her essay of 1945 on Merleau-Ponty's *Phenomenology of Perception*, she notes that 'Empiricism like intellectualism separated the world from consciousness . . . the one demanded that consciousness abdicate before the opacity of the real; the other dissolved the real in the light of consciousness.' The phenomenological attitude, she continues, 'permits man to reach the world, and to recover himself in it'.[15] The ways in which the phenomenological attitude informs other aspects of Beauvoir's philosophy will be explored later.

Before proceeding, however, it is useful to summarize some of Beauvoir's foundational principles introduced in this chapter. According to the principle of intentionality, consciousness is a relation rather than a substance; consciousness always has its object – and real-life objects, not representations of them, are the primary objects of consciousness. Although Brentano introduced intentionality in the context of psychology, his thesis carried latent ramifications for philosophy, ones which extended far beyond phenomenology and which proved crucial to the development of existentialism. But these were only slowly identified and developed.

Husserl's use of Brentano's insight was boxed in by his commitment to at least some form of Kant's universal or transcendental ego. Beauvoir's entry into the frame, however, marked the beginning of a new sociocultural dimension to the history of Western philosophy: she recognized and announced that, as a woman, she was deeply sceptical about traditional universalist male philosophical pretensions. Her innate particularism, her fondness for the concrete, her disdain for the male commitment to universalism, her woman's awareness that consciousness – like it or not – is embodied, as well as the eccentric metaphysical predilections brought forward from her childhood, all predisposed Beauvoir to the philosophical radicalism whose insights so animated the brilliant and ambitious young male philosophers who congregated around her. The remainder of this chapter will consider how Beauvoir's early recognition of intentionality's neglected implications contributed to theories of self and of conscious being that emerged in her early fiction.

Two Dimensions of Human Reality

Once again, as in the previous sections where the place of individual experience in the formulation of philosophical ideas was the issue in question, to understand Beauvoir's position on immanence and transcendence we must turn back to the history of philosophy, and especially, once more, to Kant. While Kant's revolution in philosophy shifted philosophers' attention away from cosmic reality and on to humankind, especially on to the nature of human being, philosophy's tendency to abstraction and unreality still remained. Kant's new 'humanist' focus illustrates the difficulty. While Kant is interested in human being, he excludes individual existents from his analysis. He brackets off human diversity through his notion of the transcendental ego, an *a priori* attempt to map out an eternal and universal structure of the human mind. Kant's concept presupposes a sort of standard-issue human being, a man for all times, all places, all occasions. And it was this presumed single unified totality of human nature which underwrote, so went the argument, the unity of the real-life individual self.

Kierkegaard's intervention half a century later represented not so much another revolution in philosophy as the first of the many attempts (which range from Nietzsche's to the current work of the postmodernists) to find a way through or past the traditional philosophical principles of universalism and transcendentalism. With his acceptance of the Kantian focus on humankind, the rebellious Danish philosopher's rejection of the universal ego opened philosophy's door to the indeterminacies, the concrete particularities and, most importantly, the differences in human existence. And, as has since become obvious, philosophical analysis of the human individual poses a stiffer, more intractable and more interesting philosophical challenge than the more orderly but unreal assumptions of transcendentalism.

From one point of view, since Kierkegaard, existentialism has done little other than elaborate and rephrase his ideas. Further, many reworkings of Kierkegaard's thought by philosophers of other nationalities have been credited with an originality which would be unthinkable if, for example, Kierkegaard had been German. But it is also the case that Kierkegaard's acute turn of thought merely began an enormous inquiry which not only continues, usually under banners other than that of 'existentialism', but which draws more participants with each generation. Kierkegaard's questions are, simply, *the* modern questions. Although these questions are now ubiquitous, rehearsing them here will help to focus the following discussion. What is the relation between an individual's freedom and the givenness of his or her situation? What is the nature of self-identity? How is the individual related to society? What is the ontological structure of an individual's relation to the world? How does one make moral choices without a set of universal moral absolutes? What is the relation between truth and the knowing subject? These crucial questions are all inspired by Kierkegaard, and they belong even more to today and tomorrow than to the past century and a half during which they have been discussed. They are also the key questions for Beauvoir.

By breaking free of the universalist straitjacket, Kierkegaard identified a split or divided self in the individual existent, a paradox which has been at the heart of existential thought ever since. It is also the problem with which Beauvoir began her work as a philosopher. Although succeeding generations of existentialists and post-existentialists often develop elaborate terminologies and complex metaphors to elucidate further Kierkegaard's insight, the Dane's basic paradox is best described in everyday language. John Macquarrie, in his study of existentialism, does this clearly: 'To exist is to project oneself into the future. But there is always a lack or disproportion between the self as projected and the self where it actually stands.'[16] From one point of view, one is free to make choices about one's being; from another, one is predetermined. The individual faces different possibilities, not only for tomorrow, but also for the next minute. And, indeed, about these possibilities the individual cannot keep from making choices. Similarly, making plans for tomorrow and beyond, or making no plans, both mean making choices about the person one intends to be – a doctor or a teacher, an altruist or an egoist, a mother or a father – but is not yet. And, to varying degrees, individuals identify themselves with these future selves which they choose and which they may or may not become.

But juxtaposed to the dimension of freedom are the givens of the individual's existence. For a start, individuals exist in bodies fixed in their attributes, including sex, race and heredity, and in bodies located at single and unique points in physical space. Everyone occupies a place in a particular society at a certain moment in time; everyone exhibits socially and historically determined characteristics, as well as personal habits; and everyone possesses a unique past. Everyone also, as Beauvoir stressed, holds images of themselves generated by the people they know and by the social categories to which they find themselves assigned.

Beauvoir most often referred to these two dimensions of human reality as *transcendence* and *immanence*. Her formulation of these concepts, carried out partly in cooperation with Sartre,[17] is distinguished by its comparative rigour and by the depth of its philosophical meaning. Beauvoir achieved this new rigour by tying the split in human existence to her ontological categories of conscious being and non-conscious being *and* to the principle of intentionality. Clearly, immanence is a universal property of non-conscious being, and, thus, also of conscious being. But previously the ontological basis of transcendence had remained unclear. At the start of her publishing career, beginning with the first of the deleted chapters of *She Came to Stay*, Beauvoir identified the origin of transcendence with consciousness and its property of intentionality. If transcendence is defined as a going beyond a given state of affairs – or, as

Beauvoir explained in *Pyrrhus et Cinéas*, a process of 'forever going beyond what is' – then, according to the principle of intentionality, by its very nature consciousness is a continuous process of transcendence, a deliberate positing of one object of consciousness after another.[18] The principle, Beauvoir noted in *The Prime of Life*, makes 'the existence of consciousness . . . depend on a perpetual transcending of itself towards an object'.[19]

It is this transcendent nature of consciousness that compels the human being endlessly to project his or her existence beyond the present. This projection is enacted through choices of objects of consciousness, choices which necessarily extend to projects and values, and choices of the means for realizing them, and to the use of one's body as an instrument that transcends aspects of the world. In this way, Beauvoir identifies transcendence as an essential dimension of human existence. Stasis is alien to the human manner of being. 'One never arrives anywhere,' says Beauvoir in *Pyrrhus et Cinéas*, 'there are only points of departure.'[20]

The Theory of the Narrative Self

This distinction between transcendence and immanence is fundamental to almost all of Beauvoir's thought, including her theories of the Individual and the Social Other and her analysis of the oppression of women, the colonized and the old. Also fundamental is her related theory of the *narrative self*, which, after World War II, she extended to cover social groups. Beauvoir's theory that it is narratives which are, as Hume said, missing 'principles, that unite our successive perceptions in our thought or consciousness' is carefully and clearly set out in her earliest fiction.[21] The five interlocking short stories she completed in 1937, *When Things of the Spirit Come First*, focus on young people grappling with the problems of personal identity. The collection's concluding and highly autobiographical story, 'Marguerite', is especially to the point. On the surface this first-person account of Marguerite's successful break with the Church and her ending of an unsatisfactory romance appears conventional and undistinguished. A deeper reading, however, reveals the outline of Beauvoir's vision of a self as a narrative construct.

The story centres on two points in Marguerite's life when her sense of self collapses. Beauvoir explains both breakdowns as due to the discrediting in Marguerite's mind of a narrative which she had constructed and maintained regarding the nature of her individual

self. The story associates each failed narrative with a theory of self.
The first is the Christian doctrine that the self or soul is a space that
the believer reserves for the will of God, and which conceives of the
soul as beautiful in proportion to its openness to this holy presence.
Marguerite grows up listening to stories about her soul's beauty,
and because she believes these stories and the theory of self behind
them, she becomes accustomed to picturing herself as living 'under
the eye of an all-powerful being'.[22] As a teenager, however, she
learns that her belief in the nature of her self is based on a misunderstanding of Catholic teaching. She had given her faith a Protestant
interpretation, believing that her soul was open to God Himself
rather than relying on the mediation of the priests. Confronted with
her heresy, Marguerite loses her faith, and with it her sense of self.

Marguerite, now a student at the Sorbonne, tries to reconstruct
her self under the influence of her knavish brother-in-law Denis,
who preaches the doctrines of André Breton's Surrealists' Mani-
festo. Denis promises her 'miracles' of perception by placing her in
touch with her true self, her unconscious mind and vision. He
instructs her in the principle of gratuitous action, the futility of
hope, the absurdity of life and the beauty of sin, and finally treats
her to a night in 'the place of miracles', his favourite bar. There
Marguerite is 'more deeply moved than on the day of [her] first
Communion'.[23]

Marguerite's tutelage ends prematurely when her 'spiritual'
guide disappears. Alone, the neophyte makes weekly pilgrimages
to the night-life of Montparnasse, where she worships bohemia's
more sordid dimensions, but where she engages only in flirtation
and the occasional gin fizz. In time she finds that the surrealist
narrative offers her 'only a very narrow field of action' on which to
project her life, limiting her in the main merely to 'playing with
words' and to spectating life as if it were a theatre. In consequence,
a strong sense of self, such as she had enjoyed under Catholicism,
fails to develop. But Marguerite's chrysaloid existence ends suddenly when, after eighteen months, she stumbles on Denis in a bar.
She spins his vague suggestion of need for her into a vision of a
shady but shared life together as expatriates in Saigon, a false hope
which Denis cynically exploits. Armed with this new story about
herself, she finds that the meaning her life had lost the day she lost
God is replenished. Every one of her actions becomes an attempt at
building a life for Denis and herself, with the principles of the
surrealist narrative – gratuitousness and absence of hope and desire
– falling by the wayside.[24]

When after six months Denis returns to live with his wife, Marguerite's new self implodes. Beauvoir, who has littered the text with theatrical images, makes a pointed allusion to Hume's famous theatre analogy. For Marguerite: 'Now the world was falling apart again; it was no longer a theatre and there was no longer any play going on; and once more it was only a chance collection of scattered objects.'[25] The world is no longer a theatre because Marguerite ceases to find it amusing. And a play is no longer proceeding because Marguerite is now without a narrative to unite her successive thoughts and raise her existence above Hume's 'theatre, where several perceptions successively make their appearance; pass, repass, glide away, and mingle in an infinite variety of postures and situations'.[26] For Marguerite, the lights of Montparnasse

> had lost their fascinating brilliance; and I no longer knew where to go. A vast, shapeless mass, swarming with people, stretched in all directions around me; I walked along the streets as chance led me, and my thoughts too wandered at random, forming a weak little eddy that led nowhere and that the slightest event drove from my mind.[27]

Beauvoir's first book ends with Marguerite trying to reinvent herself with a new narrative. A few months later Beauvoir explored her theory of narrative selves further through the story of a child, Françoise, in 'Deux chapitres inédits de *L'Invitée*'. This time Beauvoir is particularly concerned to show how a *self emerges as a construct out of the split between transcendence and immanence* in human existence. The first chapter describes Françoise's emerging realization of that split in herself and, by implication, in all human existence. The young girl is trying to ascertain the basis and nature of her 'identity', of her sense of self. In the days following her metaphysical encounter with her jacket on the back of a chair cited earlier in this chapter, she thinks further about how her consciousness is trapped in her body. She finds that, just as she cannot transfer her consciousness to her jacket, neither can she transfer it to another person. Consciousnesses are simultaneously embodied and irredeemably separated.[28]

At this stage of her development, Françoise believes she 'knew very well who she was'.[29] Like her old jacket, she has certain attributes recognized by her parents and by herself. She is, in her parents' eyes, precocious, morally upright and possesses a 'lovely nature'; she tells her mother everything, does not lie, likes reading, works hard at her lessons, has fits of rage when refused a pleasure, but never disobeys; she has hair that is chestnut and naturally curly;

she takes pride in her good grades, precociousness and lovely nature. These physical characteristics, past kinds of behaviour and events, and relations with her parents – in total, the immanence of her being – make her 'this little girl and not another'.[30] And when she looks at herself in the mirror she can say 'It is I.'

But, unlike the jacket, immanence is not the whole of her being. Françoise is also free. She is capable of undertaking actions, of behaving and valuing the world, and, moreover, of doing so differently today and tomorrow than she did yesterday. In Beauvoir's philosophical language, Françoise is a transcending being as well as an immanent one: she has, to some degree, the power to transcend both her past and her present situation in the world, to choose the objects of her consciousness and to decide how she will value them. Furthermore, she can never make these choices and decisions once and for all. Instead, she must keep choosing day after day and minute after minute, even if she only elects to choose and decide as she did last time.

However, like most children, Françoise lacks awareness of her freedom. She thinks of herself, like a machine engineered to perform only in prescribed ways, as predetermined to act in characteristic modes – precociously, righteously, good-naturedly, truthfully; and to perform certain fixed acts – to confide all in her mother, to read with pleasure, to stage fits of rage; and to experience certain feelings, like pride in her predetermined attributes; and, finally, never to perform some kinds of acts – lying and disobedience. Even so, Françoise is dimly aware that 'she was not always this little girl,' that, unlike the old jacket with no control of its qualities, she lacks self-identity in some intrinsic way.

A few years older, and again at her grandparents' country house, Françoise sits by herself at a table in the garden, 'exploring a problem'. As she had earlier, she encounters the problem of non-self-identity. She carefully reflects on the sequence of objects of her consciousness: her fingers detaching warts of paint from the table; her habit of doing so; her identity as the studious, diligent, docile little girl named Françoise who does her vacation lessons in the garden every year.[31]

> She stopped suddenly; *it was like a story that one tells oneself*, when one says, I am a poor orphan, and feels all sad and starving on the inside; the garden was indeed a garden, the pen was truly a pen, and Françoise was indeed she; and yet she had the impression that she was playing; just as she played sometimes at being someone else, she played at being herself.[32]

This excerpt from Beauvoir's fiction illustrates her point that the self or ego is 'like a story one tells oneself'. Prompted by others, subjects tell themselves what their characteristics are, and then choose – or choose not – to act out the part. It is in this sense that one *plays* at being one's self, and that Françoise is playing the part of Françoise.[33] The girl's metaphysical insight occurs because, by focusing on her stream of consciousness, she has inadvertently focused exclusively on the transcendent and volitional side of her being. This encounter parallels the previous episode in which Françoise feels smugly self-identical because she keeps the transcendent dimension of her being almost completely blocked from view. The narrative coordination of the two dimensions of human reality presents further difficulties for the problem of personal identity, difficulties which can be explored through addressing the concept of bad faith.

Bad Faith

The existentialist identification of immanence and transcendence as the two dimensions of human reality conceals a logical twist which gives rise to a paradox at one level of meaning. Another way of saying that there is an essential disproportion between self as immanence and self as transcendence or project is that the self is not identical with itself. Indeed, this is how Beauvoir characterizes the distinction between conscious and non-conscious being in the passage just examined. She shows the impossibility of anyone corresponding to themselves in the way that 'the garden was indeed a garden' and 'the pen was truly a pen.' For Beauvoir, the subject can never be self-identical. And on the phenomenological level, as for example in the descriptions of the young girl's consciousness, this non-self-identity is eminently intuitive, non-self-identity being a characteristic of all emergent phenomena. But on a purely logical or metaphysical level, non-self-identity is counterintuitive. It violates two of what logicians often call 'the three laws of thought'. The two 'laws' violated are:

The law of identity: if anything is X, it is X.

The law of contradiction: nothing can be both X and not X.

Even everyday discourse implicitly subscribes to these 'laws'. This makes it a simple matter to describe conscious being, given its lack of identity with itself, in a paradoxical mode. For example, it can be said that conscious being is 'in the mode of being what it is not and of not being what it is', or 'I am what I shall be in the mode of not being it', or 'we are what-we-are-not and are not what-we-are.'[34]

Such formulations were rarely used by Beauvoir, whose writing is notable for its clarity. Such complicated phrasing tends to mystify an essential structure of human reality which, when treated in its natural context at the phenomenological level, is, as Beauvoir's lucid prose shows, inherently intuitive. Beauvoir began to explore the behavioural implications of the split between immanence and transcendence in human reality in the early to mid-1930s. When set against her prior rejection of a self resident in consciousness, the relevance of this split to patterns of human behaviour looms extremely large.[35] If an individual's self (or selves) is merely a construct and an evolving one, created and maintained by a process of belief, then a self need not faithfully reflect the ambiguity at the heart of conscious being. Social conditioning or individual choice may lead subjects to deny, in general or in relation to particular situations, either their transcendence or their immanence. A subject may deny to him- / herself that he / she is free to behave or choose differently, or deny one or more of the givens of his / her existence. This ever-present possibility of the 'self' not coinciding with the invariant structure of embodied consciousness means that lived existence may in various degrees be prejudiced by a conceptual confusion.

This phenomenon, identified by Beauvoir and Sartre, has become known as 'bad faith', an unfortunate term as it gives rise to confusion on two levels. First, there is the problem that the single term 'bad faith' refers to two radically divergent forms of human behaviour, that is, to denying one's immanence or to denying one's transcendence. This, in turn, leads to the tendency to associate the term solely with the latter form of bad faith – it being dominant at the behavioural level – leaving the former kind to drift conceptually into the distance and, with it, the ontological structure of both varieties of bad faith. (The practice of sometimes calling the latter kind of bad faith 'seriousness' or the 'spirit of seriousness' without assigning a name to bad faith's other form only aggravates the terminological imbalance.) Therefore, it seems advantageous to introduce a new pair of terms. We will call the denial of transcendence the *bad faith of immanence*; while we will call the denial of immanence the *bad faith of transcendence*.

'Bad faith' is also an infelicitous term, given that Beauvoir regarded many important instances of this class of behaviour as ethically neutral. In 1946–7, in *The Ethics of Ambiguity*, Beauvoir comments on this aspect of the theory of bad faith which she set out in the previous decade:

> In [a child's] universe of definite and substantial things, beneath the sovereign eyes of grown-up persons, he thinks that he too has *being* in a definite and substantial way. He is a good little boy or a scamp; he enjoys being it. If something deep inside him belies his conviction, he conceals this imperfection. He consoles himself for an inconsistency which he attributes to his young age by pinning his hopes on the future. Later on he too will become a big imposing statue. While waiting, he plays at being, at being a saint, a hero, a guttersnipe. He feels himself like those models whose images are sketched out in his books in broad, unequivocal strokes: explorer, brigand, sister of charity.[36]

Ethically, this child's bad faith of immanence is neither good nor bad. It is merely an intellectual misunderstanding. Beauvoir views it as a universal characteristic of childhood, encouraged by adults anxious to preserve their authority and to conceal from the child both its freedom and the subjective origin of language, customs, ethics and values.[37]

Beauvoir also finds an explanation for the crisis of adolescence in the child's bad faith of immanence.[38] This difficult adolescent period accelerates the child's process of emerging from its intellectual misconception about the structure of its being and of the being of others. Increasingly the child sees that her being is not constituted so as to compel her to act in certain ways, or to hold certain values. The day comes when it dawns on her that there is nothing inherently good about her parents' dress codes or musical tastes; there exist other possibilities. Gradually the adolescent notices that the habits of adults are merely their choices and that it is through their choices (that is, their freedom) that values come to exist in the world. The teenager self-consciously experiments at making some choices of her own. Aided by her peers, she begins to establish priorities, make her own rules, set her own projects, assign her own meanings. In this way the adolescent discovers, to her astonishment, her own freedom, the transcendent side of her being.

Beauvoir stands pre-eminent among major modern thinkers in identifying adolescence as the crucial phase of character formation. Adolescents' discovery of their transcendent nature is, according to her theory, the defining, but not irreversible, 'moment' for the subject's assumption of moral being. In *The Ethics of Ambiguity* Beauvoir explains why she puts so much emphasis on this moment in adolescence:

it is not without great confusion that the adolescent finds himself cast into a world which is no longer ready-made, which has to be made; he is abandoned, unjustified, the prey of a freedom that is no longer chained up by anything. What will he do in the face of this new situation? This is the moment when he decides. If what might be called the natural history of an individual, his affective complexes, etcetera, depend above all upon his childhood, it is adolescence which appears as the moment of moral choice. Freedom is then revealed and he must decide upon his attitude in the face of it.[39]

It is only at this point, when the individual loses her childhood ignorance about the nature of her and others' being, that bad faith acquires an ethical dimension. Beauvoir's case rests on the moral idea that, once the free or transcendent side of being has been revealed, the individual should always embrace it rather than retreat back into immanence. But, as Beauvoir emphasized in *The Second Sex* and *Old Age* with regard to members of oppressed groups, even adults are capable of genuine and morally neutral intellectual confusion, especially when they have been subjected to programmes of miseducation. Therefore, even for the fully mature person, the ethical import, if any, of bad faith depends on the individual case.

The theory of bad faith, especially Beauvoir's version, belongs to a small but extremely important group of doctrines, each of which seeks to identify, explain and chart some pervasive mechanism of concealment. Freud's theory of repression, Marx's theory of ideology and Aldous Huxley's impoverished and fallacious Newspeak are, along with bad faith, influential examples of ideas which belong to this category. It was partly in reaction against what they saw as the baroque metaphysics of Freudianism that Beauvoir and Sartre begin work on bad faith in the early 1930s, seeking to explain the various concealments which Freud attributed to repression – 'semantic quibbling, false recollections, fugues, compensation fantasies, sublimations and the rest', as Beauvoir puts it in *The Prime of Life* – without resorting to the Freudian compartmentalization of human consciousness.[40] It was not until later, however, when Beauvoir applied her theory of bad faith in her fiction and within the context of her own philosophical vision, that her new theory of concealment revealed its worth.

The Philosophy of Joy

Recognition of the primary break or schism in the being of the human individual, then, has been central to existentialist thought from its beginning. It represents the first radical turning away from the Enlightenment category of the unified subject. As we have shown, Beauvoir's contribution to analysing this emerging metaphysical paradox, facilitated by her 'new dimension of investigation' and by her rigorous use of the point of view of individual consciousness, is considerable. It is, however, what Beauvoir made of the existential break and of her attitude towards it that truly sets her apart, not only from her predecessors, but also from her contemporaries and from many philosophers writing today.

Philosophy did not welcome the revelation that the subject lacks simple unity. Even now the analytical tradition, despite its grounding in and admiration for Hume, prefers to avoid the topic. This may be a victory of wisdom over valour, given that the existentialists themselves – with the exception of Beauvoir – find this, their central message, dispiriting. They – and here Kierkegaard, Heidegger, Gabriel Marcel, Jaspers and Sartre must all be included – speak habitually of the anxiety, dread, fear, anguish and the prominence of death caused by awareness of the subject's non-self-identity and corresponding freedom. With the exception of Sartre, these thinkers tend to pose as soul doctors, as medicine men for the modern psyche, bemoaning the split in the individual's being and offering remedies for what they perceive as humankind's existential agonies. In so far as they hold out hope for a reunification of being or for a discovery of the 'true' or 'authentic' self, they are philosophers of nostalgia and escape.

Beauvoir regards her male counterparts' grievances against the existential condition as little more than philosophical whingeing. She offers a tougher but more optimistic account of the human condition based on her very different reading of the capabilities of the human personality. Beauvoir's tough-minded philosophy of joy is possible because of her two major points of ontological difference from other existentialists.

Firstly, Beauvoir differs with the existentialist tradition about the source and magnitude of the anxiety, dread, fear or anguish that people feel when they confront their freedom, their indeterminateness, their non-self-identity, their need continuously to project themselves towards the future in order to be. Whereas existential orthodoxy regards this anguish as ontologically based, that is, as an irreducible and inescapable part of the human condition (barring a philosopher's cure), Beauvoir sees it as conditioned by the individual's personal and social history. As children, argues Beauvoir, our 'freedom was first concealed' from us, and for the rest of our lives we may, like Heidegger and Sartre, remain 'nostalgic for the time when [we] did not know its exigencies'.[41] But the depth of this concealment varies from child to child, as does 'the apprenticeship of freedom' that the individual undergoes at adolescence. And it is in this historical and experiential context, rather than in the ontological freedom itself, that Beauvoir locates the anguish of freedom. With disparate individual histories, adolescents and adults arrive at 'moments of moral choice' differently equipped. They experience the anguish of freedom in greatly varying degrees. For some, it will be so great that, in order to conceal their freedom, they will structure their adult lives as tightly around bad faith as if they were still small children. But for others the anguish of freedom is a 'tension' which they actively desire, which they may even embrace with joy.[42]

Beauvoir's view of self forms an integral part of the analytical apparatus of *The Second Sex*. And it is through this source that Beauvoir's (often heavily criticized) ideas on the self largely became available to the wider intellectual community. Beauvoir's rejection of existentialism's characteristic nostalgia for authenticity in favour of the idea of multiple narrative selves, was, for the most part, too disturbing to be acceptable to her immediate male contemporaries. Today, however, Beauvoir's heresy of half a century ago is the new orthodoxy. The following passage from a recent essay captures the Beauvoirian flavour of much of the current dialogue about the nature of self.

> If modernist existentialism suggests that there are a number of possible selves we can choose from as we search for our one authentic self, postmodern existentialism relativises selves and celebrates, or at least flaunts, this variety. There is (was) always the suggestion with modernist existentialism that inauthentic selfs were fraudulent copies of some original. The postmodern existential outlook has copies of selfs without originals. Another way in which we might push this changeover from modernist to postmodernist is to argue that in the modernist version there is an element of temporality, since a journey towards the essential self is involved. No such chronology affects postmodernism in that the various selfs are coextensive in time and space.[43]

Beauvoir's second early quarrel with existential philosophy extends to the whole of the phenomenological tradition. She identifies a second primary mode of intentionality in which consciousness is not the desire to be but rather the desire to reveal being. This dimension of Beauvoir's philosophy has an even stranger social history than the others. In 1945 Merleau-Ponty called attention to it in 'Metaphysics and the Novel', but it was too radical to be taken up and popularized by either himself or Sartre. The consequence was that it soon disappeared completely from cultural view. The recent rediscovery of this important aspect of Beauvoir's philosophy, as well as imaginative explorations of its wide-ranging implications, is due to Debra Bergoffen.[44] The American philosopher's disinterment of Beauvoir's reworking of the theory of intentionality is based on a neglected passage in *The Ethics of Ambiguity*. In it Beauvoir identifies not one but two primary modes or moments of intentionality, two distinct and independent ways of intending the objects of one's consciousness. Beauvoir writes: 'Thanks to [man], being is disclosed and he desires this disclosure. There is an original type of attachment to being which is not the relationship "wanting to be" but rather "wanting to disclose being".'[45] Whereas the desire to be is haunted by failure in the sense that one can never achieve self-identity (that is, one can never, absolutely, be oneself like a pen is a pen), the desire of disclosure, says Beauvoir, is characterized by unequivocal success and joy. Margaret Simons calls attention to similar passages in *America Day by Day*. Having landed in New York, Beauvoir describes her anticipation of being a tourist: 'it would be a revelation experienced beyond the limits of my ordinary life. And suddenly I was free of the monotonous cares I call my life. I was but a charmed conscience [consciousness] to which the sovereign Object would soon reveal itself.'[46] But what exactly does she mean by this disclosure of being? And what part does joy play in Beauvoir's analysis of consciousness?

Beauvoir's comments in *The Ethics of Ambiguity*, as well as Bergoffen's astute explication of them, leaves these questions unanswered. But then, when it comes to Beauvoir's own philosophical ideas, her essays are rarely her major primary texts. This is very much the case with her theory of intentionality.[47] Alerted by Bergoffen's readings of *The Ethics of Ambiguity*, earlier and much fuller accounts of Beauvoir's theory of the two modes of intentionality are discernible in her very earliest published fiction. And it is to this fictional presentation that Merleau-Ponty referred when he wrote:

> Only when I discover the landscape hidden until then behind a hill does it fully become a landscape; one cannot imagine what a thing would be like if it were not about to, or able to, be seen by me. It is I who bring into being this world which seemed to exist without me, to surround and surpass me. I am therefore a consciousness, immediately present to the world, and nothing can claim to exist without somehow being caught in the web of my experience. I am not this particular person or face, this finite being: I am a

pure witness, placeless and ageless, equal in power to the world's infinity.[48]

Merleau-Ponty's 'pure witness' encapsulates Beauvoir's idea of a joyful mode of intentionality divorced from the desire to be. How this mode relates to the mode of 'wanting to be' is a question which will be addressed further in relation to Beauvoir's ethics.

5

Embodiment and Intersubjectivity

The great modern philosophical question of the nature of intersubjectivity and its mechanisms runs through the entirety of Simone de Beauvoir's work. Her response to it is her most original and influential contribution to philosophy. Beauvoir's theory of intersubjectivity also forms the base on which her work on ethics (to be considered in the final three chapters) rests. Beauvoir herself recognized the importance of finding answers to difficult questions regarding intersubjectivity, and in her autobiography she notes that she began working on the question in her early twenties. The problem of the Other, she says, was always *her* problem. But Beauvoir's philosophical analysis of intersubjectivity depends on her equally interesting work on embodiment, and it is with this topic that this chapter begins.

She Came to Stay

In *She Came to Stay*, Beauvoir addresses two major philosophical questions: first, what is the relation of the body to perceptions and to consciousness; secondly, what, if any, are the possible relations between one's own consciousness and those of other persons?[1] This metaphysical novel, whose central lines of inquiry proceed straightforwardly, is structured around an extremely complex and unified philosophical plot. It provides a paradigmatic example of Beauvoir's philosophical method and corresponds exactly to the 'new dimension of investigation' which she and her contemporaries identified as a central modern need. One facet of Beauvoir's intentions here can be gauged from her technical choice of narrative voice. Instead of utilizing an ubiquitous or all-seeing narrator (which would reflect the philosopher's traditional pretence of a universal point of view), each section of the narrative adopts the viewpoint of one character's consciousness. Over 80 per cent takes the point of view of Françoise, who is thirty and an aspiring writer.

The published text opens with Françoise personifying traditional positions regarding the two primary questions above: the relation of body to consciousness, and the possible relations between one's own consciousness and those of other persons. Beauvoir invents a series of lived situations for Françoise which test these and other hypotheses ever more strenuously, making her philosophical argument coextensive with the metaphysical drama of her novel. From Françoise's viewpoint (and also, Beauvoir hopes, from the reader's), conclusive falsification of these traditional philosophical positions is reached near the middle of the novel. Meanwhile, new theories consistent with observed existential facts emerge or are postulated through the characters. The second half of the novel develops Beauvoir's own theories further, while constantly measuring them against the characters' experience. In this simple and obvious way *She Came to Stay* is structured precisely in the terms of a philosophical essay.

The novel takes place in the bohemian Paris of the late 1930s and concerns itself with five young people who are variously involved in the arts. Françoise and Pierre, although they occupy separate hotel rooms and remain free to pursue other sexual liaisons, have been partners for eight years. Pierre doubles as actor and director in a theatre company for which Françoise edits plays, while she works on a novel. Gerbert, ten years the couple's junior, assists Françoise with editing, and takes supporting roles in the company's productions. Elizabeth, Pierre's sister, a commercially successful but unhappy painter, shares the theatre's social life. Françoise and Pierre's relationship, as well as their individual identities, seem models of stability until Xavière, a mercurial child-woman, enters their lives, throwing them into emotional and, for Françoise, metaphysical turmoil. Out of this potent mixture a 'commonplace tale of jealousy and revenge' develops.[2] Xavière, whom Françoise first regards as her pet, threatens not only Françoise's relationship with Pierre, but also her sense of identity. In the second half of the novel, Françoise faces up to the challenges posed by Xavière. She agrees to form a 'trio' with Xavière and Pierre, and works to turn it to her advantage. Meanwhile, both Françoise and Xavière enter simultaneously into affairs with Gerbert, who, along with Pierre, is called away to fight the invading Germans. The novel concludes with Françoise gassing Xavière as she sleeps.

In terms of philosophy, *She Came to Stay* has proved by far the most influential of Beauvoir's works. Because she permitted both Sartre and Merleau-Ponty to study the manuscript of *She Came to Stay* in 1940, the impact of its arguments and ideas on the shape of continental philosophy was both immediate and profound. The next four sections of this chapter focus on those philosophical aspects of *She Came to Stay* which, besides being of interest to her emulative friends, provided a theoretical foundation for Beauvoir's subsequent books, and especially for *The Second Sex*.

The Body

For most of history the human body has scarcely figured in the philosopher's universe. Whereas physical science traditionally copes with 'the mind / body problem' – which is about how the two things are related – by ignoring mind (or consciousness), philosophy usually sees body as the troublesome term best passed over. In *She Came to Stay*, however, Beauvoir broke decisively and influentially with this philosophical tradition. Rather than bracketing off the body's existence, she made the body a central part of her philosophical vision, a lead quickly taken up and developed further by her friends Merleau-Ponty and Sartre.[3]

The previous chapter looked at the phenomenological view that consciousness is a relation between the human body and the world, and at how Beauvoir drew out the implications of this relation to posit new theories about self and about consciousness's structure. But the relational view of consciousness also implies that consciousness is embodied. In *She Came to Stay* Beauvoir explores what embodiment means.

Beauvoir is not interested in the generalized human body of anatomists, physiologists or traditional psychologists. Instead, her field is the neglected one of the body as actually lived by the subject. She demonstrates that, at the level of individual existence, the body is not primarily a thing, but rather the instrument by which individuals have a hold on and a point of view of the world. She conceives of each human body as an integrated system of perceptual powers, which include its consciousness, and as uniquely located in physical space. These factors make the body an essential element of each individual's existential situation.

In *She Came to Stay* Beauvoir presents her theory of embodied consciousness through extended phenomenological critiques of two opposed theories of perception, one based on British empiricism, the other derived from Kantian idealism. In the opening chapter, Beauvoir identifies – in a rather awkward and belaboured manner – the quasi-Kantian position with Françoise. Thinking of Pierre travelling on a distant train, she says to herself 'I am there. I am there,' indicating that she conceives of herself – or at least pretends that she does – as a disembodied subject, as one whose experience of the world is neither limited nor contextualized by her body. She also claims that 'but, for me, this square exists and that moving train,' thereby considering their existences dependent on her thinking about them, and implying that she conceives of the world as constituted by her consciousness.[4] Françoise also, as Merleau-Ponty notes, represses the idea of 'elsewhere'.[5] She says to Gerbert, ' "I'm convinced that wherever I may go, the rest of the world will move with me." '[6] This denial of the existence of elsewhere gives her, like the traditional philosopher, the illusion that she possesses a universal point of view on the world.

A few pages on, a nightclub scene offers further insights into Françoise's metaphysics. While her friends dance, she remains at their table thinking.

> Each one of these men, each one of these women present here tonight was completely absorbed in living a moment of his or her insignificant individual existence . . . 'And I – here I am at the very heart of the dance-hall – impersonal and free. I am watching all these lives and all these faces.'[7]

Rather than locating consciousness's constituting power in her personal self or selves, as she does with the people around her, Françoise sees her consciousness as 'impersonal and free' in the sense of Kant's transcendental or universal ego. This theory of perception, inspired by Kantian idealism, looks rather foolish in the context of Françoise's lived experience. Beauvoir's tactic here is to highlight the theory's inherent absurdity, an absurdity normally concealed by the abstraction and formality of traditional philosophical discourse.

Françoise's life provides an extreme example of the bad faith of transcendence. She actively pursues the illusion that she is pure transcendence, sometimes in the face of experiences which directly undermine this view. To this end, all of Françoise's waking hours are given over to structured pursuits of carefully chosen projects, which include her social engagements and her relationship with Pierre. At the same time she avoids experiences that remind her of her immanence, especially that of her body. For example, in contrast to her general self-discipline, she is very casual about her personal appearance. We are told that 'For most of the time, she was not even aware that she had a face,' and that, despite it being pretty, 'she had a vague hope that it would be invisible.' She also, in general, distances herself from sensual pleasures, like dancing, and thinks of herself as 'a naked conscious[ness] in front of the world'.[8]

Meanwhile, Xavière pursues, sometimes with frightening passion, the opposite illusion. She craves dancing as much as and for the same reasons as Françoise fears it: as a sensual experience. Dancing consumes Xavière's youthful energy while turning her consciousness inwards on the givenness of her body. But off the dance floor, Xavière's exaggerated bad faith of immanence leads her towards total passivity. She expresses no preferences and makes no plans, even to see a film or to meet a friend, because these mental activities reveal the transcendent side of her being. '"The pleasures of the mind"', she announces, '"are repulsive to me."' Unless taken out by others, Xavière scarcely ever leaves her hotel room, where she spends most of her time in a passive slump.[9]

The juxtaposition of Françoise's and Xavière's polar extremes of kinds of bad faith creates a grim metaphysical comedy, out of which Beauvoir distils her theory of embodied consciousness. Selecting a nightclub, the Pole Nord, for her existential laboratory, Beauvoir uses Xavière's heightened sensuality to critique the empiricist view of perception, especially the sense-data theory of British phenomenalism, and to set out her own view of the structure of sensory experience.[10] As noted previously, philosophy's empirical tradition conceives of perception not as an immediate relation with the world, or a sensing of its objects, but as an indirect or second-order relation based on sense-data. For the empiricist, 'sensations' do not result from awareness of the objects themselves, but from awareness of the sense-data. This theory appears most plausible when considering visual phenomena, because, in this kind of perception, there is a distance between the object and the perceiving subject. In her fiction, Beauvoir shrewdly shifts the analysis to more immediate orders of perception, describing her characters' experiences with taste, time, sound and, especially, touch.

The empiricist tradition also regards perception primarily as a problem of objective knowledge, and therefore treats the perceiving subject as if he or she were a scientist approaching an experiment. Sense organs receive data, which are stored in their respective data spaces, and which the perceiver subsequently interprets. The empiricist judges these interpretations according to their correspondence to 'real' spaces, shapes, time intervals and so on – 'real' in the sense of a physical reality which exists independently of the perceiving subject. Beauvoir does not deny this dimension to perception. But she considers the view that this is all there is to perception, or even that it is its most important aspect, as seriously deluded.

For example, Beauvoir argues through her characters in *She Came to Stay* that perception of time is not primarily about universal time, but about individuals' movements towards their projected futures.[11] This holds true even in situations where simple clock time might seem the only relevant dimension. For example, when sitting an exam, although the examinee 'works against the clock', she perceives time unfolding as the living of her exam *project*: answering questions, making calculations, composing sentences, writing letters or numerals. The subject's point of view on time is this series of present moments defined by the future which she projects for herself. Experience of time rarely focuses on time's physical dimension, and when it does, it appears absurd.[12]

Beauvoir rejects mechanistic explanations of all perceptual experiences (not just time) which leave out the perceiver. The perceiver is a subject and his or her body a unity, not just a collection of reflex mechanisms. The body's organs of perception, and power of consciousness, are interlocked, indivisible, inseparable. The body is subjectified; the subject embodied.

Beauvoir argues for the holistic character of the perceptual field. In 'Littérature et métaphysique' she explains that 'In the real world the sense of an object . . . unveils itself to us in the global relation that we maintain with it and that is action, emotion, sentiment . . .'[13] Like Kant, Beauvoir believes that human consciousness is part of this global relation, participating actively in structuring experience. But she moves away fundamentally from Kant's ontological ground. By 'consciousness' Beauvoir means the consciousness of the individual existent concretely situated – including the ambiguous unity between body and subject – and not Kant's disembodied universal subject.[14]

Whereas the empirical and Cartesian traditions attribute sense-data to the objective body and the data's interpretation to the 'mind' or subject, Beauvoir insists that there is only a single entity: embodied consciousness. In her view, it is this unity's shifting modes of existence which give rise to the confusion of dualism and to the possibility of the bad faith exhibited by Françoise. More than any other sense, touch expresses this ambivalent subject /object nature of the human body so central to Beauvoir's philosophical vision. For this reason, she sometimes loads her narratives with descriptions of tactile experiences.[15] Beauvoir identifies 'double touching', the touching of oneself, as especially revealing of the body's subject /object ambiguity. For this reason, 'Deux chapitres inédits de *L'Invitée*' features a masturbation scene, and *She Came to Stay* offers conspicuous examples of double touching, as when Xavière notes 'It's extraordinary the impression it makes on you to touch your eyelashes.'[16] Contact between any two parts of the body, where each part performs vis-à-vis the other both object and subject roles, can lead to awareness of the double-touching phenomenon, and thereby to the body's subject /object or transcendence/immanence ambiguity. But the body's dual nature becomes especially obvious when one's hand touches one's body hair, because the latter provides a physical distance between the two sensations, thereby accentuating their separateness.[17] Beauvoir's examples of Xavière's double touching reveal a further aspect of the body's subject /object split. While stroking a strand of her hair, Xavière watches 'the slow and steady movements of her fingers'.[18] Here, where vision as well as touch comes into play, the fingers perform subject and object roles for Xavière not alternately but simultaneously.

Beauvoir uses the specialized examples of touching as a way of bringing her readers to an initial awareness of the body's subject / object bimodality. To illustrate this relation more generally, and also to illustrate the transcendence/immanence split, she frequently shows her characters engaged in mirror-gazing and dancing, activities which spring directly from the subject /object and transcendence/immanence ambiguities. A person can view any part or the whole of their body in a mirror as merely an object in which they have a special interest. This is how Françoise, determined not to identify herself with her body, sees Françoise in the mirror.[19] She also finds mirrors largely an irrelevance, because they do not reflect the transcendence of consciousness. But the mirror offers another set of possibilities. Looking straight ahead, one's eyes can see themselves seeing themselves. One frowns, pulls a face, or looks askance and one sees this bodily subjectivity returned instantaneously as an object. Françoise observes that Xavière 'smiled to herself so mysteriously in mirrors'.[20] If the subject identifies strongly with their body, the individual may regard their reflection as an opening into their inner self. Xavière refuses to look at herself in a mirror in public places, but spends hours in front of the mirror when she is alone in her room. The looking-glass enchants by offering the illusion that consciousness crystallizes into body before one's eyes. In the spirit of play, dancing also celebrates the incarnation of consciousness. Dancers experience and present their bodies to others as simultaneously object and subject, making visible the experiential unity of consciousness and body. It is for this reason that there is so much dancing in Beauvoir's novel.

Beauvoir's dancers also illustrate her view that the body projects its own spatiality. But it is primarily through Françoise that Beauvoir demonstrates that space, like time, is not experienced primarily as a universal, or objective, or homogeneous phenomenon, that instead space is essentially relative and personalized, with human bodies engaged in projects acting as shifting reference points or poles around which physical space is organized. 'In the ordinary way,' writes Beauvoir, 'the centre of Paris was wherever she [Françoise] happened to be.'[21] It is this existential space centred on the psycho-physical body, rather than the independent set of points assumed by rationalism and empiricism, which Beauvoir identifies as the subject's broad sensory field.

In the middle of the novel Françoise ceases to personify philosophy's traditional disregard for the body, when she falls seriously ill and awakens to find her sweat-drenched pyjamas 'glued to her body'. Whereas before she had thought of herself as pure transcendence, she now experiences herself as 'just a body shivering with fever, without strength, without speech, even without thought'.[22] A month in a nursing home, during which she exists as a passive and bedridden body to which things happen (poultices, injections, temperature readings, X-rays) leaves her cured, in part, of her bad faith of transcendence.

Social Solipsism and Holistic Union

Beauvoir develops her theory of intersubjectivity in *She Came to Stay* by the same method she uses for her theory of embodiment. Through concrete analysis she shows that two opposing beliefs regarding the existence of other minds are untenable. One view, which presumes ontologically autonomous individuals, is personified by Françoise's relations with Xavière, and the other view, that of the quasi-mystical union of subjects, is represented by Françoise's relations with Pierre. At issue is the ancient philosophical question of the problem of other minds.

Almost without exception, people believe that other people are, like themselves, conscious beings. Moreover, far from being held passively, this belief influences many human actions.[23] Consequently, solipsism – the doctrine that other people do not have consciousness – lacks plausibility, and a philosophy which offers no argument for the existence of other minds appears radically incomplete. However, philosophical arguments for the existence of other minds remain astonishingly rare. Beauvoir (after 2,500 years of Western philosophy) faced only one argument for the existence of other minds which commanded broad philosophical respect. And even this argument is logically weak and existentially unconvincing. The argument in question is an argument from analogy, and therefore a very weak explanation of humankind's universal and unequivocal belief in the consciousness of others. John Stuart Mill's famous statement of the argument illustrates its weakness. He asks himself: 'by what considerations am I led to believe, that there exist other sentient creatures; that the walking and speaking figures which I see and hear, have sensations and thoughts, or in other words, possess Minds?' He answers as follows.

> I am conscious in myself of a series of facts connected by an uniform sequence, of which the beginning is modifications of my body, the middle is feelings, the end is outward demeanour. In the case of other human beings I have the evidence of my senses for the first and last links of the series, but not for the intermediate link. I find, however, that the sequence between the first and last is as regular and constant in those other cases as it is in mine. In my own case I know that the first link produces the last through the intermediate link, and could not produce it without. Experience, therefore, obliges me to conclude that there must be an intermediate link; which must either be the same in others as in myself, or a different one: I must either believe them to be alive, or to be automatons: and by believing them to be alive, that is, by supposing the link to be of the same nature as in the case of which I have experience, and which is in all other respects similar, I bring other human beings, as phenomena, under the same generalizations which I know by experience to be the true theory of my own existence.[24]

This argument may merit respect as a formal exercise in inductive reasoning, but that anyone, even John Stuart Mill, is really 'led to believe' in the existence of other minds primarily on the basis of such an analogy is unlikely.[25] Bertrand Russell, anticipating less generous readers than Mill's, presents the same argument more circumspectly. He writes: 'I am, of course, not discussing the history of how we come to believe in other minds . . . What I am discussing is the possibility of a postulate which shall establish a rational connection between this belief and data . . .'[26] Russell's attempt to isolate completely the question of other consciousnesses from ordinary human existence reflects the weakness of his position. Bracketing off the argument from the worldly phenomena which give rise to the question is not an acceptable philosophical procedure. More importantly, Russell's bracketing misses the primary question: what is the 'connection' or relation between a subject's experience and their belief in the consciousness of others?

The significance of this question is better understood by approaching the issues from a slightly different angle. The analogical avenue to the problem of other minds, though logically and existentially lightweight, comes heavily loaded with ideological freight, including, as will be explained later in this chapter, major methodological implications for the social sciences. This traditional approach to the other-minds-problem stems from the assumption, usually unstated, that people do not and cannot *experience* other people as conscious beings. It implies that although solipsism can be overcome at a highly abstract philosophical level, at the experiential level of personal and social relations solipsism remains an insurmountable fact of human existence. In other words, this doctrine holds that because consciousnesses cannot be perceived through any sensory mechanisms, a person has no means of experiencing or apprehending consciousnesses other than his or her own. This position can be called that of *social solipsism*.

Thus, although the social solipsist concludes that other people probably *are* conscious beings, he or she believes that, whatever people may infer and believe about other people, they can *experience* each other *only* as complex mechanisms, or, in Mill's word, as automatons. By observing people's bodies, acts and signs, individuals learn various manoeuvres by which, like jukeboxes or personal computers, other people can be manipulated. But the relation of philosophers, even analytical ones, to this position is decidedly ambivalent. Russell's remarks imply that on some level (one which he dissociates from his role as a philosopher), he believes that human relations are founded on more than just sensory experience, that is, on more than just spatio-temporal phenomena. In her theory of intersubjectivity, Simone de Beauvoir seeks to bridge this gap between the private belief of philosophers on these matters and the theories they expound.

But the refutation of social solipsism is only half – although by far the most important half – of what Beauvoir sets out to achieve through her portrayal and analysis of the interpersonal relations of her character Françoise in *She Came to Stay*. In polar opposition to social solipsism stands the belief that two or more individuals can merge their consciousnesses into a single entity. We will call this position *holistic union*. Through the writings of Martin Heidegger and through the rise of German Nazism, the notion that consciousnesses could be or were unified into a larger whole enjoyed special prominence at the time Beauvoir was planning and writing her novel. In *Being and Time*, Heidegger argued for the *a priori* existence of an 'ontological solidarity', a being-with, a predestined collective consciousness, racially and geographically oriented ('blood and soil'), and to which individual consciousnesses were, at best, subordinate. Later this idea became a key ingredient of Nazi ideology.

She Came to Stay takes place against the backdrop of historical embodiments of these two oppositional ideas of relations between consciousnesses: that is, between the ideas of holistic union and of social solipsism. The novel projects as its background, on the one hand, the rising spectre of Nazism, and on the other, the inability of the liberal French bourgeoisie, represented by the novel's five principal characters, to coalesce enough as a group to offer effective resistance to it. Beauvoir uses the relationship between Françoise and Pierre as her test case of holistic union.

Subjects and Objects

The French edition of *She Came to Stay* has an epigraph: 'Each consciousness pursues the death of the other.' The quotation comes from Hegel's parable of 'The Master and the Slave', which portrays a struggle between the consciousnesses of two radically unequal individuals. As a philosopher, Beauvoir is the antithesis of Hegel in most respects. Hegel's approach is metaphysical rather than concrete; he presumes himself to be possessed of a universal point of view; he regards the human subject as self-identical; and, ultimately, he sees the relations between his master and slave as part of the grand plan of the Absolute. Hegel also does not attempt to explain individuals' comprehension of the existence of other consciousnesses. Nevertheless, his famous parable, because it describes the *interaction* of two consciousnesses, is suggestive, with post-Beauvoirian hindsight, of a new approach to the problem of the existence of other minds. In prefacing *She Came to Stay* with the quotation from Hegel, Beauvoir not only signals her novel's murderous plot, but also tries to establish a lineage, however tenuous, for its most important thesis.[27]

As noted, the problem of other minds was for centuries bewitched by the tacit assumption that if there was no direct external (that is, sensory) relation between consciousnesses, then there could be no direct relation at all. But it is not only the minds of other people which cannot be perceived. Neither can one see, hear, smell, taste or feel one's *own* consciousness, so that if 'knowledge' and 'experience' include only what is obtained through the five senses, it follows that one lacks experiential knowledge of the existence of one's own mind no less than of the minds of others. Insistence on logical consistency here undermines one of the two terms of the argument from analogy for other minds, that is, knowledge of one's own mind. Beauvoir, however, takes her awareness of the non-sensory basis of her 'knowledge' of her own mind in a more positive direction. For Beauvoir, consciousness is (though not always) self-aware and capable of reflection. These two modes of consciousness, self-awareness and reflection, afford individuals the ability to 'observe' changes in their states of consciousness. Beauvoir's method of research involves looking for changes in conscious states which can be explained only by a *direct* or *internal* relation between her consciousness and the consciousness of another person.

Beauvoir locates the solution to the problem of other minds in the structure of social solipsism. At the beginning of the novel, Françoise personifies this position in her relations with Xavière. Françoise works at keeping herself persuaded that, rather than apprehending Xavière's consciousness, she knows of its existence only indirectly through inferences based on sensory observations of Xavière's body. This metaphysical position includes an honouring of Xavière's existence only as a physical object of Françoise's consciousness. She equates Xavière's immediate experiential relation to her with that of any sensory phenomenon, for example, the taste of coffee, the sound of music.[28] Françoise even equates the reality of Xavière's past, present and future life with her body and its place in Françoise's visual field.[29] Likewise, she seeks to persuade herself that she experiences Xavière's emotions, even when directed towards her, as purely sensory, in this case visual, phenomena.

> Her cheeks were flushed with anger. Her face was extremely attractive, with such subtly variable shadings that it seemed not to be composed of flesh, but rather of ecstasy, of bitterness, of sorrow, to which the eye became magically sensitive.[30]

In principle, an observer of another person – such as Mill in his argument from analogy for the existence of other consciousnesses – may find the roles reversed and discover his or herself as the other's object, a process called *objectification*. But, by definition, an inanimate object is incapable of making someone its object, and therefore the experience of objectification implies the existence of another consciousness. Consequently, both the relevance of Mill's analogical argument and the maintenance of Françoise's social solipsism depend on not undergoing this type of experience or recognizing its possibility. Philosophy generally has been loath to admit the ontological reciprocity of subject / object relations between individuals when considering the problem of other consciousnesses. Thus it seems philosophically significant that in *The Second Sex* Beauvoir identifies the refusal to recognize the possibility of subject / object reciprocity between the sexes as the basis of women's oppression. If it is granted that this is an essential characteristic of patriarchy, then philosophy's refusal to consider the possibility of the *objectification* of the male philosopher–observer may be read as an example of how social structures can condition what society comes to or refuses to recognize as knowledge. Likewise, as a *woman* philosopher approaching this ancient problem, Beauvoir did not suffer from the same ideological inhibitions as her male colleagues.

Beauvoir seeks to discredit the doctrine of social solipsism by demonstrating the possibility of experiencing oneself as another's object and showing that this experience is not reducible to sensory phenomena. But what, other than sensory data, can be the basis of an 'experience' of something outside one's consciousness? Far from posing a problem for Beauvoir, this question throws the strength, originality and elegant simplicity of her argument into relief. Like any philosopher approaching the problem of other minds, Beauvoir begins with two categories of being: non-conscious being and conscious being. From considering these she hopes to conclude whether or not the category of conscious being includes beings beside herself. Whereas philosophers traditionally approach the problem of other minds with the tacit assumption that the same and only the same order of knowledge pertains to both orders of being, in *She Came to Stay* Beauvoir adopts the idea that different orders of being entail different orders of knowledge as her working hypothesis. Through her characters, she entertains the possibility that people do not experience other people as conscious in the same sensory way that they experience oranges as orange, lemons as sour, rock and roll as loud. This means searching for changes in the state of consciousness, especially Françoise's, which result from relations with another person or persons but which are not attributable to sensory input, and which, therefore, can only be explained as arising from an internal relation between consciousnesses.

The Internal Relation

She Came to Stay begins with Françoise's revelation that sometimes her social solipsism is overwhelmed, that sometimes she is rendered terrified by 'the impression of no longer being anything but a figment of someone else's mind'.[31] Françoise's project, rather than exhibiting the good faith of trying to come to terms with the subject / object duality of her existence, shows bad faith in trying to maintain the illusion that she exists only as a subject. It is for this reason that she assiduously avoids awareness of her body, it being through her body as an object in another person's visual field that she (and every subject) most frequently experiences objectification.

As the plot progresses, and against her will, Françoise undergoes ever more frequent and prolonged bouts of objectification, until at last she fully acknowledges the direct relation between her and other people's consciousnesses, especially Xavière's. Beauvoir describes concrete individual experiences involving changes in states of consciousness, changes which cannot be explained on the basis of reflection and sensory perception alone. Categories examined include instances of embarrassment, of pride and, especially, of experiencing oneself as judged by another consciousness. Beauvoir also provides lengthy analyses of the more prolonged intersubjective relations of love, hate, desire, seduction, masochism and sadism, all of which presuppose the existence of another consciousness.[32]

The long process of disabusing Françoise of her social solipsism begins with her embarrassment in the dance hall on becoming aware that Xavière is observing her 'with a curious smile on her face'.[33] A flush of sudden shame or pride on finding oneself at the end of a critical or admiring *gaze* represents the archetypal subject / object reversal. Everyone (even John Stuart Mill) has *experienced* these fundamental yet instantaneous modifications of the state of consciousness. In these moments when one is caught in another's gaze, one undergoes a sudden shift from experiencing oneself as the centre of reference around which the world is organized, to experiencing oneself as an object in the world organized by another person, of 'seeing' the image of oneself in another person's eyes. The other person, as Merleau-Ponty explains, has 'the power to decenter me, to oppose his centering to my own' and 'to be a mirror of me as I am of him'.[34] These transformations are not independent structures of the subject's consciousness, nor can they be derived from the other person's status as object. They only can be explained as instances of a *causal relation internal to two people's consciousnesses*, that is, as *intersubjective* experiences. This asymmetrical *subject / object relation* became the basis of Beauvoir's social theory.

But for the determined social solipsist, like Françoise, these are only fleeting moments to be avoided. Her illusion of a world free of intersubjectivity is supported by her illusion that she and Pierre are one, that they comprise a holistic union. The interdependency of Françoise's two positions enables Beauvoir to refute them simultaneously. Beauvoir's line of attack on the illusion of holistic union is to explore this case of two individuals, Françoise and Pierre, who consider themselves 'to be one'. The argument's implicit logic is that if holistic union is impossible between two individuals (that is, in its simplest case), then it must be impossible with more than two. The novel begins with Françoise and Pierre believing that they have achieved total union of their consciousnesses. '"You and I are simply one,"' says Pierre to Françoise. '"That's the truth, you know. Neither of us can be described without the other."' Françoise concurs, '"We are simply one."'[35] She even believes that 'misunderstanding with Pierre was impossible,' and that between them 'there was but one life and at its core but one entity, which could be termed neither he nor I, but we.'[36]

The first serious cracks in Françoise's illusions of holistic union with her partner and of social solipsism with everyone else appear when, 'without warning', Pierre, in support of Xavière's opinion that the creation of art is too much trouble, abandons a view he and Françoise have long shared (that the creation of beauty in art is the most important thing in the world). Subsequently, when Xavière ridicules some of the principles by which Françoise lives, Françoise finds herself 'struck by the indictment. Usually, Xavière's insinuations left her cold; but tonight it was a different matter. The attention Pierre was paying to Xavière's opinions lent them weight.' Françoise's crisis grows in the course of the evening. She not only becomes aware that she and Pierre do not view Xavière 'in the same light', but she also hears Pierre tell Xavière that he and Françoise are 'two distinct individuals'.[37] No longer able to treat Xavière's opinions as mere objects in her (Françoise's) world, she now begins to experience herself as the object of Xavière's hostile thoughts. By the end of the evening Xavière-as-subject, as-a-being-who-could-make-Françoise-experience-herself-as-an-object, has been born. And, concomitantly, Françoise-as-object. Even after retiring to bed with Pierre, Françoise's growing awareness that other people's consciousnesses can impact directly on her own continues to haunt her. Thinking of Xavière in the room below thinking of her, Françoise concludes *on the basis of her experience of objectification* that there is no sense in continuing to deny that as a conscious being 'Xavière did exist.'[38]

Françoise can 'no longer simply close her eyes and blot out Xavière' because she no longer sees Xavière solely as a complex mechanism. Françoise apprehends that, whether she likes it or not, she *is* as Xavière, another person, sees her. Françoise has become for herself a self which another self knows. In this way Xavière has entered into Françoise's being, her-being-for-Xavière. Françoise, the social solipsist, is incapacitated, unable to convince herself that *her* experience of this other person's perceptions of her are reducible to sensory phenomena, that the other person's thoughts are merely 'objects' in her world. Later in the novel, an attempt by Françoise to resuscitate her social solipsism in the face of Xavière's hatred brings out the sublime ridiculousness of this metaphysic.

> 'And if she hates me, what then?' she thought defiantly. Was it not possible to consider Xavière's hatred exactly as she did the cheese-cakes on a plate? . . . Xavière's small round head did not occupy much more space in the world, it could be enveloped in a single glance; and if this haze of hatred issuing from it in clouds could only be forced back into its container, then it, too, could be kept under control. She had only to say the word, and, with the sound of crumbling plaster, the hatred would dissolve into a cloud of dust, to be perfectly contained in Xavière's body, and become as harmless as the familiar taste hidden under the yellow cream of the cakes.[39]

It must be understood that social solipsism entails a double concealment: of the other as subject and of oneself as object. Therefore, in the weeks following her initial crisis, as Françoise slowly emerges from her position of bad faith, she not only becomes sensitive to other people's power to cast her in the role of object, but also gains awareness of the various forms her objectivity takes in this world of intersubjective phenomena. Sitting in a nightclub again, she no longer perceives herself as a 'naked consciousness in front of the world', but rather as *in* and *part* of the world, as 'a woman among other women', and with a face which other people see and judge. Simultaneously, Françoise progresses towards realizing that her relation with Pierre is intersubjective, not intrasubjective; that she cannot really know what goes on in his mind, what exactly lies behind his words and smiles; that unobstructed communication and transparency of language are illusions; that his and her embodiment condemns them to different places in space, different vantage points on the world; that they can never really see things in the same way. She even finds herself 'keeping up appearances' in front of him.[40]

'Henceforth', writes Merleau-Ponty in his analysis of Beauvoir's novel, 'Françoise can no longer know herself from inner evidence alone. She can no longer doubt that, under the glance of that couple [Pierre and Xavière], she is truly an object, and through their eyes she sees herself from the outside for the first time.'[41] Françoise also comes to realize that her existence as an object in the world includes her membership in social categories, categories which can be defined at the whim of subjects and which cast their members as types, associating with them the indefinite article. Along with the 'past that she dragged along behind her', Françoise struggles to come to terms with this aspect of her immanence.[42]

Beauvoir portrays the process by which Françoise becomes sensitized to experiencing herself as an object as gradual and progressive. Her embarrassment at the end of a disrespectful look and her objectification as a consequence of casual conversation are steps towards regaining an awareness of other minds, like the step she took in the novel's original opening chapter when as a child she felt herself an object even when the subject was absent from the room. As always, Beauvoir's examples contain implicit appeals to the reader, asking if they too have known similarly structured experiences. One of Beauvoir's original examples of objectification – Pierre experiencing shame while peeking through Xavière's key-hole – is especially famous, it being much used by other philosophers. But Beauvoir's use of her example is particularly provocative. Pierre experiences shame with no one witnessing him and with no one in particular in mind.[43] This episode echoes earlier ones with Pierre's sister Elisabeth, who is given to experiencing herself as the object of an indeterminate public. Françoise's, Pierre's and Elisabeth's experiences in which they apprehend themselves as objects for an impersonal other indicate that Beauvoir's identification of an internal relation between consciousnesses has theoretical implications that extend far beyond the personal and into the broadest social realms.

The Blood of Others

In her second novel, *The Blood of Others* (1945), Beauvoir projects her theory of an internal relation between consciousnesses on to a broader social canvas. Her journals show that she conceived of this novel, which was to be her first commercial success (thirty-two printings in two years), as a logical progression in the development of her theory of intersubjectivity. She writes, probably in January 1941, that whereas *She Came to Stay* investigated 'the relation of the psychological to the metaphysical', she wants in her next novel to explore the relation 'of the *social to the metaphysical*', and also to illustrate the individual's metaphysical relation to others 'in its existential complexity'. Her methodology commits her to begin from 'a particular case' of the 'subject–object relation', and by late January 1941 she had opted for an instance of 'unshared love'.[44]

The principal characters in this love story are Jean Blomart and Hélène Bertrand. The novel opens late at night with Jean at the bedside of the dying Hélène. Paris is under German occupation, and Hélène has been wounded carrying out a mission for the Resistance. Jean, the resistance group's leader, must make a harrowing ethical decision by dawn. With that decision, and Hélène's death, the novel ends.

The narrative includes a number of different chronological sequences, their interaction mirroring what Beauvoir sees as the intersubjectivity of humankind. These narrative sequences divide into two primary strands, Jean's and Hélène's, and take up alternate chapters. Jean's narrative is written in the first person, but includes passages in which he designates his past self as 'he'. These third-person passages within first-person sections exemplify Beauvoir's theories of the subject/object split and of the impermanency of self. As Elizabeth Fallaize notes, the 'effect of this technique is consequently to reinforce by yet another means, the idea that our lives are lived as both subject and object, as personal experience and yet inserted in a wider social and political perspective.'[45] For example, with this technique Beauvoir shows simultaneously both the failure of Jean as a factory owner's child (and, by implication, members of dominant groups generally) to comprehend the objective side of his social being, and his possibility of overcoming this failing.

> He [Jean] was present, but at first he did not know it. I [Jean] see him now, leaning against a window in the gallery. But he did not know it, he thought that only the world was present. He was looking at the begrimed skylight through which the smell of ink and dust rose in gusts, the smell of other people's work . . . He did not know that through the fanlight, when they raised their heads, the workmen could see the solemn, fresh face of a middle-class child.[46]

As in *She Came to Stay*, in *The Blood of Others* the two central characters are, initially, metaphysical opposites. Whereas Hélène is portrayed as bounding from one pattern of bad faith of immanence to another, Jean, now in his early thirties, has long enjoyed a clean bill of existential health. His problem is an intellectual one, for which, like Hélène's bad faith, he has arrived at various false solutions over time. He recognizes his responsibility for his own acts, the necessity of respecting the freedom of others and the need to ethically reassess each new situation. From youth onwards he has been much concerned – even obsessed – with the consequences which his personal existence has for others. He possesses what Hazel Barnes describes as the awareness 'that by each choice he is affecting the arrangement of the world within which others will make their choices.'[47] This leads him to abandon his class, including his prerogatives in his family's printing firm, in favour of employment as a common typesetter, 'a worker amongst other workers'.[48] Jean joins the Communist Party, aiming to improve the socioeconomic conditions of others through active and unmitigated interventionism. But when a friend is killed in a demonstration, Jean is horrified at the consequences of his political engagement and he enters a long period of non-involvement, which extends to his personal life. This phase continues until Hélène's pregnancy (not by Jean), and the Nazi occupation of Paris leads him to a deeper understanding of the nature of freedom in a world comprised of interconnected subject-beings.

By the time of Hélène's deathbed vigil, Jean's ethics and social metaphysics are Beauvoir's. He believes that the human condition is essentially and unavoidably intersubjective; that this imposes on each individual responsibility for the freedom of others; that no individual's acts and choices (including abstention) are without adverse effects on the freedom of others; that the consequences of our actions escape us; and that our responsibilities to others must be carried out within these limits. From this ethical perspective, and with Hélène now dead, Jean decides to send another friend on a dangerous mission.

Jean's hypersensitivity to the interconnectedness of human destinies, and especially to the impact of his own being on that of others, is counterbalanced initially by Hélène's disregard for the consequences of her choices on other people and her lack of any sense of social responsibility. Hélène's narrative charts her conquest of bad faith, her eventual winning of Jean's love, her realization of the dependence of her freedom on that of others and of her responsibilities thereto, and, finally, her willing ultimate sacrifice. Beauvoir explains Hélène's moral conversion as brought about by three instances of her objectification: the reproachful stare of a child while waiting in line for petrol needed to flee the invading Germans; the image in a mirror of herself dancing with a German and the realization that this was how she looked to the French; and, finally, when she imagined her Jewish friend Yvonne's 'look fixed upon her and she was horrified with shame'.[49]

Whereas, for Beauvoir, *She Came to Stay* was the culmination of a decade of research into the problem of the existence of the Individual Other, *The Blood of Others* was her first systematic effort to explore the broad social aspects of her prior discoveries, an exploration which would lead directly to *The Second Sex* and which would occupy her for the rest of her life. That this has become such fertile ground for social research, not just for Beauvoir but for many and increasing numbers of others, stems from the way the internal subject/object relation challenges the two traditional methodologies of the social sciences. The next section examines this challenge, including the part played by the African-American intellectual heritage in the formation of Beauvoir's later thought.

Intersubjective Social Theory

With the exception of Adam Smith's *The Wealth of Nations*, no social science text has had so much influence, both in thought and in social practice, as Beauvoir's *The Second Sex*. This remarkable success, however, tends to obscure the profoundly original social metaphysics on which Beauvoir based this and other works. To appreciate the significance of this side of her contribution requires a rough understanding of the two diametrically opposed schools of metaphysics which have long dominated social thought.

In the social sciences, social solipsism and holistic union have their methodological corollaries. In fact, for over a century an acrimonious debate has raged between the partisans of these two systems of social metaphysics, that of methodological individualism and that of methodological holism. This split, which shows no signs of disappearing, centres on the nature of social explanation. A recent journal article on methodology in the social sciences illustrates the temper and substance of the dispute and summarizes the 'individualist' position. The article defines individualism as the principle that all social phenomena are by definition explicable solely in terms of individual human beings, each of whom (and here is the crux of the matter) 'is delimited as a unit by perfectly clear boundaries'. This view of the atomized individual is justified in the following manner: 'Persons, precisely, are individuated in an unambiguous way by being physically delimited in their bodily existence and by the persistence over time, from birth to death, of this unambiguous physical delimitation.'[50]

This justification, which is the standard one, begs the question. What is at issue is not the physical delimitation of individuals, but rather their delimitation as *social beings*. Methodological individualism's implicit postulate is the familiar one of social solipsism, that people experience each other only as complex physical mechanisms, that there exists no relationship between consciousnesses which makes the properties of individuals (such as, for example, consumer preferences) socially interdependent. Holism is merely methodological individualism stood on its head: individuals are explained in terms of their position in social wholes which are governed by macroscopic laws. This doctrine's paradox is that it cannot explain how social wholes can exist if there do not also exist parts which are in some sense – and, once again, not just physically – independent.

Without an agreed theory of intersubjectivity, no identifiable, let alone defendable, middle ground exists between the polar and often fanatical extremes of methodological individualism and holism. Beauvoir, probably more than any other thinker, takes up a position in this perilous no man's land. The internal subject / object relation she identified and then explored in her fiction supplies the elusive ontological basis for a structured, non-mystical account of intersubjective phenomena, not just between two individuals but across the full range of social relations, including those of the broadest social categories. When it is in play, Beauvoir's intersubjective social theory tends to invisibility, because, beyond its subject / object relation, it requires no additional conceptual baggage. This elegance stems from the peculiar properties of the internal subject / object relation.

Because conscious beings are open to the experience of objectification, that is, to becoming the object term of the subject /object relation, the boundaries of no individual's being can ever be unambiguously delimited. As Hazel Barnes notes, in *The Blood of Others*, when Hélène encounters her reflection as she dances with a German, she undergoes 'a self-revelation through the eyes of others'.[51] Merleau-Ponty too emphasizes this aspect of Beauvoir's theory of intersubjectivity:

> It is simply that all of our actions have several meanings, especially as seen from the outside by others, and all these meanings are assumed in our actions because others are the permanent coordinates of our lives. Once we are aware of the existence of others, we commit ourselves to being, among other things, what they think of us, since we recognize in them the exorbitant power to *see us*.[52]

Objectification means that the boundaries of an individual's being, far from having an independent existence, kaleidoscopically overlap with the boundaries of those people with whom one associates. Intersubjective experience, along with the intrinsic transcendence of consciousness, consigns individual being to a constant state of flux. In contrast, in terms of Beauvoir's theory of conscious being, equilibrium and unambiguous individuation are realized only with death.

As noted, Beauvoir begins her inquiry into intersubjectivity with cases where the two terms of the subject /object relation are individual conscious beings. But already in her earliest fiction her analysis extends to the situation where one term of the subject / object relation is an individual and the other a couple. Through the triangular structure of couples, Beauvoir demonstrates in her first novel not only the overlap of individual identities through the dynamically reversible subject /object relation, but also the kaleidoscopic overlap of exemplifications of the subject /object relation. Merleau-Ponty, in *The Visible and the Invisible*, on which he was working on at the time of his death in 1961, reflects on this aspect of *She Came to Stay*:

the problem of the other is not reducible to that of *the* other . . . since the relation with someone is always mediated by the relationship with third parties, that these have relationships among themselves that command those of *the* one and those of *the* other – and that this is so as far back as one goes toward the beginnings of life, since the Oedipus situation is still a triangular one.[53]

Through the permutations of subject and object pairings in her first novel, Beauvoir infers the general principle that two or more individuals may comprise the subject and/or object terms of the intersubjective relation.

Beauvoir widens the application of these principles in *The Blood of Others*, and in subsequent works extends her theory of intersubjectivity across the whole of the social realm, showing that *individuals-related-by-the-subject / object-relation* is not only the foundation of collective phenomena, but also of a morphology of socioeconomic groups. *The Ethics of Ambiguity* considers the case of individuals who forego personal choice of values in favour of choosing the values of a social group. In doing so, they project themselves as objects of a socially constituted subjectivity, like Hélène dancing with the German, which may or may not have a direct presence in their lives.

Margaret A. Simons's recent work on Beauvoir's mid-1940s collaboration with the African-American novelist Richard Wright shows how this association helped Beauvoir carry her theory of intersubjectivity to its logical conclusion in *The Second Sex*. Beauvoir's extended tour of the United States in 1947, chronicled in *America Day by Day*, confronted her both with American racism and with Wright's hypothesis that race is primarily a construct of racism, that is, socially constituted. Before her conversations with Wright, Beauvoir seems not to have realized that her analysis of internal subject / object relations also applied to cases where both terms of the relation were large social groups. But Wright's view of the basis of differences between the races in America fitted so perfectly into Beauvoir's theory of intersubjectivity, and was so obviously a predication of intersubjective phenomena, that almost inevitably it acted for her as an intellectual catalyst.[54] Her application of the subject / object relation to the broadest of all pairs of social groups, men and women, immediately followed in *The Second Sex*. When the members of one group (in this case, women) internalize the other group's (in this case, men's) valuation of them, a subject / object relation exists between the groups that parallels the subject / object relation between individuals.

Even more than that of Beauvoir, the part Richard Wright played in the development of the concept of 'the Other', now a standard intellectual concept, has been excluded from the official record. Yet in *America Day by Day* Beauvoir carefully recorded Wright's arguments. Working with ideas available to African-American intellectuals at least since the time of Frederick Douglass's *Narrative* in 1845, Wright explained that the consciousness of a black person in America is, minute by minute, 'penetrated by a social conscious[ness]' which is that of 'the white man whence the word black derives its meaning'.[55] Under the gaze of white people, black people experienced themselves 'defined as the antithesis of American civilisation'.[56]

Wright's lesson was that an entire subnation of people could, and too much of the time did, experience themselves as not being 'anything but a figment of someone else's mind', as the object term of the subject/object relation, where they were always the negatively defined object. African-Americans were always construed as 'the Other' of the white majority consciousness, which, as the subject term of the intersubjective relation, penetrated their consciousness and defined their being. Wright's and Beauvoir's message is that *the position of oppressed peoples cannot be understood without an appreciation of these intersubjective phenomena*. For this reason, social solipsism, especially as manifested by social scientists who practise methodological individualism, is an innately oppressive ideology, in that it denies the reality of the intersubjective experience by which, among other means, women and racial minorities are kept in inferior positions.

Intersubjectivism's subject/object relation is asymmetrical. If X is the relation's subject term, then X is not the object term, and vice versa. But it is also the case that the asymmetry is inherently reversible. X may cause Y to experience herself as X's object, but Y may subsequently do the same to X. This property of reversibility, especially when coupled with the intentionality of consciousness, makes intersubjective social theory integrally dynamic. The property of reversibility also means that the direction of explanation or of causality between the two terms of the relation may change. When one term is an individual and the other a group, the relation's reversible asymmetry opens up the middle ground between methodological individualism and holism. The subject/object relation's bidirectionality makes both micro and macro explanations possible. Under the terms of *methodological intersubjectivity*, social and economic phenomena may, depending on the realities of the particular case rather than on methodological dogma, be explained either in terms of individual human beings or in terms of socioeconomic wholes.[57]

The methodological extremes of individualism and holism are predicated not only on ideological dogmas, but also on their shared lack of a method of analysing intersubjective experience. This discussion has tried to show how this lack is a direct correlative of philosophy's failure, prior to Beauvoir, to identify an internal relation between consciousnesses. But the history of the past half century shows that the subversiveness of Beauvoir's – and Wright's and many others' – intersubjectivism extends far beyond the academy and its traditional modes of thought. By offering intellectual understanding of the processes of liberational change, intersubjective theory has proven highly subversive of social hierarchies (for example, colonialism, racism, sexism). The expanding awareness of the subject/object relation's efficacy in human affairs has fostered development among 'object classes' of strategies of de-objectification, of turning away from the subject group's cultural gaze so as to recentre and recreate cultural narratives, of 'building up a solid counter-universe', as Beauvoir puts it in *The Second Sex*, in order to reclaim subjectivity and to objectify oppressors.[58]

6

The Ethics of Liberation

Introduction

Philosophical problems often lead philosophers to group around contrary positions, which, if no middle ground is discovered or agreed, become more entrenched, dogmatic and self-enclosed with each generation. In previous chapters we considered how Beauvoir's works brilliantly pioneer defensible spaces in the broad philosophical centre on some main traditional battlegrounds: empiricism versus rationalism, the mind/body problem, the problem of other minds, and the problem of a methodology for the social sciences. Beauvoir's contribution to ethical theory is another such case.

Between 1942 and 1946 Beauvoir wrote two book-length essays on ethics. The first, *Pyrrhus et Cinéas*, was rushed into print following the Liberation of Paris in 1944, becoming a major vehicle for the introduction of 'Existentialism' to the French reading public.[1] Two years later, Beauvoir published the more developed *The Ethics of Ambiguity*. In this same period she wrote and published numerous other works focused on ethical problems, including the essays 'Idéalisme moral et réalisme politique' and 'Eye for Eye', the novels *The Blood of Others* and *All Men Are Mortal*, and the play *Who Shall Die?*[2] These works are all closely related, and all provide examples of Beauvoir's fully formed ethical thought.

Beauvoirian ethics has been highly influential in providing philosophical ballast for liberation movements, whose success was a salient feature of the decades following World War II. Her ethical theory is also remarkable philosophically for the extent to which it emerges, not from a basis of categorical premises or ad hoc position-taking, but rather as a logically coherent outgrowth of her ontology. Indeed, most of the facets of Beauvoir's philosophy explained in the preceding chapters form part of the derivation of her ethics. From her theory of consciousness she accounts for the origin of value. From her theories of embodiment and intersubjectivity she establishes the situational and social nature of freedom. And on the basis of these results, together with her theory of consciousness, including its two modes of intentionality, she develops her theory of social ethics. This chapter will examine these three sets of arguments.

The Origin of Value

In *Ethics: Inventing Right and Wrong*, J. L. Mackie notes the importance to modern ethics of 'the question whether values are or are not part of the fabric of the world'.[3] Philosophers who answer yes to this question are called 'cognitivists' because they attribute truth or falsity to judgements about values. Conversely, 'non-cognitivists' hold that ethical terms are not descriptive, and that the propositions which contain them are therefore neither true nor false.[4] For the non-cognitivists – and, like their opposite numbers they are an extremely diverse group – moral judgements are only recommendations or prescriptions or evocations or personal preferences or expressions of social conditioning. Beauvoir's ethics is distinguished by being situated between these two positions. She locates this middle ground and the ethics which she builds on it directly in the fundamental categories of her ontology.

In *Pyrrhus et Cinéas*, when Beauvoir asserts that no values exist in the world of non-conscious being before consciousness's putting them there, she is adopting, in part, the non-cognitivist position. But the way she arrives at this view is very much her own. In a passage reminiscent of her childhood encounter with the thingness of her jacket, she considers what it would be like to be a non-conscious being:

> If I was only a thing myself, indeed nothing would concern me; if I shut myself in, the other is also shut off to me; the inert existence of things is separation and solitude. There exists no ready-made attachment between the world and me. And in so far as I am within nature a simple given, nothing is mine.[5]

Without consciousness there can be no concern, and therefore no value. How then do values come into existence through consciousness?

In *Pyrrhus et Cinéas* Beauvoir argues that values, like transcendence, are inevitable consequences of consciousness's intentionality. Consciousness, as a binary relation projected from a human body, requires objects, other beings, for its other term. Without something to be conscious *of*, consciousness does not exist. It is in this sense that every act of consciousness is said to begin as a *lack* of being, and every 'transcendence of the given' as 'defining the present as a lack'.[6] Beauvoir identifies this lack, including a lack of justification for one's existence, as the ultimate basis of desire: consciousness emerges continuously as the project of overcoming its lack, of obtaining being. Beauvoir's hypothesis is that this goal-directed, justification-seeking spontaneity universally characterizes consciousness. The objects of consciousness and the concrete goals comprising a person's project of being, however, are a matter of their individual situation and choice. Within the limits of its worldly situation, a consciousness is intrinsically free, and this freedom requires continuous choices between alternative objects and goals. Beauvoir's ethical starting point is that it is on the basis of such choices, born of the situated freedom of consciousnesses, that all values, including self-justification, emerge in the world.

Beauvoir describes the human 'project' and the lack that haunts it as follows:

> Because my subjectivity is not inertia, not a falling back upon itself, nor a separation, but on the contrary a movement towards the other [being], the indifference between the other and myself is abolished and I can call the other mine; the link that unites me to the other can only be created by me; I create it by the fact that I am not a thing but a project of myself towards the other, a transcendence ... I am not first a thing, but a spontaneity which desires, loves, wants, acts.[7]

This view of desire and value begs to be compared (and Beauvoir herself makes this comparison) to the one which underpins the stylized notion of rationality, tendentiously called 'rational choice theory'. Although indigenous to economics, in recent decades this doctrine has colonized large parts of the social sciences and – as it is usually deployed – is a major subspecies of methodological individualism. On two separate accounts, Beauvoir's conception of desire and value reverses this currently influential mini-system of metaphysics. The latter conceives of the individual as possessed of an ordered set of desires or values, called 'preferences', and it labels an individual 'rational' or 'irrational' if her or his choices confirm or disconfirm this presumed ordering. Under this metaphysic, 'rational consumer choice', for example, is a euphemism for a kind of obedience to one's supposed essence, so that a person who takes this 'rational' approach to his or her self is an example of someone caught up in the bad faith of immanence.

Beauvoir's view of humankind does not admit a distinction between preferences and choices. One can be 'irrational' in the sense of not choosing what people in authority would like other people to choose, or in the sense of miscalculating or misremembering the most efficient way to a goal, or in the sense of exercising one's freedom to make different choices at different points in time, but not in the sense of not choosing what one prefers. For Beauvoir, the last is both an ontological impossibility and a contradiction in terms.

Beauvoir's view of the nature of individual desires also reverses that of rational choice theory. The latter conceives of human beings primarily as objects, as receptors of sensations. Men and women are inclined to rise above this passive state only in so far as they hope to increase their pleasurable sensations and decrease their painful ones. In consequence, the universal goal is 'to have everything one wants', to exist in a state where every desire is satisfied, to abide in contented, heaven-like repose. Beauvoir takes the opposite view. She conceives of the human as active, as a spontaneity engaged ceaselessly in a project, as a being whose consciousness endlessly casts itself into the world towards something, as 'a transcendence which throws itself towards the future'. The sensations of pleasure are not experienced separately from a person's projected existence. Persons do not become radically different kinds of being when they experience enjoyment. For Beauvoir, 'All pleasure is project.'[8] She illustrates this principle as follows:

> the pause is relaxation after the fatiguing exercise; from the summit of the hill I view the path travelled and it is present in its entirety in the joy of my success, it is the walk which gives value to this rest, and my thirst which gives value to this glass of water.[9]

This argument leads to a more general point: it is not possible 'to separate the end from the project that defines it and recognize in it an inherent value'.[10] Against conventional belief, in her analysis of the structure of human consciousness Beauvoir finds: 'It is desire which creates the desirable, and the project which sets up the end.'[11] She accuses those who pretend that values exist in the world before and without human beings, as if values were there to be gathered like pebbles on the beach, of the bad faith of immanence, of being guilty of a 'false objectivity'. Similarly, she labels the opposite practice of trying 'to separate the project from the end and reduce it to a simple game' as 'false subjectivity'.[12]

Beauvoir emphasizes the significance her theory of desire holds for the conduct of political affairs, where the separation of ends from means, as postulated for example by the economist's sensationalist theory of desire, provides the rationalization in whose name most modern crimes against humanity have been and continue to be committed. In 'Idéalisme moral et réalisme politique', an essay from 1945, Beauvoir writes:

> that which it is necessary to understand is that end and means form an indissoluble totality; the end is defined by the means which receive from it their meaning, an action is a significant whole which deploys itself through the world, through time, and of which the unity can not be broken. It is this singular totality that it is a matter at each instant of constructing and choosing.[13]

For Beauvoir, although the projective nature of the human being is ontologically determined, the form the project takes is not. The goals and subgoals by which lack of being is to be filled are neither given nor fixed. Out of consciousness's freedom, people create and choose their goals minute after minute, and it is through these choices, Beauvoir argues, that values are injected into the world. They are generated inexorably by the intentional structure of consciousness, by the way consciousness engages with the world, so that in this sense values are, like the lack or non-being which gives rise to them, objective and ever-present. Values are not an optional extra to be added to human existence. They are as much a part of the fabric of the world *one lives in* as the sun and the earth. This is the 'ambiguity' of the human condition: we exist simultaneously in the objective and the subjective, the one inseparable from the other.

'Freedom', Beauvoir writes in *The Ethics of Ambiguity*, 'is the source from which all significations and all values spring. It is the original condition of all justification of existence.' By crediting human freedom as the source of all value, Beauvoir remarks that, in one sense, she 'carries on the ethical tradition of Kant, Fichte, and Hegel'. But she also notes that, in another sense, her analysis of freedom and value differs radically from that of her precursors. In setting out her ethics, she, unlike the philosophers she has listed, makes no false appeal to the universal. She remains faithful to her self-imposed injunction not to feign access to a universal point of view. Likewise, she reminds her reader that: 'Universal, absolute man exists nowhere.' In her ethics, she writes, 'it is not impersonal universal man who is the source of values, but the plurality of concrete, particular men [and women] projecting themselves toward their ends on the basis of situations whose particularity is as radical and as irreducible as subjectivity itself.'[14] Elizabeth Fallaize notes that in these circumstances, '"Humanity" consists not of a totality aspiring to the same aim . . . but of a mass of individuals each with his or her own freedom and aspirations.'[15] This generative structure for value is homologous to Beauvoir's theories of temporality and spatiality. We have noted Beauvoir's explanation of how human bodies engaged in projects act as shifting reference points around which physical space is organized. Here her argument is that an individual's engagement with the world also leads her or him to create ever-shifting fields of value.

In common with other existentialists, Beauvoir identifies the subject's non-self identity as giving rise to anxiety and, in turn, to the seeking of justification for their existence. This means establishing and embracing values. But, given that these values do not exist independently of human consciousness, it is Beauvoir's thesis that values come into being only through the projects which a person freely chooses. A freely adopted goal is itself a declaration of the existence of a value. This makes a person's values, and thereby justification of their existence, ultimately dependent on their freedom. Beauvoir gives this as the reason why a person might choose to embrace their freedom rather than the bad faith of immanence. In any case, if freedom is the source of all values, and if a person values anything, then it follows that she values her freedom.

The Structure of Freedom

'Freedom' is a notoriously slippery word, especially in the hands of philosophers. Beauvoir embarked on a hazardous path when she developed an ethics in which freedom was the concept around which everything turns. That she succeeded in inventing an ethics of freedom which both triumphs over philosophical banality (and confusion) and finds wide relevance in human affairs owes much to the care she took in theorizing its central concept. Three aspects of that theory need careful treatment here: freedom's situational nature; situations as more or less freedom-enhancing; and the interdependence of consciousnesses.

From the early 1940s onwards, Beauvoir emphasized the distinction between 'an abstract notion of freedom', one 'emptied of all content and all truth', and her concept of *freedom in situation*.[16] 'A man', she writes in *Pyrrhus et Cinéas*, 'is simultaneously freedom and facticity; he is free, but not in the sense of that abstract freedom expounded by the Stoics; he is free in situation.'[17] This view that freedom, like physical area, is a two-dimensional phenomenon, is central to Beauvoir's ethical and social thought. Everyone is originally free, in the sense that they always project themselves spontaneously into the world towards something through the intentionality of their consciousness. This is what Beauvoir calls 'the subjective and formal aspect' of freedom, because it follows from what she identified as the fundamental structure of consciousness.[18] But the Beauvoirian individual is also situated in a world of givens, including her own immanence. Her situation includes her past, her physical, historical and social place, her economic circumstances, her body, and her objectification by others, both as a unique individual and as a member of various recognized categories. On one hand, it is *against* these givens that imagined ends are intended by a consciousness (for example, eating a piece of chocolate cake which is now on the plate), and on the other, it is *by* these givens that ends are realized (for example, cutting and lifting a piece of the cake with a fork). It is this ability to change the given situation (getting the cake from the plate into one's mouth), rather than merely being able to dream of doing so, that Beauvoir means by 'freedom.'

The conception of the human being as project, as perpetual transcendence, is refreshingly immune to the excesses of utopianism. In terms of the Beauvoirian vision, a situation in which all desires are satisfied, in which all conditions are ideally perfect, is consistent only with death. Life requires dissatisfaction; success requires resistance. 'The resistance of the thing sustains the action of man as air sustains the flight of the dove.' Freedom becomes manifest as 'a movement of liberation' beyond something judged as limiting freedom itself.[19] Beauvoir's best state of affairs is not the apathy of contentment or the perfection of paradise, but rather the exhilaration that comes when situations yield to wilful exertions of freedom, and when goals which have been reached appear as points of departure for new acts of surpassing and for new values:

> The creator leans upon anterior creations in order to create the possibility of new creations. His present project embraces the past and places confi-

dence in the freedom to come, a confidence which is never disappointed. It discloses being at the end of a further disclosure. At each moment freedom is confirmed through all creation.[20]

By way of contrast Beauvoir considers the case of someone who persists in beating their fist against a stone wall. Here the individual's 'freedom exhausts itself in this useless gesture without succeeding in giving itself a content. It debases itself in a vain contingency.' The given situation, the stone wall, fails to destruct, so the person's project, with its chosen value and attempt at self-justification, collapses in on itself. This person would be well advised to choose a different goal. However, it is not uncommon for people to find themselves surrounded by stone walls, real and metaphorical, which have been erected by other people and which do not leave them the option of choosing other goals. Beauvoir considers their plight:

> In case his transcendence is cut off from his goal or there is no longer any hold on objects which might give it a valid content, his spontaneity is dissipated without founding anything. Then he may not justify his existence positively and he feels its contingency with wretched disgust.

Obviously, human situations vary greatly in terms of their congeniality to freedom in Beauvoir's sense. She calls a situation 'privileged' if it tends to permit a person to realize their goals indefinitely, and a situation one of 'oppression' if it cuts a person off from their goals.[21]

Beauvoir is especially interested in the part intersubjectivity plays in creating and sustaining situations of oppression between social groups. And her analysis of this aspect of intersubjectivity informs her work on women in *The Second Sex*, on the aged in *Old Age*, on race in *America Day by Day*, as well as major elements in her fiction. She identifies the subject /object relation between consciousnesses as the ontological foundation and generative basis of many socially asymmetrical situations. Members of oppressed object groups tend to internalize subject groups' negative objectification of them. But the intersubjective worlds conceived and described by Beauvoir which affect ethics extend much wider than this. Preconstituted spheres of intersubjectivity exist where one finds 'realities which resist consciousness and possess their own laws'.[22] People are thrown into these worlds of *collective intentionality*, wherein social habits and social hierarchies have assigned values and meanings to various objects and groups of people. Beginning as a child, one 'emerges in a world filled with meanings which impose themselves'. Each value and each individual's values take on their meaning within these cultural fields of values. In this way, says Beauvoir, her 'situation is defined through its relation to the society to which I belong'.[23] Collective intentionality even extends to specifying what kinds of characteristics do and do not count in defining and evaluating an individual. And, whatever the criteria, an individual is defined by herself and by others in relation to other individuals whose identities also are determined relative to others.[24] We each exist, in part, as the ongoing product of this interdependence of subjectivities.

The Ethics of Ambiguity identifies an extreme but not uncommon situation of intersubjective oppression where collective intentionality has succeeded in 'mystifying' the member of the oppressed group to such a degree that 'his situation does not seem to him to be imposed by men, but to be immediately given by nature, by the gods, by the powers against whom revolt has no meaning.'[25] As Sonia Kruks explains, because the Beauvoirian subject is 'intrinsically intersubjective', this kind of 'oppression can permeate subjectivity to the point where consciousness itself becomes no more than a product of the oppressive situation', and in this way 'situations can become conditions that impose their meaning on the subject.'[26]

But Beauvoir's vision of intersubjectivity has an alternative side. We have been considering its less optimistic side, whereby individuals and groups, engaged as terms of the subject/object relation, struggle with one another for, or concede, subjective domination. This is the mode of *subjection* in intersubjective relations. But the reversibility of the subject/object relation's asymmetry entails the possibility of a second mode, where the parties to the relation choose to treat each other and themselves both as subject and object, as equal freedoms which are simultaneously original sources of value and of meaning. Beauvoir calls this second mode of intersubjectivity, where the parties agree to alternate in serving as the subject and object terms, that of *reciprocity*. In *The Second Sex* she identifies 'exact reciprocity' as a situation where 'each is at once subject and object.'[27] Reciprocity pertains not only between individuals, and between groups (collective reciprocity), but also, as will be explained in the next section, between the individual and society and between groups and society (civic reciprocity). This second mode of intersubjectivity is a natural complement to Beauvoir's conception of freedom as situated and it assumes a central role in her social and ethical thought.

Historically, as Bob Stone notes in considering Beauvoir's ethics, it has been standard practice to view freedom as 'a sort of property or possession, that is, something I can *have* in isolation from everyone else'. Stone continues:

> But for Beauvoir I am not related to my freedom as a thing is to its properties since I am not a thing; rather, I *exist* my freedom as my own constant self-transcendence of my 'properties'. Indeed it is this perpetual intentionality within and toward the world and others that decides what 'self' and 'other' are to be. Thus understood, freedom is inherently opened onto other people.[28]

Linda Singer also notes the importance and originality of Beauvoir's 'sense of a freedom which realizes itself in engagement with and for others'. Commenting on the tradition of treating freedom 'as a quality or attribute of persons, rather than relationships', she says that Beauvoir's 'rewriting has the effect of shifting the locus of freedom from that of isolated autonomous individuals to freedom emergent from a situation of relatedness and affinity.'[29]

Social Ethics

The traditional map of moral philosophy is as ordered as a French formal garden. The map neatly splits between deontological theories, which hold that certain formal rules of conduct should be followed regardless of their consequences, and teleological theories, which hold that the moral worth of an act must be judged by its consequences. Beauvoir's disbelief in the existence of universal categoricals would seem to place her with the teleologists, who come in two varieties, the egoists and the universalists, or, as they usually are called, the utilitarians. The egoists hold that one should always do what will promote one's own greatest good, whereas the universalists believe that one should obey those moral rules which will bring the greatest good to the greatest number of people. Both groups contain many and diverse notions of what constitutes 'good' or the moral end. Popular foundational notions of the good include that of the greatest balance of pleasurable sensations over painful ones, that of self-realization, that of knowledge or power, as well as various assortments of these.

What is so noteworthy about moral philosophy's traditional landscape is that there is no room in it for Beauvoirian ethics. That there is no place for a woman's ethics in a design laid out exclusively by men and produced by patriarchal societies scarcely qualifies as surprising. Yet the manner in which Beauvoir's ethical theory differs from those of her male counterparts is, although profound, not immediately obvious. When considering philosophical ethics, thinkers formed within patriarchal ethics are conditioned to think of all human relations as originating in social solipsism or in the mode of subjection of intersubjectivity. Beauvoir's innovation was to develop an ethical discourse *founded* on the mode of reciprocity. One effect of this shift is to establish for ethics a domain free of the is/ought dichotomy. Beauvoir offers four arguments in support of respecting and promoting other people's freedom. Her arguments need to be explained on their own ground, to show how the ethical landscape they project differs from the traditional one.

The central thrust of Beauvoir's social ethics is that success in justifying and finding meaning for one's existence and in disclosing being is maximized in a world of free and equal individuals. 'Man can find a justification of his own existence only in the existence of other men.' Underpinning the whole of her case is her intersubjective hypothesis: 'The me–others relationship is as indissoluble as the subject–object relationship.'[30] The bare bones of her argument are as follows: we all rely on others for this justification and meaning and for the creation of cultural being; others can serve us in this way only to the extent that they are free; therefore, it is in our self-interest to guard and to promote the freedom of others. Beauvoir develops this case through the explication of four ways in which people's freedoms are reciprocal, that is, positively interdependent.

'A man alone in the world', says Beauvoir in *Pyrrhus et Cinéas*, 'would be paralysed by the manifest vanity of all his goals.' To reduce and make bearable the contingency of one's existence requires the validation by others of one's projects. 'Only the freedom of others can make necessary my being. My essential need is therefore to have free men facing me.' Because the other person's freedom is the source of that valuation, one must value the other person's freedom in order for her valuations to be seen as significant. To deny the value of someone's freedom is to deny oneself the validation which that freedom might otherwise provide.[31]

Beauvoir carries this argument further and develops it into one for equality. She notes that we value the valuations of our peers more than the valuations of those who are not our peers. It is only one's equals who can truly appreciate and understand one's existence:

Others can accompany my transcendence only if they are at the same point on the road as I. In order that our appeals [for justification] are not lost in the void, it is necessary to have near me men prepared to hear me; these men must be my peers.[32]

Therefore, it is in a person's self-interest to promote equality, to have free and equal subjects to valorize their existence. This principle not only holds obvious and radical implications for personal relations, but also extends, by way of the idea of the general interdependence of subjectivities, into the broadest social realms. For example, in denying women equal rights and opportunities, societies also deny most men the opportunity of sharing their lives with women they see as their equals. 'He would be liberated himself in their liberation,' notes Beauvoir of men in relation to women's freedom in *The Second Sex*, a work full of empirical detail regarding the material and social conditions which pertain to the project of obtaining freedom and equality for women. Similarly, Beauvoir's earlier *Pyrrhus et Cinéas* gives empirical content to her more general arguments for freedom and equality, especially by linking them with needs. 'For people I ask for health, knowledge, well-being, leisure so that their freedom is not consumed in fighting illness, ignorance, misery.' Similarly, doing violence to a person deprives us of their peership and, thereby, 'possibilities for expansion of our being'. Beauvoir's essay 'Eye for Eye' (1946) explores further the relation between violence and her ethical theory.[33]

Individuals also, argues Beauvoir, require the freedom of others if they are not to be devitalized by awareness of their individual finitude. A logical consequence of consciousness's intentionality is that the 'fact of transcendence precedes any end, any justification'. This is an elemental structure of human temporality which makes the justification of projects, beyond the satisfaction of basic biological needs, inherently problematic. If a project has no justification beyond itself, then its realization abolishes its justification. In 'the light of reflection, any human project seems absurd, because it only exists through the limits it assigns to itself.' For this reason 'A man alone in the world would be paralysed by the self-evident vanity of all his goals; he could not bear to live.'[34]

Twentieth-century literature has made the negative existential consequences of this structure of consciousness one of its central themes. (*The Stranger* (1942), by Beauvoir's friend and sometime colleague Albert Camus, is one celebrated example.) Beauvoir, however, argues that the malaise documented by Camus and others is allayed by an interlinking of the projects of free individuals across space and time. Women and men, she writes:

> are free and I am thrown into the world among these strange freedoms. I need them, because once I have surpassed my own goals, my acts will fall back upon themselves inert, useless, if they are not carried by new projects towards a new future . . . The movement of my transcendence appears vain to me as soon as I have transcended it; but if through others my transcendence prolongs itself always further than the project I presently form, I will never be able to surpass it . . .[35]

Beauvoir notes that a person's need for others to join them in their projects has practical implications.[36]

> The other's freedom can do nothing for me unless my own goals can serve as his point of departure; it is by using the tool which I have invented that the other prolongs its existence; the scholar can only talk with men who have arrived at the same level of knowledge as himself . . . I must therefore endeavour to create for all men situations which will enable them to accompany and surpass my transcendence. I need their freedom to be available to use me, to preserve me in surpassing me.[37]

Sonia Kruks notes that in *The Second Sex* Beauvoir extends her argument for the need for the interlinking of human projects to 'the perpetuation of the species', without which all linkage would cease. In this way Beauvoir sees 'the phenomenon of reproduction as ontologically founded'.[38]

Beauvoir identifies a reciprocity between the individual and civil society as another basis of personal freedom. In order for collective undertakings to have meaning, society must affirm at every opportunity the importance and even sacred character of its individual citizens, the dignity of each man, woman and child, taken one by one. 'This is what democratic societies understand,' writes Beauvoir, 'they strive to confirm citizens in the feeling of their individual value; the whole ceremonious apparatus of baptism, marriage, and burial is the collectivity's homage to the individual; and the rites of justice seek to manifest society's respect for each of its members considered in his particularity.' In return for being validated as 'a unique and irreducible value',[39] for having personal relations honoured, and for providing a framework in which freedom is secured, enhanced and celebrated, the individual offers reciprocation, ranging from extreme sacrifices in times of collective crises, to the daily consideration given to the well-being of one's immediate civic environment. Having experienced the onslaught of

Fascism and watched the rise and spread of communist states, Beauvoir was especially sensitive to the perils of breaking the civic covenant between individuals and of the allure of the rhetoric of holistic union. Her play *Who Shall Die?* (1945) addresses the question of what happens when people fail to observe civic reciprocity.

In chapter 4 we noted Beauvoir's theory that the intentionality of consciousness has two modes: the desire to be and the desire to disclose being. The present chapter has considered three ways in which people's freedoms are reciprocal, that is, positively interdependent: firstly, through mutual validation; secondly, through the interlinking of projects; and thirdly, through civil society. Each of these pertains primarily to the mode of intentionality of the desire-to-be. But the fourth category of reciprocity relates fundamentally to the desire for disclosure of being. In *The Ethics of Ambiguity* Beauvoir identifies this mode of intentionality as our 'original type of attachment to being', but argues that in the confusion of life, the desire for disclosure is subsumed in the desire to be.[40] Or, as Debra Bergoffen usefully puts it, it is 'contextualized' in terms of the projects of the desire to be.[41] Beauvoir says that wanting freedom and desiring being 'are two aspects of a single reality. And whichever be the one under consideration, they both imply the bond of each man with all others.' Why? Because in a civilized world this being which consciousness desires is mostly humanly made. This is the case not just in a material or economic sense, but, more importantly, in cultural and interpersonal ones. We all live in worlds in which each object, even the moon and the stars, 'is penetrated with human meanings. It is a speaking world from which solicitations and appeals rise up.' One's own freedom, properly informed, wants freedom for others so that they can join in the creation of the being which consciousness desires. 'To will that there be being is also to will that there be men by and for whom the world is endowed with human significations. One can reveal the world only on a basis revealed by other men.' As Bergoffen notes, the 'desire of disclosure is also the ethical will of liberation.' As Beauvoir stresses, 'To want existence, to want to disclose the world, and to want men to be free are one and the same will.'[42]

In patriarchal societies men seek the domination of women. Such societies, by definition, make the mode of subjection of intersubjectivity their archetypal mode of human relations, that is, the one not only demanded between men and women, but also favoured generally. (The same point would hold, in principle, for matriarchal societies.) It seems wholly natural, therefore, that such a society's systems of and discourses on ethics should be predicated on the mode of subjection in human affairs. Indeed, it would be most unexpected for such societies to promote awareness of the non-essentiality on which their ethical discourse was predicated, as this would call directly into question the fundamental relation on which those societies depend for their continued existence. It is for these very plain reasons that ethics, in Western philosophy, has consisted primarily of declaring limits to or rationalizing the subjection of one's fellow human beings.

Philosophical ethics is traditionally pursued as the study of systems of restraints on conduct. This negative outlook is captured well by J. L. Mackie when, after having surveyed 'the object of morality' as manifested by philosophers through the ages, he sums up his findings as follows:

> Protagoras, Hobbes, Hume and Warnock [G. L.] are all at least broadly in agreement about *the problem that morality is needed to solve*: limited resources and limited sympathies together generate both competition leading to conflict and an absence of what would be mutually beneficial cooperation.[43]

Of course, resources are limited. But, by itself, this fact generates competition neither more nor less than it does cooperation. No one contends that historically, as resources have become more generally plentiful, cooperation has superseded competition. The balance between these two responses to the existence of Others surely depends not on the quantity of resources, but rather on the relative emphasis which the society, including its philosophers, places on the two modes of intersubjectivity. How can sympathies between a society's members and factions not be in short supply if that society is founded on the mode of subjection in human relations?

Beauvoir disagrees fundamentally with her precursors 'about the problem that morality is needed to solve'. Without denying the need for restraints in patriarchal societies, she sees the ethical problem primarily as one of overcoming a particular kind of ignorance, one encouraged and protected by philosophers and teachers of philosophy who present the problem of morality only within the context of the mode of subjection or the subject/object mode of intersubjectivity. It is in this restricted context that ethical discourse meets the is/ought dichotomy – the logical impossibility of deriving an 'ought' or normative statement from a statement of facts, or a fact from a normative statement. By calling attention to the possibility of the mode of reciprocity, Beauvoir, rather than saying that one 'should' behave in certain ways, seeks to show why it *is in fact* in one's self-interest to act in ways which are generally thought to be altruistic. 'The respect of the liberty of others is not an abstract rule: it is the first condition of the success of my effort.'[44] As Linda Singer notes, 'Freedom, on this view, finds in others not only obstacles, but also its sites of realization and recognition.'[45]

It should be clear by now why Beauvoir's ethics have scarcely been recognized. The ethics of reciprocity are not to be found on 'official' maps of moral philosophy. Beauvoir's ethics have been excluded from the record not just because it is the invention of a woman, but also because it is a dangerous ethics, dangerous not only to several thousand years of philosophical tradition, but also to society as presently constituted. Just how much this is the case can be seen in the programmes for change she proposed in her two major works of applied ethics, *The Second Sex* and *Old Age*, and in her critiques of the ethical status quo which structure her late fiction.

7

Applied Ethics I: The Second Sex

Introduction

With her passionate commitment to the principle that philosophy and experience were of a piece, Beauvoir was exceptionally well placed to provide ethical analysis of major human abuses which depended on fallacious deployment of the notions of subject and object, of embodiment, and of intersubjectivity. After the more general orientation of *Pyrrhus et Cinéas* and *The Ethics of Ambiguity*, Beauvoir put her philosophical discoveries to more practical use than any philosopher since the age of revolutions when the thought of Locke and Rousseau served as foundational sources for the rise of modern democracies. The final chapters of this study examine the ways in which Beauvoir put her philosophy to work in the service of the elderly, the colonized and, most famously, women.

The second sentence of *The Second Sex*, the twentieth-century's classic and pivotal analysis of women's condition, consists of a prescient statement of just how annoying its contents were likely to be.[1] 'For a long time I have hesitated to write a book on women,' writes Beauvoir by way of introduction. 'The subject is irritating, especially to women, and it is not new.'[2] With these deft words, and with her characteristic lucidity, Beauvoir embarks on her monumental project of irritation on behalf of women, noting her own hesitant attitude at the prospect of her undertaking, and signalling her historical place in a debate which she is joining rather than initiating. It is also clear that the first reader to be irritated by what follows in the substance of the book is Beauvoir herself, whose disgust at the levels of imbecility and injustice unearthed by her research into the condition of women throughout human history both tried her patience and prompted from her a philosophical and cultural response of such complexity that its intricacies are still not fully mapped. As Jo-Ann Pilardi demonstrates in her excellent recent study of the history of *The Second Sex*'s reception, Beauvoir's text is so rich and multifaceted that it has provoked a range of partial and variant responses, each in tune with the characteristic interests of its time. There is no reason to believe that this process has been completed. It is, quite obviously, one of those rare classic statements on the human condition whose power only grows as its many dimensions are discovered and interrogated.

The Second Sex was received as a major publication from the first, and early responses to it ranged from personal attacks on Beauvoir for her unwomanliness to praise for its seriousness and stylistic excellence. Beauvoir's forthrightness about maternity as a cultural practice rather than a solely biological fact attracted particular attention amid the simplistic psychologizing of the anti-feminists of the 1950s. The obsession with sexual behaviour of the 1960s cited Beauvoir's book alongside *The Kinsey Report* as evidence on sexual practices. With the re-emergence of liberal feminism in the United States in the late 1960s and early 1970s, *The Second Sex* was claimed as a foundational text by key activist writers such as Kate Millett and Shulamith Firestone. In the 1980s and 1990s the book has attracted distinguished philosophical commentators such as Michèle Le Doeuff, Monique Wittig and Judith Butler, who build on Beauvoir's work in significant ways, but also serious criticism by the new wave of feminist critics who have attacked the text for its reliance on Sartrean existentialist ideas, for its rational 'masculine' orientation (which is linked to its failure to glorify maternity in particular and feminine gender difference in general), for its insensitivity to class and cultural diversity, for its lack of celebration of the female body, and for a universalism unacceptable to those allied with postmodernist theory. *The Second Sex* has attracted and continues to attract the kind of ferocious, productive debate which only characterizes texts of the utmost importance.[3]

The Second Sex needs to be read in the light of Beauvoir's literary–philosophical method. As ever, Beauvoir's philosophical arguments are grounded in lived experience: the distinction between the subjective and the objective is not simply elided but rejected. And, given Beauvoir's strong conviction that history forms the central constituent element in the construction of experience, the historical research which so massively informs the project should be read as the collective voice of the culture which shapes possibilities for those individuals it assigns to the category of 'woman'. The point here is that the scholarship behind Beauvoir's writing and her great care in recording the voices of the past in relation to women should be read somewhat differently from the way in which historical evidence usually is treated. For Beauvoir, history's voice is not dead but living. It produces effects which tend to allow or disallow given ethical and ontological possibilities. The philosophical effects of the dominant historical voice within a culture carries meanings which must be understood before they can be questioned.

The Second Sex

The Second Sex is full of such voices speaking at, about and to women. Beauvoir orchestrates this historical and contemporary cacophony by means of a philosophical plan which pulls together arguments from the deep and repeatedly forgotten history of feminist thought and from elements in the work of Merleau-Ponty, Sartre, Lévi-Strauss, Husserl, Kierkegaard and, especially, her revisionary view of Hegel, which support her own theories of situation, intersubjectivity and the Social Other. Before looking in some detail at the philosophical structure of the work, the complex personal genealogy which led Beauvoir to its composition demands consideration.

It is altogether fitting that the philosopher of ambiguity should give mixed accounts of the effects of her own experience as a woman. On one hand, in the introduction to *The Second Sex*, she notes that 'if I wish to define myself, I must first of all say: "I am a woman"; on this truth must be based all further discussion.'[4] One recalls the importance of her gender position to the young Beauvoir: the need to find a career as an alternative to the socially propitious marriage her family could not secure; the importance of previous women philosophers to her ability to imagine herself in that role; the wish to be a female pioneer in a discipline which seemed to be the almost exclusive preserve of men. On the other hand, Beauvoir often makes statements in her autobiographies and interviews about the negligible effect of her sex on her life. A few examples of this tendency, which has attracted considerable criticism, and, at times, dismay among Beauvoir's most sympathetic readers, indicate her purpose in making these remarks. Beauvoir wrote all the volumes of her memoirs and gave most of her interviews *after* the publication of *The Second Sex*. When she writes or speaks of herself in these later contexts, which form part of the larger project of constructing a philosophy which is simultaneously a witnessing of experience, she does so with the arguments of *The Second Sex* fully formed as a strong portion of her intellectual background. Remarks on the lack of the impact of her sex on her life sometimes serve as illustrations of her own previous blindness to the obvious, sometimes glossed further by Beauvoir as indications of the subtle forms gender oppression may take.

One exchange of this type in an interview with Alice Schwarzer serves as an example of the strategies Beauvoir employs in analysing her own position while locking it into ideas regarding the position of women in general and the impact of history on women's possibilities. The question Schwarzer asks is a familiar one:

'You said in a commentary on *The Second Sex* that the problem of femininity had not touched you personally, and that you felt you were in a "highly impartial position". Did you mean that a woman can, as an individual, escape her feminine condition? On the professional level and in her relations with others?'

Beauvoir responds:

'Escape her condition as a woman? No! But actually I've been very lucky. I've escaped most of woman's bondages: maternity, the life of a housewife. Also in my day there were fewer women who pursued advanced studies. To have a postgraduate degree in philosophy was to be in a privileged position as a woman. I received immediate recognition from men – they were ready to accept friendship with a woman who had succeeded on their own level, because it was so exceptional. Now that many women are advanced students, men are afraid of losing their own status.'[5]

Beauvoir's answer to Schwarzer's question, one often put to her in various forms, centres on the way she slipped through a historical net, gaining her degree in philosophy when her token status as a pioneering woman was not yet felt as threatening by her male colleagues, and avoiding what she feels remain the unreconstructed aspects of feminine roles. This is not so much a statement of *personal* exceptionalism as an account of being the fortunate beneficiary of particular *historical* circumstances which she, as an individual, embraced. This intense awareness of herself (and all individuals) as situated in history is typical of Beauvoir, and informs *The Second Sex* (and also her later book, *Old Age*) in ways that are sometimes overlooked, but which must be kept in mind if the full implications of Beauvoir's social philosophy are to be understood.

The genesis of *The Second Sex* has its own deep history. Although the idea of a book on women was one which Beauvoir discussed with her friend and colleague Colette Audry when they were both young teachers in Rouen in the 1930s, the project interested Audry rather than Beauvoir.[6] For her part, the young Beauvoir still resisted the need to insert herself into the category 'woman' at all. For example, when she suffered a diminution in her sense of purposefulness following the completion of her education and the beginning of her liaison with Sartre, she refused to attribute her distress and remorse to her female position. 'I had refused to be labelled "a child",' she writes, 'so now I did not think of myself as "a woman": I was *me*.' It is the older Beauvoir, writing her memoirs, who recognizes the particularly female aspect of her own youthful dilemma – that is, that women are not supposed to have individual lives, but, preferably, should accept a state of pure alterity which excludes positive experience. At the time, Beauvoir can only report that such an idea was alien to her, and that therefore the notion of feminism did not seem to apply to her circumstances, or to offer any means of understanding them. This is entirely in keeping with Beauvoir's view of the importance to her of her youthful sense of her own exceptionalism, which she at times stresses with respect to class and age as well as gender, and which she sees both as self-delusion and as a necessary fiction which made her violation of predetermined norms possible.

Another example of this, pertinent to the origin of *The Second Sex*, occurs in Beauvoir's account of the enlargement of her circle of friends in the wake of existentialism's first post-Liberation success. She notes how she always regarded her and her women friends' problems as pertaining solely to individuals. The war made an immense impact on her ethical orientation. It taught her that cultural objectifications and definitions – she cites the overwhelming example of Jews and Aryans – are not incidental. The new women she meets, all over forty, have all lived as ' "dependent persons" '. She listens to their stories with interest while still feeling that their common position has nothing to do with hers.[7]

Beauvoir portrays her realization of the significance of her female status as a moment of awakening. Casting about for a project after the completion of *The Ethics of Ambiguity*, Beauvoir says that she wanted to write about herself. She realized that the first question she needed to address was the meaning of her position as a woman:

at first she thought the question negligible. However, encouraged by Sartre to consider it further, the impact of her sex struck her as 'a revelation'. The astonishingly brief two years it took her to write her book about the female condition re-emphasized the centrality of her philosophy of intersubjectivity, and, she says, she considered *The Other, the Second* and *The Other Sex* as titles for the book, until Jacques Bost, Beauvoir's friend and lover, suggested the final title, *Le Deuxième Sexe.*[8]

As Beauvoir extended her analysis of the question of intersubjectivity with regard to sex and gender, various circumstances surrounding the composition of the book also need to be kept in mind. In 1946, when she started her research, she had, as has been noted, just completed *The Ethics of Ambiguity*, her most extended conventional treatment of ethics. World War II was only just over when the book was begun, and the war's impact in terms of Beauvoir's intellectual recognition of the force of history on the individual had been absorbed. In many ways, *The Second Sex* can be read as a product of the great euphoria which came with the Liberation of France, in which the imagined political and social possibilities for a new future were very much under discussion, not only among Beauvoir's close associates, but in Europe in general. The questions of religion and race were also very much on Beauvoir's mind: Paris had been shocked when the survivors of the Nazi death camps returned to haunt it; the first detailed knowledge of the Holocaust gave an urgency to finding new ways to address the question of the Other.

Further, during the period of the composition of the book, Beauvoir was deeply immersed in an important love affair with the American author Nelson Algren, whose ideas about women were conventional. Beauvoir met Algren when she visited the United States for the first time in 1947, and she registers her disappointment with the lack of freedom shown by American women in the volume she wrote about her lecture tour of the United States, *America Day by Day*, which she produced simultaneously with *The Second Sex*. As we have noted, this book also contains long sections about the condition of black Americans, a topic much on her mind at the time and related to her contemporaneous friendship with the great black novelist Richard Wright, which opened out Beauvoir's thought regarding intersubjectivity from that of individuals to that of social groups.

It must be mentioned, too, that Beauvoir's relationship with Sartre was seriously under threat during the composition of her study of women because of his strong attachment to another woman: there was a real danger that the association between the two philosophers might end. All these factors feed into Beauvoir's analysis of women, which is also an analysis of herself. Finally, and in anticipation of her later, cognate work on the old, it is important to note that Beauvoir was increasingly aware of her own ageing as she wrote the book.

The Second Sex, then, was written against a background composed of this concatenation of personal and historical exhaustion, shock, exhilaration and uncertainty. When viewed in this light its sharpness of focus and authority of argument are all the more impressive. The treatise shares a structure with *Old Age*, with each book moving through vast amounts of data on its topic. In both studies, Beauvoir begins with biology, moves through ethology and history, and takes in myth, legend and strategies of representation. Psychological formation and cultural practice are treated at great length in both volumes, while each ends with a concluding section that points the way out of the oppressive cultural formations which the books describe. In each case the purpose of the work is intellectually activist as well as historical and descriptive. The politics of each work, however, are of a particular order. It is not unfair to label these the politics of a philosopher who never separates experience from intellection, and whose investment in whatever matter is at hand is at once personal and impartial. What is definitely the case is that each volume is governed by a philosophical framework into which all aspects of the discussion fit. And while the detail in each volume has attracted sometimes hostile debate, it is the nature of the philosophical argument supporting the edifice of these texts which is most important for this study.[9]

Beauvoir first lays out this argument clearly and precisely in the introduction to *The Second Sex*. All her points contribute to the defence of the text's overarching principle, stated economically at the beginning of Book 2, that 'One is not born, but rather becomes a woman.'[10] She begins by asking the most fundamental of questions, 'What is a woman?', after noting the continuing babel of questioning, exhortation and exasperation which surrounds the still extensive public discussion of the topic (a circumstance which has not altered in the fifty years since *The Second Sex* was published). She cites a range of common definitions, each of which is rejected and each of which will receive extended treatment in the course of the book.

The biological definition ('"woman is a womb"') is the first mentioned and found wanting. If biology were the sole or even main determinant of womanliness, there would be no need for further discussion: it would be redundant to persuade biological females to be women, and there would certainly be no justification for the common discussions of whether certain possessors of a uterus are women or not. Beauvoir then considers the notion of femininity as an essence, whether biological or Platonic. She cites the prevalence of this definition in the time of Aquinas and notes the semi-mystical penumbra which surrounds its invocation. In a comparative point, she argues that the biological and social sciences reject the notion of fixed essences, and uses the linked examples of Jews, blacks and women as categories which must not be treated as consisting of fixed entities with unchanging characteristics. However, she also characteristically rejects the claims of those who hold positions she characterizes as 'of the enlightenment, of rationalism, of nominalism', who declare that 'woman' has nothing but the arbitrary meaning assigned to it, and that all human beings are the same.[11] This position, Beauvoir argues, is too abstract: it ignores individuals' concrete experiences and neglects to take into account the situation of specific women – unlike science, which is always alert to the impact of environment on the shaping of individuals' characteristics.

Before moving on to Beauvoir's own definition of woman, the implications of her opening statements need further comment. First, by rejecting equally functionalist biological arguments focused on reproductive capacity as well as arguments based on vague and mysterious notions of '"the eternal feminine"' as starting points, she clears the ground for her own definition, which is based on cultural practice. Secondly, her early citation of other groups who have suffered gravely from idealist definitions of fixed essences marks the potential of her method for use in other areas, such as the discussions of colonialism, race and age to which Beauvoir herself contributed. Finally, Beauvoir's last point must be noted closely, as her arguments in *The Second Sex* are sometimes dismissed for failing to recognize the difference between men and women, and for arguing for the collapse of the feminine into the more general category of the human, which, almost always, denotes only the masculine. This is, patently, not Beauvoir's argument, and the fact that it is not needs reiteration.

The next part of her argument indicates Beauvoir's awareness that her position might be misread in this way. After insisting that, if she wishes to define herself, she must begin by declaring she is a woman, she underlines the asymmetry of women's need to mark their gender position with men's lack of any need to do so. Men, she says, do not feel the need to declare their sex: the masculine is assumed to be so utterly primary that it is equated with the human in an absolute sense. The feminine, in turn, is treated as deviant from the absolute human type, which is by implication always masculine. Beauvoir argues, anticipating points made by Hélène Cixous, that the terms in the binary oppositions which follow from this sexual polarity between male and female are not of equal value. They are 'without reciprocity', with the female 'representing only the negative', and therefore the not-quite-human, given the unspoken elision of the male and the human categories. Under this regime, women are associated with the emotive and the blindly biological, while men theorize and imagine their bodies as vehicles of direct, purposive connection to the world.

Calling up the ghosts of Aristotle and Aquinas, and citing the Old Testament, Beauvoir glances at the history of the definition of women as 'lack', as 'defectiveness', as imperfection, as 'an "incidental" being'.[12] Beauvoir encapsulates her discussion in a crucial brief statement by arguing that man is regarded as the Absolute Subject, while woman is imagined as the inessential Other.[13] This is the philosophical formulation which Beauvoir intends to dismantle in the course of her treatise, and she has ready to hand the philosophical tools with which to do this in her concepts of subjection, reciprocity and situation which featured so strongly in *Pyrrhus et Cinéas* and *The Ethics of Ambiguity*.

How she means to proceed is illustrated by her remarks on Lévinas's essay 'Temps et l'Autre'. Beauvoir criticizes Lévinas's comments on the 'full flowing' of 'otherness' in the feminine by remarking that this position is entirely governed by an unspoken masculine point of view, that woman, too, is possessed of consciousness and ego, and that alterity can only be discussed properly with attention to 'the reciprocity of subject and object'. While noting that the category of the Other is 'primordial' for human consciousness, and citing Hegel's argument that consciousness itself is hostile to all other consciousness (a position to which the Sartre of *Being and Nothingness* holds), Beauvoir goes on to emphasize the means by which the relativity of consciousness is made manifest in ways which counter the idea of the supremacy of the Absolute Subject. In her view, one aspect of human culture is a series of enactments of the reciprocity of consciousness. Travel, war, festivals, trade, diplomacy, and contests among groups all work to strip both individuals and groups of illusions of absoluteness and to school them in the knowledge of the relativity of all human existence.[14]

Beauvoir's account of the interrelationship of consciousnesses as fundamental parts of their nature stresses the ontological position seen in her writing since the composition of *She Came to Stay* in the late 1930s. She now brings her theory of intersubjectivity into play in her analysis of the position of women. In this, her rejection of the idea of the Absolute Subject is of the first importance. Her alternative ontological starting point is, as Sonia Kruks puts it, the 'situated subject: a subject that is intrinsically intersubjective and embodied, thus always "interdependent" and permeable rather than walled.'[15] Further, this intrinsically intersubjective subject is always located in history, and it is to the history of women that Beauvoir now turns to explain why women, unlike possessors of other despised attributes (again she cites people of colour, the colonized and Jews as cognate examples of unjustly dominated groups), have submitted so quietly to their relegation to the category of Absolute Other.

The answer to this question lies, argues Beauvoir, in women's history. Unlike the groups noted above, women have never formed a separate collectivity, and therefore possess no cultural memory of a time before domination. No single event can be remembered as the key to their subjugation. This is an interesting point, especially in the light of certain kinds of recent feminist attempts to exhume such a women's past moment from the tangle of prehistory. Beauvoir, most pointedly, does not pursue this point (though she is highly interested in the representations of women which emerge from prehistory via myth and legend). Instead, she sees women's collective situation as most like that of the proletariat, where the oppressed and oppressor do not live as separate groups, but are intermingled and interdependent.

The comparison, like Beauvoir's earlier analogies between women and other oppressed groups, is a traditional one for certain kinds of feminist, and it has been used often both before and after *The Second Sex*. It is useful to note that Beauvoir read Engels (whose analysis of women's history in *The Origin of the Family, Private Property, and the State* she criticizes later in the text), among others, in preparation for writing the book, and equally useful to recall that Beauvoir, like many leftist thinkers, believed for decades that the improvement of women's position was secondary to, though inextricably linked with, the evolution of socialism. This was, in fact, the chief reason for her refusing the label of 'feminist' until 1971, a decision which followed her revised view that the key issues of socialism and those of feminism were separate.[16] The reasons for this shift, however, which she would not make in her private views for several decades, are already in play in the late 1940s in *The Second Sex*, where she articulates the differences between class and gender clearly.

The proletariat, she notes, is a historical phenomenon. It has not always existed, and therefore there is no reason to think it must persist. However, there have always been women: their femaleness is anatomical and physiological. And, as far as the human record knows, their subordination to men is not the result of an event. Instead it is apprehended as a condition, and, as such, exempt from contingency and from other events which might overturn or modify it. Beauvoir does not let matters rest at this. In a point which is crucial to her argument she argues that 'the nature of things is no more immutably given, once for all, than is historical reality.' What is important, she says, emphasizing a point central both to her ontology and to her ethics since the late 1930s, is assuming the position of subject. Again, she insists that this position is intersubjective. Beauvoir does not say, as might be expected, that women must learn to say 'I': instead, she says, women must learn to say 'we'.[17]

The precise kind of recognized historical intersubjectivity she has in mind is illustrated by the examples she gives of the success of groups which have been defined as subservient turning the tables on their oppressors: the proletariat in Russia; the blacks in Haiti; the Indo-Chinese who were currently fighting against French colonialism. These reversals have only been possible, argues Beauvoir, through each respective group's members' transformed apprehension of themselves as subjects, of their communal refusal to be relegated to permanent subservience and (non-reciprocal) Otherness. In agreeing to say 'we', these groups transform their oppressors into 'Others', who can, therefore, be challenged. Action is dependent on this transformation in consciousness taking place.

Beauvoir's illustration of the linkage between consciousness of the self as partaking simultaneously of individual and social elements feeds directly into her analysis of the difficulties faced by women as a caste. And, especially because *The Second Sex* often attracts criticism for its individualist principles, it seems all the more important to note that Beauvoir sees women's lack of belonging to a recognizable social unit, which can define itself against a correlated but opposing social unit, as one of women's chief difficulties. Women are not possessed of the kinds of historical experiences which tend to make for group identity: she says, bleakly, that women have 'no past, no history, no religion of their own'. Their various solidarities of class, race and religion align with those of the men to whom they are appended and not to women as a group. Further, argues Beauvoir, borrowing a term from Heidegger, men and women are bound together in 'a primordial *Mitsein*', a biologically fundamental and unbreakable togetherness.[18]

Woman's position as one half of the totality of this fundamental human *Mitsein* – which Beauvoir, giving her own strong emphasis to the commonality involved in such associations, treats as potentially advantageous to women precisely because of the shared nature of the totality formed by the component parts – could have worked to women's benefit. However, it most patently has not. To explain this circumstance, Beauvoir's takes Hegel's master–slave dialectic as the starting point for her analysis. While woman is not precisely in the position of slave to man (and, importantly, unlike Hegel's slave, she does not desire his destruction), she has, however, always been man's dependent. This dependency is ensured by society, which hampers her through legal, economic, educational and customary practice. Further, in such circumstances, to relinquish the one advantage seemingly granted by the culture – that is, men's protection, both economic and moral – is extremely difficult for women, who are left exposed on all sides by refusal of the traditional gendered bargain.

The risks run by women who choose the subject position are both 'economic' and 'metaphysical', by which Beauvoir means the risks arising from the assumption of responsibility as both an economic and an ethical agent, each of which carries a high possibility of failure. It is, she says, easier to decline the bargain than to accept it, and at times, because of the cultural and material constrictions noted above, it is impossible for women to even attempt to choose the status of subject. Beauvoir held to this position fiercely throughout her life, stressing particularly the need for economic independence for women as a condition of their assumption of full status as a subject.[19] Many women, however, cannot or will not avoid the primary kind of concrete dependency. Woman accepts her definition as the Other for three main reasons, thinks Beauvoir: her lack of resources; the *Mitsein* which binds her to man even under disadvantageous terms; and, most disturbingly, because she may actively enjoy and embrace her definition as the Other.[20]

Discouraging (although powerful) as Beauvoir's analysis is, she nevertheless points to the slow change occurring in the condition of women. Digging again into the history of the philosophical and political discussion for the origins of woman's relegation to the disempowered position in the duality of the sexes, she argues that men's explanations of women's inferiority must be suspect. She turns here, as she does at many points in the book, to statements by women to support her case. And it must be emphasized that Beauvoir's text is full of the voices of women who are her predecessors and contemporaries, from Mary Wollstonecraft to Susan B. Anthony, from Mme de Staël to Virginia Woolf. At this point, she lets the seventeenth-century feminist Poulain de la Barre carry the argument about men's lack of disinterestedness in putting women's case.[21] Concurring with de la Barre's point, Beauvoir returns again to the list of culturally significant forces which have been ranged against women. From legend to the law, from religion to science, from philosophy to literature, all have participated enthusiastically in the subordination and objectivization of women.

It is only in the eighteenth and nineteenth centuries, says Beauvoir, that things begin to shift. She links this slow change explicitly to changes in economic conditions attendant on the industrial revolution which brought increasing numbers of women into the labour market. Concurrently, the rise of democratic ideology led a few men to challenge traditional hostile views of women (Beauvoir mentions Diderot and John Stuart Mill as two of these honourable exceptions). As with nineteenth-century racist theorists, the anti-feminists of this period used the most prestigious discourses of the day – in this case the new sciences and social sciences – to promote the notion of separate 'equalities' for male and female. Beauvoir reads the formulation 'equal but separate' as wholly pernicious, and as the basis for justifying extreme discrimination. Again, her cognate cases are those of the Jews and of people of colour. Her antagonism to this position is ontological. By positing separate essences for despised groups, members of those groups appear to be fixed in the historical (and thus alterable) characteristics of inferiority which pertain at the time of definition. The Hegelian sense of the verb 'to be' loses its dynamic properties which denote possibilities of change, and instead takes on an idealist cast. The importance of situation to social conditions is forgotten, and alterity, instead of being understood as a fluctuating reciprocal property of intersubjectivity, is assigned as an essence to the oppressed group.

In all this, Beauvoir deploys her revised Hegelian ideas *contra* Hegel, noting that Hegel, like St Paul, Lenin and Nietzsche, stands with the enemies of women's equality.[22] Further, she outlines precisely what men have to lose in abandoning the conventional illusion of women's essential alterity. If women are no longer automatically defined as the Other, the assumption of the position of subject becomes all the more difficult for men. For men who fear their own powerlessness, the loss of automatic inferiors augments their terror. However, if men have (generally suspect) things to lose by recognizing women as subjects, they also have a good deal to gain. Firstly, and this is very much a philosopher's point, logical consistency will be served. Democratic ideas so infuse modern thought that the very postulation of unequal groups is troubling. Men of the democratic era, argues Beauvoir, no longer postulate women as inferior, and the logical inconsistency in treating women as the Other makes less and less sense within the dominant political and ideological framework.

Difficulties here reside in covert male defence of masculine privilege, which is often not even perceived as such. Beauvoir gives the example of women's general difficulty in entering the professions being taken by men as a sign of natural sexual inferiority with no regard to investigating other reasons why this case should pertain. Subordination, she says, takes subtle forms: differences which appear unimportant can have far-reaching effects. Only woman can fully understand her own situation. She must cultivate the ability to disregard male accounts of her position, whether these take the form of violent attack or suspect praise of feminine difference. Equally, she notes, feminist interventions have often proved counterproductive and allowed men to turn the question of woman's status into useless quarrels. In a move which echoes that of each new wave of feminist thought, Beauvoir declares the language of previous discussions of the issue hopelessly corrupt. She wants to clear the ground, to start afresh.

This is, as she immediately admits, impossible. The best that can be done, she says, is to listen to the accounts given of their situations by women who have transcended some of the limitations imposed on their caste, and who may be in a position to speak with some impartiality. It is difficult to say whether Beauvoir is simply trying to hearten herself and her readers when she announces that, as women, 'by and large we have won the game.' Ever historically alert, she points to the importance of the United Nations' positive view of the increase in women's equality, and she points as well to the achievement of a group of women, in which she includes herself, who have not had to find their femininity 'an inconvenience or

an obstacle'. Following her own argument, she declares herself a
member of a female collectivity which possesses an identity, which
can say the word 'we', and which has a responsibility to help its
'younger sisters' think with 'clarity and understanding' about the
future.[23]

Typically, with her developed theories of ambiguity and uncertainty brought into play once again, Beauvoir immediately critiques
her own argument. While noting the emergence of a group of
women who can practise impartiality, she then denies the possibility of discussing the position of woman, or any human question,
free from bias, and she goes on succinctly to state her own. Any
objective discussion, she notes, 'implies an ethical background'. The
ethics of *The Second Sex*, she says, implies a society in which the
public good is defined in terms of the creation of institutions which
promote concrete opportunities for individuals. Her definition is
situational and materialist in orientation, and she pointedly dis-
cards the romantic notion of 'happiness' from her ethics. Happiness,
she says, is a matter for individual consciousness alone, and it has
been used too frequently to justify vested interests to serve as a
useful principle in ascertaining the public good. The 'existentialist
ethics', which she declares the underlying ethical ground of her text,
takes liberty as its foundational value. The self-transcending subject, moving from the facticity of immanence to the responsibility of
pursuing 'freely chosen projects', provides the model for agency on
which Beauvoir's ethics is based. To simply accede to the given, to
refuse liberty, is to be lost in 'absolute evil'.[24]

With this ethical judgement in mind, Beauvoir turns again to her
sensitivity to woman's situation. Beauvoir emphasizes the fact that
woman is driven not only by the shared human ontological desire to
regard herself as a subject, but also by the elements of ideological
and material *compulsion* which equally form part of her situation,
and which are designed to force her to accept her definition as the
Other. In addition, when Beauvoir's principle of the intersubjective
nature of subjectivity is applied to this text, her stated project of
analysing women's possibilities in terms of liberty rather than happiness is one which is necessarily undertaken on behalf of and, in
some sense, in concert with the collective 'we' of women who, along
with Beauvoir, reject definition as absolute Other.[25] Significantly,
Beauvoir completes her map of the territory she is investigating
with a philosophically exact gesture of solidarity with her chosen
group, inserting her own 'I' into the collective 'we' and 'they' of
women in general as she reaches towards futurity.

The argument which has just been outlined represents the philosophical core of *The Second Sex*, with the detailed material presented at great length in the text serving as an exhaustive fleshing out of these principles. The vastness the text demanded was a surprise to Beauvoir, who did not expect such a massive result from her research on women. That research was, she said, a 'journey into history', from which she returned confirmed in her material principles, convinced that the history of woman was bound up with that of 'inheritance' and was 'a by-product of the economic evolution of the masculine world'.[26] This conclusion made her look at the world afresh, and Beauvoir's own sense of astonished discovery of an unperceived aspect of the familiar world is one reason for the text's energy. *The Second Sex* is one of that handful of books which tends to be a revelation for its readers: it served, first of all, as a revelation for its author, who provides it with a rigorous argument of great force and supports it with a wealth of detail from an encyclopedic range of sources.

In the third volume of her memoirs, *Force of Circumstance*, Beauvoir provides a narrative account of the reception of the book which itself is designed to underline the contentiousness of her production and to shadow its main arguments. She notes its phenomenal initial success as an economic commodity. This is important in the light of her key argument in the volume (one she reiterated repeatedly in interviews throughout her life) that women can only assume the status of subject from a position of economic independence. Next she foregrounds comments made to her about her courage in writing the book, an attitude which, she says, did not cross her mind as necessary when writing the book, but one well in keeping with the account she gives of women who challenge their relegation to the position of the Other. And, while she implicitly ranges the men associated with *Les Temps Modernes*, in which lengthy extracts from the book first appeared, along with Diderot and John Stuart Mill as males who were friendly to the emancipation of women, and who therefore welcomed her book, she stresses the outraged attacks her work attracted from others. In a famous sentence she lists the personalized attributes which informed these attacks: 'unsatisfied, frigid, priapic, nymphomaniac, lesbian, a hundred times aborted, I was everything, even an unmarried mother.'[27]

Beauvoir's tactics in this narrative continue her drive to reject a divide between her life and her philosophy, between abstraction and experience. The differences in men's responses to *The Second Sex* point again to the ideological rather than natural status of the ascription of the place of the Other by men to women. The insults she records illustrate the invocation of biologistic factors as the determining ones in the oppressive definition of woman as simply body (in this case, body gone wrong) as opposed to man's intellect. She rehearses the logical inconsistencies in the attacks on her work ('women had always been the equal of men, they were forever doomed to be their inferiors')[28] in illustration of a main point in *The Second Sex* of the inconsistency of masculine accounts of women, with their sole constant being women's position at the inferior pole of the binary opposition of gender. Noting the hostility of both the Catholic Church (which put the book on its blacklist) and the Communist Party, Beauvoir illustrates the unified endeavour of institutionalized religion and politics, left and right, in insisting on women's subservience. By gracefully citing Colette Audry's published defence of the book, she makes a reciprocal gesture of solidarity to the woman who had first proposed the project and who belongs to that group of privileged women, of which they are both members, who make up the nucleus of the identifiable group to which women can belong. After again insisting on the uselessness of a feminism that does not address the need for a revolution in the position of women in economic production, she records her pleasure in the enormous, if sometimes disturbed, response she has received from women readers.

Finally, Beauvoir ends where she began *The Second Sex*, with irritation, but this time an irritation overcome, in finding in women her 'most serious public'. In overcoming this highly damaging, but typical part of women's condition which leads even other women to consider members of their own sex as inferior, Beauvoir again uses herself as an illustration of the processes she philosophically analyses in *The Second Sex*. Further, and more generally, her work on women, she says, helped to keep her attuned to the real and saved her from the philosopher's vice of 'drifting in the universal'.[29]

It is, indeed, Beauvoir's short-circuiting of the universalism permeating the Cartesian mind–body split through her insistence that consciousness and material existence are indivisible, and the ways she employs her concept of the situatedness of the subject in *The Second Sex* which provide the basis for some of the most vibrant recent work on gender. Two key recent writers provide examples of the continuing impact of Beauvoir's declaration that 'One is not born, but rather becomes a woman.'

In 1981, Monique Wittig's essay, 'One Is Not Born a Woman', took Beauvoir's insistence that 'woman' was a cultural rather than a natural category as the starting point for a powerful argument for the privileging of lesbian society as a way to escape the hierarchical master/slave dichotomy inherent in the persistence of the political categories of 'women' and 'men'. Wittig's influential essay provides one of the landmarks in the current flourishing of Queer Theory and is an impassioned call for the dissolution of the myth of universal 'woman' and an undoing of the pernicious hierarchical social relationship which the collective classification as 'women' means. While stressing the effects on consciousness of belonging to the 'class' designated as 'women' for any individual subject who is defined within that class, Wittig argues the case for the exemplary practice of the lesbian as an 'escapee' from binary concepts of gender politics, well placed to work for the destruction of the social system of heterosexuality which has proved so destructive for its female members.[30]

Judith Butler, the most eloquent and influential of the current inheritors of Beauvoir's work in *The Second Sex*, also grounds her writing in Beauvoir's distinction between sex and gender. Like Wittig, she stresses Beauvoir's point that gender is not a natural but a cultural phenomenon. She powerfully reformulated Beauvoir's point in 1986 in 'Sex and Gender in Simone de Beauvoir's *Second Sex*' with her statement that 'all gender is, by definition, unnatural,' drawing out its corollary that, if this is the case, the body must be seen as 'a field of cultural possibilities',[31] open to any number of interpretations which provide escape from gender polarities. In the intense recent debates on gender identity and embodiment, Butler takes Beauvoir's ideas to their radical conclusions by stressing the completely conventional (and therefore transformable) nature of the link between sex and gender. In her major work, *Gender Trouble: Feminism and the Subversion of Identity*, Butler grounds her own view of the contingent and active nature of gender as performance, activity or becoming in Beauvoir's philosophical principles. (And Butler argues that Wittig has misread Beauvoir in that she has elided the distinction between sex and gender, and that further, unlike Beauvoir, she mistakenly places the lesbian outside gender categories. Most importantly, Butler rejects Wittig's instatement of the lesbian as a discrete category, as this requires equally fixed heterosexual categories to sustain the definition.)

Butler's own programme is to promote individuals' possibilities for cultural and social agency by reconceptualizing gender politics in terms that reject notions of static, gendered selves in favour of understanding the subject as 'a point of agency'.[32] Butler argues that the most effective gender politics supports the proliferation of possibilities generated by the material structures of signification (rather than identification within them). Gender does not provide identity but a repertoire of actions which can be performed subversively. The proliferation of subversive gender acts can, she argues, break down the divide between the Self and the Other in precisely the ways suggested by Beauvoir. Butler emphasizes the bodily fissuring of the signs of gender in ways which call attention to its unnatural and therefore political status.

It is important to note that these writers working on the question of women in the tradition initiated by Beauvoir are not writing solely as academics, or theoreticians, but as intellectuals who have regard for the application of the ethics their thought invokes. Both Butler and Wittig end with philosophically informed calls to political action with regard to gender which can only be of the greatest benefit to women. In this, they are entirely faithful to *The Second Sex* and to Beauvoir's ethical programme on behalf of the half of humankind she refused to define as Other.

8

Applied Ethics II: Les Belles Images, The Woman Destroyed *and* Old Age

Autobiography dominated Beauvoir's writing in the 1950s and the early 1960s. In her massive, autobiographically based, Prix Goncourt-winning novel of 1954, *The Mandarins*, in the first three volumes of her memoirs, in her accounts of her travel to China and of her mother's death, Beauvoir put her literary-philosophical method to extensive use. She had, indeed, found a way to textualize her life as well as an extensive international audience which welcomed her books. In this intense autobiographical phase, Beauvoir's writing is always shaped by her method to work simultaneously as literature and as philosophy. It is a circumstance which sometimes misleads readers who read Beauvoir against the dominant conventions of autobiography as straightforward confessional and as the self-revelation of a coherent subject. Despite the vast quantities of words Beauvoir produced on the topic of her own life during this period, she is less personal, and (as has become more and more obvious with the information that has emerged since her death in 1986) less veracious than those conventions suggest. Instead, Beauvoir treats herself as an exemplary situated historical figure. She often bends the details of her experience into shapes that illustrate her philosophical and historical arguments, which nevertheless remain closer to experience than the fiction which Beauvoir always regarded as part of the same writerly continuum.

Beauvoir returned to autobiography in the last of the four volumes of her memoirs, which was published in 1972. Her memorial to Sartre, *Adieux*, appeared in 1981. But in the mid- to late 1960s, between her two autobiographical periods, Beauvoir turned back to the major genres of fiction and of the exhaustive sociophilosophical study. Her fictions – the short novel *Les Belles Images* of 1966, and the three *nouvelles* which make up *The Woman Destroyed* of 1967 – remain two of her most widely read texts. Her study of the aged and ageing, *Old Age*, published in 1970, has yet to find the readership it deserves, but may prove one of the foundational texts for a First World population whose demographical composition is shifting towards the aged. All of these texts are concerned with Beauvoir's characteristic topics of the split between subject and object, the questions surrounding embodiment, and the play of inter-subjectivity in individual and social terms.

Les Belles Images

Les Belles Images was Beauvoir's first novel since *The Mandarins* in 1954, and it was her last. The text she produced on returning to the genre after more than a decade is not only a beautifully crafted literary artefact but a timely and prescient attack on technocratically based consumerist culture. Composed in the mid-1960s, before the student revolts of 1968, it might have been written in the 1980s, for it portrays a social world where humans try to live as glossy automatons for whom life has become solely concentrated on the material pursuit of style. Discussing the book in *All Said and Done*, Beauvoir said that she culled the contemporary media for examples of 'processes of thought and formulas' whose inanity provided her with 'a collection of nonsense as dismaying as it was amusing'. This research allowed her to reproduce the exact 'sound' of the consumerist style-machine, in a book she structured around the themes of noise and silence.[1] The novel also took on the most fashionable Parisian intellectual theories of the day, particularly those of the *Tel Quel* group and Foucault, which Beauvoir criticized in an interview about *Les Belles Images* for suppressing history, praxis, the human, misery and evil, while assigning power only to the impersonal workings of systems.[2] Her novel is most concerned to reinstate the centrality of ethics amid the chatter of the media and of utopian dreams of a machine-made future.

The characters Beauvoir constructs to enact her contemporary fable were more distanced from her personal experience than any in her previous fiction, except in the crucial sense that they figure as inhabitants of the historical and cultural milieu of postwar modernity in which Beauvoir herself was located. The novel charts the contemporary obsession with flawless objects, such as the newly done-up farmhouse, with its perfect flowers and decor, with which the text opens, and which has been given the final kiss of reality by virtue of having been photographed for several glossy magazines. The hyperreality of even the plants and the photogenic food and drink consumed at the farmhouse is matched by accounts of characters who themselves appear simply as living exponents of the opinions of the mass media of their day. Their professions are typically postindustrial: architecture, electronics, acting, health services. (There are examples, as well, of more old-fashioned bourgeois types – the lawyer, the dentist, the Christian. These reconcile themselves easily with their newer privileged variants.) The central character, Laurence, who works in advertising, feels stranded among the adults in her – only partial – unease with the values of this culture, with which she thinks she is happy to conform.

Her dissatisfaction, and her inability to articulate it or the reasons for it, as well as the ways in which her technocratic culture of unnatural perfection disallows the vocabulary of moral revulsion are Beauvoir's central themes. Interestingly, Beauvoir said that she found her characters in *Les Belles Images* stupid, repulsive, morally base.[3] And while superficially Beauvoir's presentation of these media-informed characters abuts Baudrillard's descriptions of postmodern humans as simulacra, just beneath the stylish surface of Beauvoir's fictional landscape lie the ancient vices of selfishness, greed and cruelty, which bubble away as the motivations beneath her cool characters' active choices.

Les Belles Images pits the aesthetic of inhuman technological perfectibility (which implies a stasis which for Beauvoir itself theoretically precludes desire, transcendence, and therefore subjectivity) against an ethical response to a world which has become inarticulate. The attempt to recover the ethical in a culture which denies its existence is represented by Laurence, a young, successful wife and mother. She has had a breakdown in the past, and has tried to assuage her radical unease and the deadening of her sensibilities with the fashionable antidote of a love affair, and with the distractions of work. Laurence seems rich in everything her culture values: material success, an enviable marriage, clever children, a father she adores. Her uncertainty about her state, however, is captured in the narrative in which her consciousness is portrayed as engaged in a constant alternating turmoil of doubt and reassurance about all the elements of her situation.

This radical unease is crystallized by her young daughter's questions about happiness, triggered by a poster of a hungry child. As Laurence considers the questions of evil, oppression, insufficiency and greed (all evoked by Beauvoir's characteristic trope of hunger as the sign of evil, a sign which recurs in her autobiography connected with war and famine, as it does in dramatic form in *Who Shall Die?*) the narrative swings through repeated episodes which show the absence of reciprocity in intimate and in larger social human relations dominated by the technocratic code. The characters treat each other solely as objects, to accumulate or discard as they judge to their advantage, with youth, sex, wealth, status and the bad faith of media-derived social pressure as their sole concerns.

Beauvoir noted that the problem of the book, for her, was to make the inability to articulate what is wrong with this culture, in which the possibility of reciprocity is rejected in favour of the supreme dominance of the object, the topic of the text itself. 'It was', she said, 'a question of making the silence speak.'⁴ She offers a double resolution to this question by showing Laurence take refuge in the silence of a new breakdown, in her compulsive, anorexic vomiting of the sustenance provided by her culture, followed by her demand that her daughter be allowed to visit the home of her Jewish friend who is clearly attuned both to suffering and to the profound moral choices which structure the human world. Laurence cannot articulate the nature of the void her world presents to her. But she tries to ensure that her daughter, on the verge of adolescence (for Beauvoir the age of moral awakening), will find a friend and an ethics to lead her out of the unspeakable impasse of the nullity of consumerist values.

The Woman Destroyed

One of the most vivid (and repellent) characters in *Les Belles Images* is Laurence's mother Dominique, a fifty-one-year-old actress who is deserted by her (extremely rich) lover for a much younger woman, and who is devastated as much by her declining market value as a desirable sexual object as by the signs of ageing on her body. Expressing her genuine suffering in rage, vindictiveness, scheming and self-delusion, Dominique provides a prototype for several characters in the three *nouvelles* which make up Beauvoir's next volume of fiction, *The Woman Destroyed*. The themes of this collection, said Beauvoir, link back to *Les Belles Images* in that the characters in two of them are actively engaged in lying to themselves, in weaving the darkness which engulfs them, and all three stories are concerned with isolation and failure for women who lose their illusion of reciprocity with the men who are their husbands. The collection also draws on ideas from *The Second Sex* in its treatment of the dependent position of women, and the dangers to them if they acquiesce in it, and looks forward to *Old Age* in its attention to the internalization of helplessness which often characterizes ageing.

Beauvoir noted that the reception of this book was both mixed and contradictory, with some readers understanding and praising her three tales of complicity in the enactment of 'failure, error and bad faith', while others took them as simple instances of male-bashing, and still others as downmarket romances. Finally, some feminists were disappointed that Beauvoir had not provided an uplifting text. For her part, Beauvoir pointed out that a feminist reading of *The Woman Destroyed* was quite legitimate, but declined, as usual, to write to the demands of any programme but her own.[5] Like *Les Belles Images*, *The Woman Destroyed* was a bestseller: Beauvoir had again drawn her audience into consideration of serious ethical issues in her last work of fiction.

The three *nouvelles* which make up the volume are linked in their attention to women's suffering as they face different crises all related to their delusions about themselves and their feminine roles. Formally, they each feature separate narrative techniques which allow for the direct fictional portrayal of subjectivity. The first story, 'The Age of Discretion', consists of the first-person narrative of an ageing author whose son has assumed his own identity and who feels that she faces the void as she loses her illusions that she controls him and that he has infused her with his youth. Equally, she sees her husband, a scientist past his prime, as a spent force who will not help her sufficiently in reclaiming their son for the kind of life she wants for him. At the same time, her latest book, which she had thought her best, simply repeats her old work, and is seen to do so. Her body lets her down. She finds she must abandon her previous belief in progress and control, and she conceives of ageing only as collapse and dread.

The second tale, 'Monologue', with its epigraph from Flaubert, presents a direct transcription of an interior monologue and a telephone conversation by Murielle, a woman abandoned by her men, who has driven her daughter to suicide and been separated from her son, and who blames everyone rather than herself for her situation as an outcast. The contents of her consciousness consist of a long, violent, enraged cry of self-justification and demands for revenge which illustrate various aspects of bad faith.

The final story, 'The Woman Destroyed', uses the diary form to trace the reaction of Monique, the perfectly domesticated woman, whose husband leaves her for a younger (and predatory) female colleague who has not subsided into dependence. In facing this unwanted situation, Monique seems to lose her identity, and her self-justification, which was, she tells herself, to create happiness for her husband and daughters, but which meant, in effect, her embracing of the idea that her subjectivity could be submerged in that of others. This self-interested pseudo-relinquishment of self has now been revealed as false, and Monique is left with nothing but the fear of the future as an autonomous subject which it was her main project in life to evade.

'Failure, error and bad faith' were Beauvoir's terms to describe the common elements shared by these three accounts of ontological and ethical delusion, kinds of delusion which are not limited by sex, race or age. She might also have mentioned fear, defeat and derangement. These are, indeed, bleak tales and Beauvoir has been criticized especially for her harshness towards these female characters while letting her male figures off lightly. However, it can also be said that it is to women's condition that Beauvoir is most concerned to speak in these contemporary cautionary tales of female desolation which exactly reverse the tradition of tales that school women in the moral necessity of docile wifehood and dependency. Each of the women in the stories faces either isolation or self-diminution as they experience the insufficiency of the female gender roles they have used to screen off their inescapable freedom and responsibility. The roles have been justified as the self-sacrifice of motherhood or wifely dedication, but they have given these three women no protection from the necessity of recognizing their position as subjects, that is, as active ethical agents with all the social and personal elements that involves. Each wishes, in some way, to assert a bond of dependency which carries its own guarantee of control: each is blocked in her attempt by the contrary choices of other subjects who refuse inertia and manipulation. And each suffers from hostility to her own embodiment as a middle-aged or elderly woman, a physical state which carries no positive cultural meanings for them, and which marks a theme in the text that links it closely with Beauvoir's next published work, *Old Age*.

Old Age

Old Age can best be read as a companion volume to *The Second Sex*. And if *The Second Sex* has performed impressively as an ethical, intellectual and political irritant in the fifty years since its appearance, Beauvoir's second vast work of applied ethics, *Old Age*, published in 1970 when she was sixty-two, is a text still waiting for its time to come. As the century ends and as the demographic swing from youth to age in the population of the West becomes more pronounced, the power of Beauvoir's radical reassessment of the position of the elderly is likely to command its deserved attention.

Interestingly, as in *The Second Sex*, Beauvoir introduces her project with a statement of intent to irritate. She cites the outrage she caused by broaching the 'forbidden subject' of her own old age in 1963 at the end of the third volume of her autobiography, *Force of Circumstance*. Her aim in *Old Age*, she says, is 'to break the conspiracy of silence' about ageing.[6] She intends to disturb society's peace of mind on this subject which it pretends does not exist: she says she will 'compel' her readers to listen to the voices of the old, to recognize the 'barbarous' treatment the elderly suffer.[7] She intends to irritate and proceeds to do it with all the intellectual resources of her philosophical armoury.

Beauvoir became less and less susceptible to the slide away from concrete experience as she aged. In an inversion of more usual life patterns, her activism increased with her years, and after she had attained celebrity in the aftermath of World War II, she used her fame to champion various radical political projects. As an author, and as a highly visible French intellectual, this support was best expressed through her writing. It is for this reason, for example, that the Cold War and the Algerian War for independence saturate the events recounted in the third volume of her autobiography, *Force of Circumstance*, as much as World War II does the second volume, *Prime of Life*; in the same way, support for the students' and workers' protests of 1968, interest in Cuba and China, as well as a growing commitment to feminist activism feature strongly in the fourth volume, *All Said and Done*. All of these affiliations are underpinned by Beauvoir's ethics, and noting the philosophical ground of her activities is a frequent dimension of her autobiographical accounts of her political commitments.

In addition, Beauvoir produced an impressive amount of occasional writing specifically targeted at political issues. Her introduction to *Djamila Boupacha*, an impassioned case history of a young

Algerian woman who had been raped and tortured by the French, which Beauvoir put together with her friend and associate, the lawyer Gisèle Halimi, in 1962 is an excellent example of this kind of work.[8] Beauvoir's interest in applied ethics ranged over the entirety of the most dangerous issues of her day: racism, colonialism, socialism. But her two most constant areas of concern were those which elicited major studies from her. As well as her deep attention to the condition of women, which generated *The Second Sex* and remained in play throughout her fiction, Beauvoir displayed a continuing interest in the process of ageing and the place of the old, an interest which found its fullest expression in the text under consideration here.[9]

Beauvoir found the taboo against discussion of ageing as strong as that against making serious claims for women's equality. Her memoirs, which, it must be recalled, began to appear in the year she reached the age of fifty (the fourth volume came out when she was in her mid-sixties), are as attentive to her experience of ageing as to her position as a woman. And just as she threads analysis of the effects of her gender through her autobiographical narrative in elements which predate her overt awakening to its true significance, so she ascribes the first signs of the onset of old age to remarkably early points in her experience. By doing this, Beauvoir treats ageing as a process rather than an event, a becoming instead of a fixed moment in an argument which directly parallels her account of femininity. For Beauvoir, old age, like sexual identity, is a cultural effect which is not, strictly speaking, determined by a biological state. In terms of applied ethics, she analyses the fixed meanings ascribed to old age as a prelude to positing an alternative to what she sees as another example of human oppression so widespread as to appear, fallaciously, natural.

The topic is one to which Beauvoir frequently returns in her autobiographies, and she always uses these occasions to present parts of her argument regarding ageing. For example, in *Prime of Life*, writing about herself in 1934 when she was twenty-six, Beauvoir tells of her sense of her life being, in some sense, over. With her career secure and her friendships formed, she felt that nothing would ever again happen to her. She apprehended her situation as monotonous and fixed. Her characteristic 'hankering for the Absolute' and her equally characteristic apprehension of the vanity of life in the face of certain annihilation both drove her into depression and frequent tears. Further, she writes, 'I had another worry besides this: I was getting old. Neither my general health nor my facial appearance bore witness to the fact, but from time to time I felt that everything was going grey and colourless around me, and began to lament the decrepitude of my senses.' Her 'curiosity seemed stifled; excitement drained out of life; life seemed to move in a tight circle.'[10]

She picks up the theme of ageing forcefully in 1963 in the next volume of her memoirs, *Force of Circumstance*. Comments on the process of ageing are scattered throughout the text, more frequently than in *Prime of Life*, but Beauvoir sums up the significance of the process of ageing most pointedly in the epilogue to the book, which covers the period from the aftermath of World War II until the celebration of Algerian independence in 1962 (just as the Liberation of Paris and the end of World War II had closed *Prime of Life*). 'Since 1944,' she writes, 'the most important, the most irreparable thing that has happened to me is that . . . I have grown old. That means a great many things.' The meanings she then enumerates include the narrowing of the world and her growing sense of the finitude of its contents; the loss of any sense of the mystery of individuals; the absence of sudden apprehensions of the real which feel close to revelations. Beauty, she finds – and here she uses the aesthetic example of her response to a recording of a Beethoven andante – seems as often a loathsome attempt to justify the world's suffering as a pleasure. She is now aware that 'the truth of the human condition' is that 'two-thirds of mankind are hungry.' Hunger is, for Beauvoir, the bar to the assumption of any kind of liberty. As we have noted previously, she invokes it in many of her works as shorthand for absolute oppression, for utter material evil. And it fills most of the world. She no longer wants to travel much in an earth 'emptied of its marvels'. 'To grow old', she says, 'is to set limits on oneself, to shrink.'

She would like to know what will happen in a future in which only her ideas may live in the young in whose eyes she sees herself 'already dead and mummified'. Her contemporaries are old: she sees ghosts of their younger selves in their ageing faces. She cannot believe in her own ageing, only the mirror (that important Beauvoirian symbol of the subject's immanence) and its reflection of her own face convinces her of her age. As in her early presaging of age when she was twenty-six, the world appears grey, her powers of pleasure and revolt are diminished. The list grows of things which will never again be part of her experience: walking in the mountains, sexual intercourse with a man, skiing, the pleasure of rest after strenuous physical exertion. The only important novelties

will be misfortunes, deaths. In a final paragraph which is an enraged lament at the prospect of the annihilation of her consciousness, Beauvoir ends with a vehement statement as she takes stock of
her life: 'The promises have all been kept. And yet, turning an
incredulous gaze towards that young and credulous girl, I realize
with stupor how much I was gypped.'[11]

Understandably, Beauvoir's final sentence in *Force of Circumstance*
prompted extensive speculation. In an interview with Deirdre Bair
she commented further that her statement was made against her
alienation and despair at the Algerian conflict, during which she
received death threats and had to hide from right-wing bombers.
'"It was as if everything Sartre and I had worked for meant nothing.
We had very little hope in our lives, and I expressed it in my
writing."'[12] But this is clearly not the whole story (elsewhere, she
characterized the final sentence as her summary of her 'very
deep distress, my revolt at the horror of the world').[13] More specifically, Beauvoir's memorable cry of rage comes at the end of her long
account of ageing which constitutes her preliminary attempt to
think through both what ageing in general means and what emotions it evokes in her. The resonance of her final statement gives a
foretaste of the passion she will bring to her extended examination
of the subject in *Old Age*.

She returns to the subject of ageing, and her writing about it, in
All Said and Done. And she begins by discussing the reception of
Force of Circumstance. As always, she says, her intention in the book
was that of 'bearing witness' via the construction of the distanced
writer's 'I' which confounds genre and seeks to treat the personal as
a vehicle of general intersubjective communication. As with *The
Second Sex*, Beauvoir says explicitly that when she wrote *Force of
Circumstance* she 'hoped the book would give offence', and it did,
but not on the grounds she intended in savaging the French reaction
to the Algerian struggle for independence. 'I did give offence,' she
notes, 'but for a completely different reason: I spoke about old age
without glossing it over.' Just as her realization of the importance of
her gender came to her as a blinding shock after she was forty and
radically changed her apprehension of the world, so her discovery
of the convention of silence and euphemism which surrounds ageing startled her at the age of fifty-five. 'I did not then know', she
says, 'to what a degree the subject was taboo nor how shocking was
my sincerity.' The 'violent reproaches' coupled with an overwhelming parade of 'platitudes' about age which constituted the major
response to the book caught her attention. Surprisingly, she said,

even the readers who usually enjoyed her 'desire for intellectual clarity' protested.[14] The passion and unexpectedness of the response provided one spur to take on the topic of old age as the focus of her final extended book of applied ethics.

Like *The Second Sex*, Beauvoir's analysis in *Old Age* uses an organizing principle based on her theories of the Individual Other and the Social Other. The materialist orientation of her analysis has deepened since the composition of the earlier book (and, indeed, Beauvoir said that if she were to change *The Second Sex* it would be to shift its theoretical foundation to a materialist ground).[15] But Beauvoir's intersubjective ontology and her materialist principles are not only compatible but mutually reinforcing. There is no need to choose between them. The effect of the shift in balance between them, however, makes *Old Age* a more openly angry production than *The Second Sex*, and one whose invitation to activist response is more immediate.

Beauvoir opens *Old Age* with an evocation of the Buddha and his discovery of ageing as part of the entirety of the human condition which he chose to assume. This story, she says, violates the norm, which is to suppress knowledge of old age to the extent of denying its existence. Her intention is 'to break the conspiracy of silence' on the subject. Citing the Frankfurt School philosopher, Herbert Marcuse, and his observations on the quieting of guilt as necessary in consumer culture, she declares that her intention is to show that with regard to the aged, society 'is not only guilty but downright criminal'.[16] As in the opening to *The Second Sex*, Beauvoir stresses her purpose of annoying, of acting as an ethical abrasive against the complacency of unexamined cultural habit which oppresses significant numbers. Unlike the case of women, however, where evidence of society's need to justify its supposedly natural attitudes exists in overwhelming abundance, the position of the old is often one of invisibility.[17] The law, the media, the aged themselves appear to treat the old as part of a seamless category of responsible individual adults. In economic terms, however, society treats the old as if 'they belong to an entirely different species'.[18] Only trade unionists seem interested in material provision for those who no longer work at paying jobs: otherwise, the elderly are treated as a burden on those who still count in terms of economic activity.

Like women, the elderly have no group with whom they can make common cause. Ontologically, they are imagined, not as individuals with particular strengths and weaknesses, but as examples of 'another being', outside the fully human. The absolute alterity of the aged is taken for granted, and it is on this ground that the material provision needed for human life is denied them. Those who are not old cannot imagine ageing: death is a clearer prospect, and the idea of absolute nothingness provokes fewer problems for consciousness (and may even provide a few metaphysical thrills) than the notion of great age. Because consciousness refuses to ac-knowledge the metamorphosis attendant on ageing, the experience itself is denied, ignored, silenced. Old age regarded sentimentally as a time of freedom and old age regarded as the scrapping of surplus and useless persons are both scandals, a pernicious dualism which Beauvoir means to expose in order to reach a point where it is no longer 'almost tautological to say "old and poor"'.[19]

The situation of the consciousness of the old is particularly one in which the relationship with time is bound up with the material state of the body. The intersubjective constitution of the self in the aged is deeply affected by conventions pertaining to the attitude of the Other to the aged self in any given society at a given historical moment. 'Every human situation', writes Beauvoir, 'can be viewed from without – seen from the point of view of an outsider – or from within, in so far as the subject assumes and at the same time tran-scends it.'[20] The gaze of the Other, in the case of the old, tends to be entirely objectifying: encounters tend not to be reciprocal. The old are perceived not as Individual Others but as bundles of conven-tions, identityless instances of a condition regarded as unchanging and powerless. Only the tiny minority of the old who are wealthy escape this objectification by virtue of their economic force which allows the display of active engagement with the culture. Other-wise, the old are reduced to definition by the condition of their bodies, whose decrepitude is close to guaranteed by the poverty in which the great majority are kept. The failure to recognize that the condition of the old does not exist as an absolute, that the meaning of age is as much culturally specific as it is part of a biological process, which itself is complex, relative and ambiguous, forms the nexus of ideas that Beauvoir's book confronts.

In the course of her study, in which Beauvoir examines the bio-logical, ethnological and historical record concerning old age, she notes repeatedly that there is no extant contemporary society which adequately values and cares for the old. Everything, in her view, must change before the disgraceful manner in which the human race treats such a large part of itself can be corrected. In particular, the shared capitalist and socialist obsession with economic produc-tivity as the dominant gauge of human value must shift, while the recognition that the essence of life is the ability to formulate projects and act on them at any age must replace the idea that orientation towards futurity ends with the coming of age.

The intersection of Beauvoir's ontological and material analysis of ageing is nowhere so apparent as in the second half of the study where she examines the experience of ageing from the point of view of the old. Rejecting the cliché that consciousness can avoid age if it will, that 'you are as young as you feel', Beauvoir puts her theories of the intersubjective self to profound use. Insisting on the total inwardness of the phenomenon of ageing, she says, displays

> a complete misunderstanding of the complex truth of old age: for the outsider it is a dialectic relationship between my being as he defines it objectively and the awareness of myself that I acquire by means of him. Within me it is the Other – that is to say the person I am for the outsider – who is old: and that Other is myself.[21]

Consciousness itself, she says, is unaware of age: time is a factor external to it and knowledge of its impact must be refracted from outside itself. For consciousness, time is either the immanence of stasis, or the orientation towards the future constituted by transcendence in the conceiving and the pursuit of projects.

Consciousness of being categorized as old is a cultural matter which originates outside the self and, like other forms of alienation from the self which result from social classification, it comprises an internalization of the view of the self by the Other. Beauvoir makes this point lucidly: 'since it is the Other within us who is old, it is natural that the revelation of our age should come to us from outside – from others.' That it should do so can be shocking (Beauvoir cites Proust, Mme de Sévigné, Oliver Wendel Holmes, Casanova and herself as examples of those who have been startled by others' remarks on their ageing).[22] The shock comes from the unwillingness of the self to assume the definition of old age, which currently means relegation to the less than human. And there is no mystery as to why this should be so. The assumption of the definition and its ascription to the self means the internalization of otherness within the self, and in all modern cultures the acceptance of an internalized definition of a self which is less than human. Under these conditions, it is no wonder that old age is treated as a matter of shame, silence and evasion. It means the closure of possibilities of reciprocity, the end of the mutual exchange between Self and Other, and the agreed subsidence into a culturally dictated situation of objectification and immanence.

Beauvoir's passionate call for the revision of notions of social value which are based solely on profitability ends her analysis. Old age itself, she says, must be radically reconsidered. Ageing must not be thought of as 'an activity': it is a biological process dictated by the passing of time. Life is, on the contrary, action. 'There is only one solution if old age is not to be an absurd parody of our former life,' she writes, 'and that is to go on pursuing ends that give our existence a meaning – devotion to individuals, to groups or to causes, social, political, intellectual or creative work.'[23] Old age, she says, contrary to received wisdom, should not be about passivity but passion. The old, like everyone else, must turn outwards to others in the reciprocity which is the mark of human value. *Old Age* is itself an enactment of this passion for 'love, friendship, indignation, compassion' which, in a characteristic mix, are the identifying marks of the entirety of Beauvoir's life and thought.

In all of her fiction, all of her formal philosophical essays, in both *The Second Sex* and *Old Age*, Beauvoir builds on her radical notions of the ontology of reciprocity and embodiment of consciousness first formulated in the 1930s with the writing of *She Came to Stay* and extended and glossed in all her subsequent writing. Her early construction of philosophical foundations provided Beauvoir with a powerful and flexible tool for ethical analysis of some of the most deeply rooted human abuses. In her attention to the effects of culture on consciousness and its ability to orient itself towards agency, freedom and mutuality, she produced a body of work which provides one of the most important extended examples of ethical engagement grounded in philosophical passion of the modern period.

Notes

Book epigraph from Margaret A. Simons and Jessica Benjamin, 'Simone de Beauvoir: An Interview', *Feminist Studies*, 2 (Summer 1979), p. 339.

Introduction

1 Interest in Beauvoir's philosophy has always been at least a muted part of the reception of her work. And in recent years, and especially in the wake of work by Margaret A. Simons and Linda Singer, this interest has grown to the point that one may speak of a philosophical renaissance in Beauvoir studies. In addition, the critical literature on other aspects of Beauvoir is often of very high quality. See, for example, in addition to our own *Simone de Beauvoir and Jean-Paul Sartre: The Remaking of a Twentieth-Century Legend* (Hemel Hempstead: Harvester Wheatsheaf, 1993; New York: Basic Books, 1994) and 'Whose Ethics, Sartre's or Beauvoir's?', *Simone de Beauvoir Studies*, 12 (1995): Sonia Kruks, 'Simone de Beauvoir and the Limits to Freedom', *Social Text* (Autumn 1987), pp. 111–22, 'Gender and Subjectivity: Simone de Beauvoir and Contemporary Feminism', *Signs*, 18.1 (Autumn 1992), pp. 89–110, and 'Excerpts from "Simone de Beauvoir between Sartre and Merleau-Ponty"', *Simone de Beauvoir Studies*, 5 (1988), pp. 74–80; María Teresa López Pardina, 'Simone de Beauvoir as Philosopher', *Simone de Beauvoir Studies*, 11 (1994), pp. 5–12; Michèle Le Doeuff, *Hipparchia's Choice: An Essay Concerning Women, Philosophy, etc.*, trans. Trista Selous (Oxford: Blackwell, 1991) and 'Operative Philosophy: Simone de Beauvoir and Existentialism', trans. Colin Gordon, *Ideology and Consciousness*, 6 (Autumn 1979), pp. 47–57; Margaret A. Simons, 'Beauvoir and Sartre: The Philosophical Relationship', *Yale French Studies*, 72 (1986), pp. 165–79; Linda Singer, 'Interpretation and Retrieval: Rereading Beauvoir', *Women's Studies International Forum*, 8.3 (1985), pp. 231–8; Chantal Moubachir, *Simone de Beauvoir ou le souci de différence* (Paris: Seghers, 1972); Toril Moi, *Simone de Beauvoir: The Making of an Intellectual Woman* (Oxford: Blackwell, 1994); Debra A. Bergoffen,

'Toward a Feminist Ethic: First Steps', *Simone de Beauvoir Studies*, 8 (1991), pp. 163–73, 'Simone de Beauvoir: Cartesian Legacies', *Simone de Beauvoir Studies*, 7 (1990), pp. 15–28, 'From Husserl to Beauvoir: Gendering the Perceiving Subject', *Metaphilosophy*, 27.1–2 (Jan.–Apr. 1996), pp. 53–62; Eleanore Holveck, 'Simone de Beauvoir: Autobiography as Philosophy', *Simone de Beauvoir Studies*, 8 (1991), pp. 103–10, and *'La Cérémonie des adieux*: Simone de Beauvoir's Philosophical Interpretation of Death', *Simone de Beauvoir Studies*, 6 (1989), pp. 69–79; Elizabeth Fallaize, *The Novels of Simone de Beauvoir* (London: Routledge, 1988); Monika Langer, 'A Philosophical Retrieval of Simone de Beauvoir's *Pour une morale de l'ambiguïté'*, *Philosophy Today* (Summer 1994), pp. 181–90; as well as the special feature on Beauvoir in *Women and Politics*, 11.1 (1991). See also essays on Beauvoir as philosopher by Karen Vintges, Julien Murphy, Julie K. Ward, Kruks, Le Doeuff, Holveck, Bergoffen, and Fullbrook and Fullbrook in Margaret A. Simons, ed., *Feminist Interpretations of Simone de Beauvoir* (University Park: Pennsylvania State University Press, 1995). An excellent list of the general orientation of books about Beauvoir is provided by Moi, *Simone de Beauvoir*, p. 268. Two excellent studies of Beauvoir's thought have just been published: Debra B. Bergoffen, *The Philosophy of Simone de Beauvoir: Gendered Phenomenologies, Erotic Generosities* (Albany: State University of New York Press, 1997), and Eva Lundgren-Gothlin, *Sex and Existence: Simone de Beauvoir's 'The Second Sex'*, trans. Linda Schenck (London: Athlone, 1996).

2 Margaret A. Simons 'Two Interviews with Simone de Beauvoir', in Nancy Fraser and Sandra Lee Bartkey, eds, *Revaluing French Feminism: Critical Essays on Difference, Agency, and Culture* (Bloomington: Indiana University Press, 1992), pp. 27–8. For an alternative translation see Simone de Beauvoir, *The Prime of Life* (1960), trans. Peter Green (Harmondsworth: Penguin, 1965), pp. 220–1.

3 Simons, 'Two Interviews', p. 34.

4 In her review in 1945 of Merleau-Ponty's most important work, *The Phenomenology of Perception*, Beauvoir notes that 'Merleau-Ponty does not invent a system.' See *'La Phénomenologie de la perception de Merleau-Ponty'*, *Les Temps Modernes*, 1.2 (Nov. 1945), pp. 363–7.

5 Margaret A. Simons and Jessica Benjamin, 'Simone de Beauvoir: An Interview', *Feminist Studies*, 2 (Summer 1979), p. 338.

6 Simone de Beauvoir, *Force of Circumstance* (1963), trans. Richard Howard (Harmondsworth: Penguin, 1968), p. 6.

Chapter 1   The Education of a Philosopher

Epigraph from Simons, 'Two Interviews', p. 34.

1 See also Toril Moi's important chapter on the education of Beauvoir in *Simone de Beauvoir*, pp. 37–72, as well as Catharine Savage Brosman, *Simone de Beauvoir Revisited* (Boston: Twayne, 1991), pp. 7–12; Claude Francis and Fernande Gontier, *Simone de Beauvoir*, trans. Lisa Nesselson (London: Mandarin, 1989), pp. 49–92; and Margaret A. Simons, 'Introduction' to Simons, *Feminist Interpretations*, pp. 1–3. Information in this chapter is taken from Beauvoir's autobiographies as well as from the sources noted here.

2 Simone de Beauvoir, *Memoirs of a Dutiful Daughter* (1958), trans. James Kirkup (Harmondsworth: Penguin, 1963), p. 41.
3 Ibid., p. 75.
4 Ibid., p. 129.
5 Deirdre Bair, *Simone de Beauvoir: A Biography* (London: Jonathan Cape, 1990), p. 623.
6 Bertrand Russell, *History of Western Philosophy*, 2nd edn (London: Allen and Unwin, 1961), p. 444.
7 *Memoirs*, p. 157.
8 Ibid., p. 158.
9 Ibid., p. 160. In addition, see Moi, *Simone de Beauvoir*, pp. 50–1.
10 For details of Beauvoir's higher education see *Memoirs*, esp. pp. 168, 179, 184, 204, 137, 245; Moi, *Simone de Beauvoir*, p. 50; Brosman, *Simone de Beauvoir Revisited*, pp. 8–12; Simons, 'Introduction' to *Feminist Interpretations*, pp. 2–3; Francis and Gontier, *Simone de Beauvoir*, pp. 51–92.
11 See Brosman, *Simone de Beauvoir Revisited*, p. 8, and *Memoirs*, p. 68.
12 *Memoirs*, p. 171.
13 Moi, *Simone de Beauvoir*, p. 1.
14 John Gerassi, *Jean-Paul Sartre: Hated Conscience of his Century*, vol. 1: *Protestant or Protester* (London: University of Chicago Press, 1989), p. 91.
15 See Annie Cohen-Solal, *Sartre: A Life* (London: Heinemann, 1987), pp. 74, 75; see also Moi (*Simone de Beauvoir*, p. 31) who cites the French version of Cohen-Solal's interview with Gandillac, who remarked of Beauvoir: '*La philosophie, c'était elle.*'
16 See Fullbrook and Fullbrook, *Simone de Beauvoir and Jean-Paul Sartre*, pp. 53–4, 61; and Bair, *Simone de Beauvoir*, who cites Gandillac, pp. 145–6.
17 *Memoirs*, p. 179.
18 Ibid., pp. 238, 260.
19 Ibid., p. 238,
20 *Force of Circumstance*, p. 12.
21 *Memoirs*, pp. 173, 180.
22 Ibid., p. 181.
23 Ibid., pp. 191, 181, 190.
24 Ibid., p. 173; see also Michèle Le Doeuff on the dynamics of the transmission of knowledge and power between teachers and students, in 'Women and Philosophy', *Radical Philosophy*, 17 (1977), pp. 2–11.
25 See *Memoirs*, pp. 185, 204, 223, 259.
26 Ibid., pp. 260, 222–5.
27 Ibid., p. 226.
28 Ibid., pp. 223, 207.
29 Ibid., pp. 223, 217, 257.
30 The best study of Beauvoir's concern with death remains Elaine Marks, *Simone de Beauvoir: Encounters with Death* (New Brunswick: Rutgers University Press, 1971).
31 *Memoirs*, p. 231.
32 *Prime of Life*, p. 18.
33 *Memoirs*, p. 234.
34 Ibid., p. 235.
35 For a good recent brief commentary on surrealism and Dada, see Peter Nicholls, *Modernisms: A Literary Guide* (London: Macmillan, 1995), pp. 223–

50, 279–300; for Beauvoir on surrealism see *Memoirs*, pp. 234–5, 237, 244, 273.
36 *Memoirs*, p. 247.
37 Ibid., p. 248.
38 Ibid., p. 261.
39 Ibid., p. 263. Additional thanks must go to Margaret A. Simons for her illuminating comments on Leibniz and Baruzi.
40 Ibid., p. 267.
41 Ibid., p. 340. Gerassi, *Jean-Paul Sartre*, vol. 1, p. 74. On Brunschvicg see Bair, *Simone de Beauvoir*, p. 628. Brunschvicg so imposed himself on the imaginations of Sartre and his friend Paul Nizan that he served as something of a bête noir in their early writing. For them, to use a crude Freudian analogy, he was clearly the philosophical father who needed to be overcome. See Ronald Hayman, *Writing Against: A Biography of Sartre* (London: Weidenfeld and Nicolson, 1986), p. 330, and Gerassi, *Jean-Paul Sartre*, vol. 1, pp. 83–5.
42 *Memoirs*, p. 266.
43 See Hayman, *Writing Against*, pp. 70, 68; Cohen-Solal, *Sartre*, p. 88.
44 Bair, *Simone de Beauvoir*, pp. 654–5.
45 For accounts of other instances of Beauvoir's tendency to disguise aspects of her life see Fullbrook and Fullbrook, *Simone de Beauvoir and Jean-Paul Sartre*.
46 Francis and Gontier, *Simone de Beauvoir*, pp. 118–20; *Prime of Life*, pp. 52–3.
47 Bair, *Simone de Beauvoir*, p. 628.
48 Ibid., pp. 279, 283.
49 Ibid., pp. 288, 327, 294, 295.
50 Ibid., p. 305.
51 Ibid., pp. 313, 314.
52 Ibid., pp. 314, 323.
53 Ibid., pp. 329, 332, 339.
54 Ibid., pp. 344–5.
55 *Prime of Life*, pp. 15, 16, 20–2.
56 Ibid., pp. 22, 25.
57 *Memoirs*, p. 230.
58 See Shadia B. Drury, *Alexandre Kojève: The Roots of Postmodern Politics* (London: Macmillan, 1994), p. ix, and *Force of Circumstance*, p. 43.
59 See *Prime of Life*, pp. 220–1, for Beauvoir on her own habits of philosophical thought. Note, too, that she declares herself to have been Sartre's 'disciple' only 'intermittently'.
60 Ibid., pp. 40, 47–51, quotation from p. 51.
61 Ibid., p. 79; grave doubts remained about Heidegger for Beauvoir in 1939 when Sartre was excited by Heidegger's work (see p. 355).
62 Ibid., p. 144. On Kierkegaard see pp. 48, 135; on Hegel, p. 48.
63 Ibid., p. 456. See Simone de Beauvoir, *Journal de guerre: Septembre 1939– Janvier 1941*, ed. Sylvie le Bon de Beauvoir (Paris: Gallimard, 1990), p. 297, for the full text of the passage Beauvoir copied from Hegel.
64 *Prime of Life*, pp. 469–70.

Chapter 2   Writing for her Life

1 *Prime of Life*, p. 225.
2 Ibid., pp. 327, 327–8.

3 Bair, *Simone de Beauvoir*, p. 206.
4 Ibid., pp. 207–8.
5 Ibid., p. 209.
6 Beauvoir cites these comments from Grasset's reader, Henry Müller, in *Prime of Life*, p. 327.
7 The best source of information on Beauvoir's publishing career is *Les Écrits de Simone de Beauvoir* (1979), ed. C. Francis and F. Gontier (Paris: Gallimard, 1979). In addition, for information on material by and about Beauvoir in English see Joan Norquist, *Simone de Beauvoir: A Bibliography* (Santa Cruz: Reference and Research Services, 1991).

Chapter 3   Literature and Philosophy

1 Maurice Merleau-Ponty, 'Metaphysics and the Novel', in *Sense and Non-sense*, trans. Hubert L. Dreyfus and Patricia Allen Dreyfus (Evanston, Ill.: Northwestern University Press, 1964), pp. 26–40.
2 Ibid., p. 27.
3 Ibid.
4 Simone de Beauvoir, 'Littérature et métaphysique' (1946), in *L'Existentialisme et la sagesse des nations* (Paris: Nagel, 1948), p. 116. All translations from this essay are our own.
5 Eleanore Holveck, 'Can a Woman be a Philosopher? Reflections of a Beauvoirean Housemaid', in Simons, *Feminist Interpretations*, p. 70.
6 See *Prime of Life*, p. 221, and 'Littérature et métaphysique', pp. 106–7.
7 Simone de Beauvoir, *Pyrrhus et Cinéas* (Paris: Gallimard, 1944), pp. 34–5. Unless otherwise indicated, translations from this text are our own.
8 Ibid., p. 58.
9 Simone de Beauvoir, 'Preface', to *America Day by Day* (1948), trans. Patrick Dudley (London: Duckworth, 1952).
10 Margaret A. Simons. 'Joining Another's Fight: Beauvoir's Post-Modern Challenge to Racism in *America Day by Day*', paper delivered to the Midwest Division, Society for Women in Philosophy, Oct. 1994, p. 5.
11 Merleau-Ponty, 'Metaphysics and the Novel', p. 27.
12 Ibid., pp. 27–8.
13 'Littérature et métaphysique', p. 114.
14 Ibid., p. 119.
15 Holveck, 'Can a Woman be a Philosopher?', p. 72.
16 'Littérature et métaphysique', p. 105.
17 Ibid., pp. 105–6.
18 Ibid., p. 106.
19 Ibid., p. 106.
20 Ibid., pp. 106–7.
21 Ibid., p. 109.
22 Ibid., pp. 123–4.
23 Mary Warnock, *Existentialism* (Oxford; Oxford University Press, 1970), p. 133.
24 Ibid., p. 136.
25 'Littérature et métaphysique', pp. 118–20.
26 Ibid., p. 119.

27 Simone de Beauvoir, *All Men Are Mortal* (1946), trans. Leonard M. Friedman (New York: Norton, 1992), p. 7.
28 Ibid., p. 117.
29 Ibid., pp. 149, 151, 152, 153, 157.
30 Ibid., p. 163.
31 Ibid., p. 173.
32 Ibid., pp. 187–8.
33 Ibid., pp. 201, 202.
34 Ibid., p. 276.
35 Ibid., p. 327.
36 *Force of Circumstance*, p. 71.
37 *All Men Are Mortal*, p. 328.
38 *Force of Circumstance*, p. 74.
39 *All Men Are Mortal*, p. 339.

Chapter 4   Narrative Selves

1 Immanuel Kant, *Critique of Pure Reason*, trans. J. M. D. Meiklejohn (London: Dent, 1934), p. 69.
2 Structuralism in the 1960s and 1970s may be viewed as a further attempt at reviving the Kantian programme.
3 From Kierkegaard's *Repetition*, cited in Paul Roubiczek, *Existentialism: For and Against* (Cambridge: Cambridge University Press, 1964), p. 57. As Roubiczek notes on the same page, this passage closely resembles the following from Pascal's *Pensées* (No. 205): 'I am frightened, and am astonished at being here rather than there; for there is no reason why here rather than there, why now rather than then. Who has put me here? By whose order and direction have this place and time been allotted to me?'
4 *Prime of Life*, pp. 304–5.
5 David Hume, *A Treatise of Human Nature*, Book 1, pt 4, sec. 6 (Oxford: Clarendon Press, 1978), p. 252.
6 Ibid., pp. 252, 253.
7 Ibid., p. 636.
8 Kant, *Critique of Pure Reason*, pt 2, ch. 2, sec. 2, no. 14, p. 98.
9 'Littérature et métaphysique', p. 115.
10 See Simone de Beauvoir, 'Deux chapitres inédits de *L'Invitée*' in *Les Écrits*, pp. 275–6; *Memoirs*, p. 49; and *She Came to Stay* (1943), trans. Yvonne Moyse and Roger Senhouse (London: Flamingo, 1984), pp. 115–16. Beauvoir also refers to the incident in *Memoirs*, p. 159, and *She Came to Stay*, p. 118.
11 *She Came to Stay*, pp. 115–16. This passage was first written for the subsequently discarded chapters of the novel, and copied into the later text. See 'Deux chapitres inédits de *L'Invitée*', pp. 275–6.
12 *Memoirs*, pp. 112, 139.
13 Margaret A. Simons, 'Beauvoir and the Problem of the Other', paper presented at the American Philosophical Association, Pacific Division, San Francisco, March 1995.
14 *Memoirs*, p. 157.
15 '*La Phénoménologie de la perception* de Maurice Merleau-Ponty', p. 364. Our translation.

16 John Macquarrie, *Existentialism* (Harmondsworth: Penguin, 1973), pp. 202–3.

17 *Prime of Life*, pp. 128–9.

18 *Pyrrhus et Cinéas*, p. 35.

19 The quotation from *Prime of Life* is translated by and cited in Peter Caws, *Sartre* (London: Routledge and Kegan Paul, 1979), p. 51.

20 *Pyrrhus et Cinéas*, pp. 53–4.

21 Hume, *A Treatise of Human Nature*, p. 636.

22 Simone de Beauvoir, *When Things of the Spirit Come First: Five Early Tales* (1979), trans. Patrick O'Brian (London: Flamingo, 1983), p. 163.

23 Ibid., pp. 170–1.

24 Ibid., pp. 173, 186, 190.

25 Ibid., p. 200.

26 Hume, *A Treatise of Human Nature*, p. 253.

27 *When Things of the Spirit Come First*, p. 201.

28 'Deux chapitres inédits de *L'Invitée*', pp. 277–8.

29 Ibid., p. 277.

30 Ibid., p. 277.

31 Ibid., pp. 277–8.

32 Ibid., p. 278 (emphasis added).

33 Perhaps Sartre knew this passage from Beauvoir's rejected manuscript from 1937 when he wrote his celebrated paragraph on the café waiter for *Being and Nothingness* in the early 1940s. For example, consider the following: 'the waiter in the café cannot be immediately a café waiter in the sense that this inkwell *is* an inkwell, or the glass is a glass . . . I can be he [the waiter] only . . . as the actor is Hamlet, by mechanically making the typical gestures of my state . . .' Jean-Paul Sartre, *Being and Nothingness: An Essay on Phenomenological Ontology*, trans. Hazel E. Barnes (New York: Philosophical Library, 1956), pp. 59–60.

34 Ibid., p. 181; *Being and Nothingness* cited in Caws, *Sartre*, p. 83; Joseph S. Catalano, *A Commentary on Jean-Paul Sartre's Being and Nothingness* (London: University of Chicago Press, 1974), p. 88.

35 In Beauvoir's and Sartre's work it is important not to confuse the rejection of a self or ego, whether transcendental or empirical, resident in consciousness, with the explication of such a rejection within the context of Husserl's phenomenology. When this distinction is not lost, Sartre's *The Transcendence of the Ego* appears as a contextual interpretation of a philosophical position already held by Beauvoir when she met Sartre.

36 Simone de Beauvoir, *The Ethics of Ambiguity* (1947), trans. Bernard Frechtman (New York: Citadel Press, 1970), p. 36.

37 Ibid., p. 39.

38 Ibid., pp. 38–9.

39 Ibid., pp. 39–40.

40 *Prime of Life*, pp. 128–9.

41 *Ethics of Ambiguity*, p. 40.

42 Ibid., pp. 37, 12–13.

43 Steven Earnshaw, 'Love and the Subject' in Jane Dowson and Steven Earnshaw, eds, *Postmodern Subjects/Postmodern Texts* (Amsterdam: Rodopi, 1995), p. 60.

44 See Debra Bergoffen, *The Philosophy of Simone de Beauvoir*; 'From Husserl to

Beauvoir'; and 'Contesting Intentional Anxieties', Silverman Phenomenology Series, Duquesne University Press, Pittsburgh.
45 *Ethics of Ambiguity*, pp. 12–13.
46 *America Day by Day*, p. 18, cited by Margaret A. Simons in 'Joining Another's Fight', where Simons also cites similar passages.
47 Beauvoir's original exposition of her theory of two modes of intentionality is in 'Deux chapitres inédits de *L'Invitée*'. In its first chapter, the narrative deliberately shifts back and forth between the two primary intentional modes of Françoise's consciousness (see especially pp. 297–8). Beauvoir sets out her case for the existence of a mode of disclosure or pure witnessing in a series of examples featuring solitude and childhood innocence. The reader repeatedly observes Françoise alone in the countryside, foregoing her usual playing at being herself. Instead she confronts the mere existence of the world around her in pure and selfless and joyous wonderment. Although adults are less likely to experience such intensity of joy in revealing the being of things disconnected from their worldly pursuits, Françoise's example suggests a general truth. Everyone has experienced joy, delight, simple pleasure from the mere fact that some things – a sunset, a cup of coffee, a piece of music, the smile on a child's face – *wholly without value to our projects to be or to achieve any end* become present to our consciousness. These and countless other objects of consciousness which evoke this characteristic human experience of the groundless welling-up of delight suggest that the disclosure of being can be an end in itself, a primary mode of intentionality.
48 Merleau-Ponty, 'Metaphysics and the Novel', p. 29.

Chapter 5   Embodiment and Intersubjectivity

1 Beauvoir's intentions are recognized by Merleau-Ponty in 'Metaphysics and the Novel', when, after studying the manuscript of Beauvoir's novel in December 1940, he noted its concern with the relation of body to consciousness. (See 'Metaphysics and the Novel', pp. 29, 33–4; and Simone de Beauvoir, *Letters to Sartre* (1990), trans. Quintin Hoare (London: Radius, 1991), pp. 356, 364.) His own theory of embodied consciousness in his influential *Phenomenology of Perception* (1945) closely resembles Beauvoir's. In addition, in *The Literature of Possibility* (1959), Hazel Barnes, the English translator and a respected critic of Sartre's *Being and Nothingness*, described *She Came to Stay*'s theory of intersubjectivity at length and observed its exact correspondence with Sartre's theory in *Being and Nothingness*, a book not formally begun until about the time Beauvoir submitted *She Came to Stay* to its publisher in October 1941. See Hazel E. Barnes, *The Literature of Possibility: A Study in Humanistic Existentialism* (London: Tavistock, 1959), pp. 113, 121–2, 385; Beauvoir, *Prime of Life*, pp. 484, 497, 501. For a fuller account of the origins of the ideas appearing both in *She Came to Stay* and in Sartre's *Being and Nothingness* see Fullbrook and Fullbrook, *Simone de Beauvoir and Jean-Paul Sartre*, and Fullbrook and Fullbrook, 'Sartre's Secret Key', in Simons, *Feminist Interpretations*.
2 Mary Evans, *Simone de Beauvoir* (London: Sage, 1996), pp. 49–50.
3 See note 1 to this chapter.

4 *She Came to Stay*, p. 4.
5 Merleau-Ponty, 'Metaphysics and the Novel', p. 30.
6 *She Came to Stay*, p. 5.
7 Ibid., p. 21.
8 Ibid., pp. 13, 32, 146.
9 Ibid., pp. 94.
10 Ibid., pp. 46–58.
11 Ibid., pp. 51–2, 113–26, 161, 171, 180, 231, 243, 354–5. These pages include analyses and discussions of the perception of time which, taken together, frame a theory of temporality. Sartre, who had studied Beauvoir's novel the previous week, is referring to the passage on pp. 354–5 when he writes to her in his letter of 18 Feb. 1940:

> I'm beginning to see glimmers of a theory of time. This evening I began to write it. It's thanks to you, do you realize that? Thanks to Françoise's obsession: that when Pierre is in Xavière's room, there's an object living all by itself without a consciousness to see it. I'm not sure if I'll have the patience to wait for you to see it when someone takes you my notebooks.

See *Quiet Moments in a War: The Letters of Jean-Paul Sartre to Simone de Beauvoir 1940–1963*, ed. Simone de Beauvoir, trans. Lee Fahnestock and Norman MacAfee (New York: Scribner, 1993), p. 61.
12 *She Came to Stay*, pp. 126, 353.
13 'Littérature et métaphysique', p. 1.
14 *She Came to Stay* offers many pointed illustrations of these individual and situational aspects of perception. For example, its comparison of Françoise and Xavière's perceptions of the sound of a saxophone (p. 23) shows how objects perceived tend to reflect back to the perceiver aspects of himself or herself. Similarly, Xavière's recollections of childhood sensitivity to changes in colour and Françoise's nausea at the sight of an enormous cake in a nightclub (pp. 54, 53) show that the logic of perception is such that the qualities of objects in the individual's perceptual field are dependent on the other objects in that field.
15 An important example is a nightclub scene early in *She Came to Stay* (pp. 52–9) in which a woman tells how she abhors being touched; a man's hand pounces on a woman's hand; Xavière brings her arm to her lips and blows on the down on her skin; women caress a child's head; a man's hand strokes a woman's arm; Xavière touches her eyelashes and plays twice with strands of her hair; a handshake is refused; people kiss; Françoise declines to reach out her hand to touch Pierre.
16 *Les Écrits*, p. 279; *She Came to Stay*, p. 54.
17 When one's finger touches one's eyelashes the roles of subject and object shift back and forth between the eyelid, which feels the movement of the finger on the lashes, and the finger, which feels the lashes.
18 *She Came to Stay*, p. 56.
19 For example, 'She powdered her nose a little, by force of habit, and turned quickly away from the looking-glass. Whatever face she wore tonight did not really matter: it did not really exist for herself' (*She Came to Stay*, p. 32). Beauvoir underlines her point by repeating it: 'Françoise was heedful of her face only in so far as she took care of it as something impersonal' (ibid., p.

146). On another occasion: 'For a moment she stood before the looking-glass, staring at her face, it was a face which conveyed no meaning: it was stuck on her head like a label: Françoise Miquel' (p. 172).

20 Ibid., p. 172.

21 Ibid., p. 114.

22 Ibid., pp. 174, 176.

23 Bertrand Russell not only locates all philosophers in the category of males, but also in the category of believers:

> A philosopher might pretend to think that he knew only this [the space–time structure of the physical world], but let him get cross with his wife and you will see that he does not regard her as a mere spatio-temporal edifice of which he knows the logical properties but not a glimmer of the intrinsic character. We are therefore justified in inferring that his skepticism is professional rather than sincere.

See Bertrand Russell, *Human Knowledge: Its Scope and Limits* (New York: Simon and Schuster, 1948), repr. in Joseph Margolis, ed., *An Introduction to Philosophical Inquiry: Contemporary and Classical Sources* (New York: Knopf, 1968), p. 392.

24 John Stuart Mill, *An Examination of Sir William Hamilton's Philosophy*, 6th edn (New York: Longmans, Green, 1889), pp. 243–4, cited in Norman Malcolm, 'Knowledge of Other Minds', in Margolis, *An Introduction to Philosophical Inquiry*, pp. 396–7.

25 Mill's presentation makes the best of a logically feeble situation. The argument from analogy for the existence of other consciousnesses by definition is based on only one known instance, the consciousness of the person presenting the argument. More recently, however, attempts have been made to make the argument more respectable by linking its justification to modern doctrines in the philosophy of science. For example, see A. J. Ayer, *The Central Questions of Philosophy* (Harmondsworth: Penguin, 1976), pp. 132–6.

26 Russell, *Human Knowledge*, repr. in Margolis, *An Introduction to Philosophical Inquiry*, p. 394.

27 Commentators have frequently assumed that Beauvoir's theory of intersubjectivity, particularly its theory of the Other, was inspired by Hegel's parable of 'The Master and the Slave'. But her posthumously published letters show that this was not the case. They show that she did not read Hegel's *Phenomenology of Mind* until July 1940, when her novel was already into its final draft. A passage from her letter to Sartre on 14 July 1940 is particularly to the point: 'I sat down at the Dôme and read some selected passages from Hegel. I found one sentence that would do marvellously as an epigraph for my novel: "In so far as it is the Other who acts, every consciousness pursues the death of the Other..."' (*Letters to Sartre*, p. 328).

This is also the point at which to note that Husserl postulated an abstract and general category of other consciousnesses which influenced experience in a general or impersonal sense. But regarding the central problem – one's concrete experiences of other consciousnesses (individually, in groups and in general) – he offered nothing.

28 'Xavière was absorbed in the dancing girl. She could not see her own face, its beauty heightened by the state of her excitement... Xavière's gestures,

her face, her very life depended on Françoise for their existence. Xavière here and now at this moment, the essence of Xavière, was no more than the flavour of the coffee, than the piercing music or the dance . . .' (*She Came to Stay*, p. 11).

29 '. . . her childhood, her days of stagnation, her distastes, were a romantic story as real as the delicate contour of her cheeks. And that story ended here in this café, among the vari-coloured hangings, and at this very instant in Françoise's life, as she sat looking at Xavière and studying her' (*She Came to Stay*, p. 11).

30 Ibid., p. 55.

31 Ibid., p. 7.

32 These concrete relations will not be discussed since, in addition to Beauvoir's texts, there already exist excellent accounts of them. Still the best and most complete critique of what were originally Beauvoir's theories of these basic binary human relations is Sartre's chapter, 'Concrete Relations with Others', in pt 3 of *Being and Nothingness*. But a more accessible and direct account, dealing directly with Beauvoir's text, is Hazel Barnes's summary in *The Literature of Possibility*, esp. pp. 121–36. Elizabeth Fallaize's synopsis in *The Novels of Simone de Beauvoir*, the best book yet to be written on Beauvoir's fiction, is also very good.

33 *She Came to Stay*, p. 22.

34 Maurice Merleau-Ponty, *The Visible and the Invisible*, trans. Alphonso Lingis (Evanston, Ill.: Northwestern University Press, 1968), p. 82.

35 *She Came to Stay*, p. 17.

36 Ibid., pp. 23, 44.

37 Ibid., pp. 48–50, 56, 57.

38 Ibid., p. 61.

39 Ibid., p. 239.

40 Ibid., pp. 146, 127–8.

41 Merleau-Ponty, 'Metaphysics and the Novel', p. 33. Recently (in addition to the other as couple identified by Merleau-Ponty and Barnes) a larger group Other has been identified as playing an important role in *She Came to Stay*. Christine Everley, in 'War and Alterity in *L'Invitée*' (a paper presented to the Simone de Beauvoir Conference, Dublin, Sept. 1996), notes that the theatre audiences of Pierre and Françoise are a collective Other entering into the novel's structure. This dimension begs further research.

42 *She Came to Stay*, p. 143. Françoise also reflects that she would never be 'the type of woman who had absolute mastery over her body'; she was thirty, 'a mature woman . . . a woman who did not know how to dance, a woman who had had only one love in her life, a woman who had not shot the Colorado Canyon by canoe, who had never crossed the Tibetan plateau' (ibid.).

43 Ibid., p. 310. It is interesting to note just how concerned Beauvoir was as a novelist that some of her readers should perceive and appreciate her philosophical arguments. When her argument for the existence of other consciousnesses reaches its climax in pt 2, ch. 5 of *She Came to Stay*, she, through her characters. Françoise and Pierre, reiterates her methodology. The narrative reminds the reader that the manner of approaching a metaphysical problem has been concrete rather than theoretical; it notes that the phenomenological solution establishes the existence of other consciousnesses 'for certain', rather than reasons their probable existence; and it

alludes to lack of success by Beauvoir's predecessors – 'The problem is as great a mystery as birth or death, in fact, it's such a problem that all philosophers break their heads over it' (ibid., p. 302).

44 *Journal de guerre*, pp. 366, 364.
45 Simone de Beauvoir, *The Blood of Others* (1945), trans. Yvonne Moyse and Roger Senhouse (Harmondsworth: Penguin, 1964), p. 46.
46 Ibid., pp. 8–9.
47 Barnes, *The Literature of Possibility*, p. 83.
48 Alex Hughes, *Le Sang des Autres* (Glasgow: University of Glasgow, 1995), p. 11.
49 *The Blood of Others*, pp. 202, 214, 227.
50 Tore Sandven, 'Intentional Action and Pure Causality: A Critical Discussion of Some Central Conceptual Distinctions in the Work of John Elster', *Philosophy of the Social Sciences*, 25.3 (Sept. 1995), pp. 299–300.
51 Barnes, *The Literature of Possibility*, p. 80.
52 Merleau-Ponty, 'Metaphysics and the Novel', p. 37.
53 Merleau-Ponty, *The Visible and the Invisible*, p. 81.
54 Wright's influence on Beauvoir goes further than this. In her paper on the relationship between Wright's and Beauvoir's ideas, 'Joining Another's Fight' (1994), Margaret A. Simons writes:

> Wright's concern, as will be Beauvoir's in *The Second Sex*, is that the mystification of difference sustains oppression. Wright's lesson to Beauvoir is that destroying the confinements of an oppressive social role is more important than preserving cultural differences, although political change is impossible without fully appreciating and utilizing those differences . . .

Beauvoir also reports that Wright believes that 'the obvious differences that exist between the castes [blacks and whites] spring from historical, economic and social causes which could be abolished – at least in theory. But this is a truth of which the white Americans, even those with the best will in the world, are never anxious to convince themselves' (*America Day by Day*, p. 268).

55 *America Day by Day*, p. 50.
56 Ibid., p. 268.
57 In the late 1980s intersubjective concepts and analysis began to find their way into economics, where the ultra-orthodox methodological individualism of the 'neoclassicalists' has long held sway over the holism of the 'institutionalists'. This fresh infusion of thought, which includes direct material from Beauvoir's works, has resulted in a new grouping of economists, called the Intersubjectivists, who are centred in Paris.
58 Simone de Beauvoir, *The Second Sex* (1949), trans. H. M. Parshley (Harmondsworth: Penguin, 1972), p. 628.

Chapter 6 The Ethics of Liberation

1 Francis and Gontier, *Simone de Beauvoir*, p. 210.
2 Ibid., p. 216.

3 J. L. Mackie, *Ethics: Inventing Right and Wrong* (Harmondsworth: Penguin, 1977), p. 15.
4 Wittgenstein, with admirable brevity and characteristic imperiousness, stated his version of the non-cognitivist position in 1921 (the first English translation appeared in 1922) as follows: 'The sense of the world must lie outside the world. In the world everything is as it is, and everything happens as it does happen: *in* it no value exists – and if it did exist, it would have no value' (*Tractatus Logico-Philosophicus*, trans. D. F. Pears and B. F. McGuinness (London: Routledge and Kegan Paul, 1922), sec. 6.41, p. 71). Wittgenstein went on to declare that 'ethics cannot be put into words' (sec. 6.421, p. 71), that ethics is transcendental, and that ethics and aesthetics are the same.
5 *Pyrrhus et Cinéas*, p. 14.
6 Ibid., p. 47. Beauvoir had developed this theory previously in *She Came to Stay*.
7 *Pyrrhus et Cinéas*, p, 16.
8 Ibid., pp. 56, 23.
9 Ibid., p. 23.
10 Ibid., p. 29.
11 *Ethics of Ambiguity*, p. 15.
12 *Pyrrhus et Cinéas*, p. 29.
13 Simone de Beauvoir, 'Idéalisme moral et réalisme politique' (1945), in *L'Existentialisme et la sagesse des nations*, pp. 99–100. Our translation.
14 *Ethics of Ambiguity*, pp. 24, 17, 112, 17–18.
15 Fallaize, *The Novels of Simone de Beauvoir*, p. 76.
16 *Ethics of Ambiguity*, p. 29.
17 *Pyrrhus et Cinéas*, pp. 85–6.
18 *Ethics of Ambiguity*, p. 26.
19 Ibid., pp. 81, 32.
20 Ibid., p. 28.
21 Ibid., pp. 28, 30, 32, 81.
22 Simone de Beauvoir, 'Merleau-Ponty and Pseudo-Sartreanism', trans. Veronique Zaytzeff and Frederick Morrison, *International Studies in Philosophy*, 21 (1989), p. 10.
23 Ibid., pp. 7, 11.
24 *Ethics of Ambiguity*, p. 156.
25 Ibid., p. 85.
26 Kruks, 'Gender and Subjectivity', pp. 98, 100, 95.
27 *The Second Sex*, p. 436.
28 Bob Stone, 'Simone de Beauvoir and the Existential Basis of Socialism', *Social Text* (Autumn 1987), p. 125.
29 Linda Singer, 'Interpretation and Retrieval', p. 232.
30 *Ethics of Ambiguity*, p. 72.
31 *Pyrrhus et Cinéas*, pp. 65, 96, 99–101, 116–17.
32 Ibid., pp. 114–15.
33 *The Second Sex*, p. 728; *Pyrrhus et Cinéas*, pp. 115–16; Simone de Beauvoir, 'Eye for Eye', trans. Mary McCarthy, *Politics* (July–Aug. 1947), pp. 134–40.
34 *Pyrrhus et Cinéas*, pp. 96, 10, 65.
35 Ibid., p. 110.

36 See Kruks, 'Gender and Subjectivity', pp. 99–101.
37 *Pyrrhus et Cinéas*, pp. 113–14; Kruks's translation in 'Gender and Subjectivity', p. 99.
38 *The Second Sex* as cited by Kruks, 'Gender and Subjectivity', p. 105.
39 *Ethics of Ambiguity*, p. 107.
40 Ibid., pp. 12–15.
41 Bergoffen, 'Contesting Intentional Anxieties'.
42 *Ethics of Ambiguity*, pp. 70, 71, 74, 86–7.
43 Mackie, *Ethics*, p. 111 (emphasis added).
44 *Pyrrhus et Cinéas*, p. 112.
45 Singer, 'Interpretation and Retrieval', p. 236.

Chapter 7 Applied Ethics I: *The Second Sex*

1 The book sold over 1 million copies in French and between 2 and 3 million in the more than twenty languages into which it has been translated. It provided Beauvoir with a sufficient income for life. See Bair, *Simone de Beauvoir*, p. 652.
2 *The Second Sex*, p. 13.
3 See Jo-Ann Pilardi, 'The Changing Critical Fortunes of *The Second Sex*', *History and Theory*, 32 (1993), pp. 51–73.
4 *The Second Sex*, p. 15.
5 From an interview in *Ms*, July 1972, republished in Elaine Marks and Isabelle de Courtivron, eds, *New French Feminisms* (Hemel Hempstead: Harvester Wheatsheaf, 1981), p. 145. For another example of this kind of response see *Prime of Life*, p. 367.
6 See Bair, *Simone de Beauvoir*, pp. 379–80. In an interview Audry told Bair about Beauvoir approaching her at the Café Flore in the summer of 1948, saying ' "You know that book you were always talking about when we were in Rouen? The one about women? Well, I'm the one who's going to write it." ' Audry remained an associate of Beauvoir throughout her life and was a significant campaigner for women's rights in France. See Francis and Gontier, *Simone de Beauvoir*, pp. 126, 290. Beauvoir quotes Audry extensively in *The Second Sex*.
7 *Prime of Life*, pp. 62, 572.
8 *Force of Circumstance*, pp. 103, 178. In a footnote (p. 196) she notes that the book 'was begun in October 1946 and finished in June 1949; but I spent four months of 1947 in America, and *America Day by Day* kept me busy for six months.'
9 With regard to *The Second Sex*, for example, this debate has recently centred on the related questions of Beauvoir's treatment of motherhood, lesbianism, the body and sexual passion, as well as querying the book's historical and class limitations, and its Western and French viewpoints: see, for example, Hazel Barnes, 'Simone de Beauvoir and Later Feminism', *Simone de Beauvoir Studies*, 4 (1987), pp. 5–34; Margaret A. Simons, 'Reclaiming *The Second Sex*', *Women's Studies International Forum*, 8.3 (1985), pp. 169–71; Moi, *Simone de Beauvoir*, pp. 73–92; Le Doeuff, *Hipparchia's Choice*, pp. 55–6.
10 *The Second Sex*, p. 295. This idea has been of immense importance to feminist

discussions from the 1960s to the present and stands behind work ranging from Kate Millett's *Sexual Politics* (1970) to Judith Butler's *Gender Trouble* (1990); it informs, often in submerged ways, much of the current work on the performativity of gender.

11 *The Second Sex*, p. 14.
12 Ibid., pp. 15–16.
13 Ibid., p. 16.
14 Ibid., pp. 16–17.
15 Kruks, 'Gender and Subjectivity', p. 98.
16 See Beauvoir's account of her decision to assume the label of feminist in *All Said and Done*, trans. Patrick O'Brian (Harmondsworth: Penguin, 1977), p. 491.
17 *The Second Sex*, p. 19.
18 Ibid. The strength of this point for Beauvoir gives the reason for her interest in Shulamith Firestone's *Dialectic of Sex* (1970), which proposes artificial insemination as a universal substitute for sexual intercourse, thus offering a utopian view of a radical revision of the terms of the biological imperative holding men and women together. On this matter see Beauvoir's interview with Alice Schwarzer in Marks and de Courtivron, *New French Feminisms*, p. 146.
19 See Beauvoir's statement about the importance of her own economic independence in *Prime of Life*, p. 367.
20 See *The Second Sex*, p. 21.
21 Beauvoir's attention to previous women's work is diminished in the English translation of *The Second Sex*, because of editorial decisions about abridging the text. For a history of these decisions and an account of what has been lost see Margaret A. Simons, 'The Silencing of Simone de Beauvoir: Guess What's Missing from *The Second Sex*', *Women's Studies International Forum*, 6.5 (1983), pp. 559–64, and Yolanda Astarita Patterson, 'Who Was This H. M. Parshley? The Saga of Translating Simone de Beauvoir's *The Second Sex*', *Simone de Beauvoir Studies*, 9 (1992), pp. 41–7.
22 *The Second Sex*, p. 25.
23 Ibid., pp. 27–8.
24 Ibid, pp. 28–9.
25 Michèle Le Doeuff, in her superb study of Beauvoir, *Hipparchia's Choice*, is absolutely correct in emphasizing the point that, unlike much recent feminist thought, Beauvoir's is not concerned with women's happiness but their subjectivity and their agency (pp. 115–16).
26 *Force of Circumstance*, p. 195.
27 Ibid., p. 197.
28 Ibid., p. 198.
29 Ibid., p. 203.
30 See Monique Wittig, 'One Is Not Born a Woman', *Feminist Issues*, 1.2 (Winter 1981), pp. 47–54.
31 Judith Butler, 'Sex and Gender in Simone de Beauvoir's *Second Sex*', in *Simone de Beauvoir: Witness to a Century*, special issue of *Yale French Studies*, 72 (1986), pp. 35, 49.
32 See Judith Butler, *Gender Trouble* (London: Routledge, 1990), pp. 111–28, 143.

Chapter 8   Applied Ethics II: *Les Belles Images,* *The Woman Destroyed* and *Old Age*

1 *All Said and Done*, p. 137.
2 See 'Simone de Beauvoir présente *Les Belles Images*', an interview with Jacqueline Paiter, *Le Monde*, 23 Dec. 1966, extracts repr. in *Les Écrits*, p. 224.
3 *All Said and Done*, p. 139.
4 Ibid., p. 138.
5 Ibid., pp. 140–4.
6 Simone de Beauvoir, *Old Age* (1970), trans. Patrick O'Brian (Harmondsworth: Penguin, 1977), pp. 7–8.
7 Ibid., p. 8.
8 See Julien Murphy, 'Beauvoir and the Algerian War: Toward a Postcolonial Ethics' in Simons, *Feminist Interpretations*, pp. 263–97, for an in-depth analysis of Beauvoir's anticolonialist principles as illustrated in the Boupacha case.
9 For further discussions of *Old Age* and Beauvoir's treatment of ageing see Kathleen Woodward,'Simone de Beauvoir: Aging and its Discontents', in Shari Benstock, ed., *The Private Self: Theory and Practice of Women's Autobiographical Writings* (London: Routledge, 1988), pp. 90–113; Brosman, *Simone de Beauvoir Revisited*, pp. 144–6.
10 *Prime of Life*, pp. 207–8.
11 *Force of Circumstance*, pp. 669, 670–1, 674.
12 Bair, *Simone de Beauvoir*, p. 470 (interview from 1982).
13 *All Said and Done*, p. 132.
14 Ibid., pp. 129 and esp. 130–1; for Beauvoir's reaction to gender after she turned forty, see *Force of Circumstance*, p. 195.
15 See *All Said and Done*, p. 483, and *Force of Circumstance*, p. 202.
16 *Old Age*, p. 8.
17 In *All Said and Done* (p. 147) Beauvoir recalls how difficult it initially was to locate documentary material on the old, in complete contrast to her research on women. And again, as in the case of *The Second Sex*, Claude Lévi-Strauss was very useful in furthering the project.
18 *Old Age*, p. 9.
19 Ibid., pp. 10–11, 13.
20 Ibid., p. 16.
21 Ibid., p. 316.
22 Ibid., pp. 320–1.
23 Ibid., p. 601.

Glossary

Words in italics have their own entries in the glossary.

bad faith An ontologically based form of conceptual confusion in the conduct of an individual's life. The dual nature of *conscious being*, as both *immanence* and *transcendence*, makes it possible for subjects to deny to themselves that they are free to behave or choose differently (the **bad faith of immanence**), or to deny one or more of the givens of their existence (the **bad faith of transcendence**). Bad faith may take the form of a vacillation between its two types.

being Beauvoir's *ontology* identifies two primary kinds of being: *non-conscious being* and *conscious being*.

collective intentionality Spheres of *intersubjectivity* wherein cultural ways and social hierarchies have assigned values and meanings to various objects and groups of people. Individuals take on personal meanings and values within the context of these cultural fields.

conscious being is *being* related to the world by *consciousness*. For Beauvoir's purposes, conscious being is synonymous with human being. A person's non-conscious being includes his or her past and body. Conscious being is simultaneously both *immanence* and *transcendence*.

consciousness is identified by Beauvoir as a relation humans have with *being*, a way of being related to the world. It has three fundamental characteristics. First, it is not being but a *lack* of being, a nothingness or emptiness or void. Thus consciousness is a perpetual striving for being. Secondly, because consciousness is a void it is consciousness of something other than itself. This characteristic, of always positing an *object* for its content, is called *intentionality*. Thirdly, intentionality implies a process by which the content of consciousness is 'determined'. This process is held to be one of free choice within the context of one's situation-in-the-world. See *freedom*.

embodiment refers to the positional state of consciousness, and to the part played by one's body in the perception and construction of one's world.

the essence at the heart of human existence is the invariant primary structure of conscious being, or core metaphysical reality shared by all human beings, which Beauvoir seeks to identify. *Embodiment, intentionality, lack,* and the split between *immanence* and *transcendence* are elements of this structure.

freedom Beauvoir makes a sharp distinction between the freedom of *consciousness*, **ontological freedom**, and the freedom of a *conscious being*, **freedom-in-situation**. The former is inalienable in the sense that consciousness is always a process of choosing projects, including the meanings one assigns to the world. But Beauvoir maintains that even these individual choices are often socially imposed or conditioned, and that the free choice of a project for which there is no possibility of realization, that is, no possibility of worldly transcendence, is an empty freedom. For these reasons, she regarded ontological freedom as an ethically meaningless concept. When she speaks of 'freedom' she usually means freedom-in-situation. See *transcendence*.

the gaze When caught in another's gaze or look, one may undergo a sudden shift from experiencing oneself as the centre of reference around which the world is organized, that is, as a subject, to a state of experiencing oneself as an object in the world organized by another person's subjectivity. This sudden shift in the state of consciousness, as with an apprehension of shame or pride, is the characteristic *subject / object reversal*.

holistic union The belief, opposed by Beauvoir, that two or more individuals can merge their consciousnesses into a single entity.

immanence The opposite of *transcendence*, the nature of *non-conscious being*. Sometimes the term denotes the non-conscious being of conscious being, for example, one's body and past. Choosing oneself as immanence, for example, as thing-like, is a form of *bad faith*, and means regarding oneself as without the power of transcendence. Occasionally 'facticity' is used as a synonym for immanence.

intentionality This hypothesis, originating with Brentano and central to *phenomenology*, holds that *consciousness* is a relation human beings have to objects, both real and imagined. This relational view of consciousness, crucial to Beauvoir's thought, contrasts with the more traditional view of consciousness as a kind of receptacle for perceptions and images. See *modes of intentionality*.

internal subject / object relation between consciousnesses A direct causal relation between consciousnesses, identified first by Beauvoir, which provides the elusive ontological basis for a non-mystical explanation of intersubjective phenomena between individuals, and between individuals and groups. This relation is the basis of Beauvoir's social and cultural theory.

intersubjective social theory Social and cultural theory based on Beauvoir's theory of intersubjectivity.

intersubjectivity Individuals and groups of individuals related by the *internal subject / object relation*.

lack Beauvoir carries the principle of *intentionality* to its logical conclusion: if *consciousness* is a relation, then it 'contains' nothing, not even an ego. This purely relational nature means that consciousness forever requires objects to be conscious of. 'Lack' refers to this constant need of consciousness, which Beauvoir identifies as the foundation of all desire.

methodological holism A doctrine in social science, related to *holistic union*, that individuals are explained in terms of their position in social wholes which are governed by macroscopic laws.

methodological individualism A doctrine in social science, premised on *social solipsism*, which holds that all social phenomena are, in principle, explicable solely in terms of autonomous individual human beings, each of whom is individuated unambiguously.

methodological intersubjectivity The social science methodology used by Beauvoir in *The Second Sex*, premised on the *internal subject / object relation between consciousnesses*, which recognizes the existence of bi-directional causality between individuals and social wholes.

modes of intentionality Beauvoir identifies two primary modes of *intentionality* for consciousness: the mode of desiring-to-be and the mode of desiring-to-disclose-being.

narrative self The idea that a person's self or selves are narratives, told by and / or to that person.

négatité Any perception which involves a negative judgement, for example, an empty glass. Every *project* begins with a négatité, in the form of a decision that the present state of affairs is in some way wanting and can be transcended.

non-conscious being Includes not only materiality, but also anything which can be made an *object* of *consciousness*, such as a concept or a memory.

non-self-identity Beauvoir holds that a *conscious being* can never be self-identical, in the way that a shovel is a shovel, because it exists always as an emergent phenomenon. See *transcendence* and *intentionality*.

object Anything of which a consciousness is conscious. See *intentionality*.

objectification The experiencing of oneself as another person's object. See *internal subject / object relation between consciousnesses*.

ontology That branch of philosophy concerned with being, especially with being's possible and primary categories.

phenomenology A major twentieth-century philosophical movement, founded by Edmund Husserl, seeking, in reaction to nineteenth-century philosophical idealism, to bring philosophy back into contact with material existence. By a process of analysis, it aims to remove the preconceptions one brings to the objects of one's perceptions, thereby revealing the structures of experience. A key idea of phenomenology is the principle of *intentionality*.

point of view This is the keystone of Beauvoir's philosophical method. She believes that because all consciousnesses are embodied and are situated historically, socially and culturally, all observation and evaluation, including that by philosophers, takes place from a particular and concrete point of view. From this methodological position, all intimations by philosophers that they command a universal point of view are regarded as fraudulent. See *embodiment*.

project A person's choice of a future end and their choice of the way she or he projects her- or himself towards it. See *transcendence*.

reciprocity (mode of intersubjectivity) When parties (either individuals or groups) to the *internal subject / object relation* treat each other and themselves as both subject and object, as equal freedoms, and as sources of value and meaning. See *subjection (mode of intersubjectivity)*.

social solipsism The belief or assumption, usually implicit, that an indirect approach to other minds is required because people do not and cannot experience other people as conscious beings. It appeals to the fact that consciousnesses cannot be perceived through any of the sensory mechanisms, and on this basis concludes that a person has no means of apprehending consciousnesses other than his or her own.

spatiality Beauvoir's theory that space is not experienced primarily as a universal, or objective, or homogeneous phenomenon, but rather as one which is essentially relative and personalized, with human bodies engaged in projects acting as shifting reference points or poles around which physical space is organized. It is this configuration of oriented spaces that Beauvoir presents as the subject's broad sensory field, rather than the homogeneous space assumed by rationalism and empiricism. See *temporality* and *embodiment*.

subject Generally, it is any conscious being exercising his or her *subjectivity*. However, this term has special import when the subject's object is another person or group of persons. See *internal subject / object relation*.

subjection (mode of intersubjectivity) When individuals and groups, engaged as terms of the *internal subject / object relation*, struggle with one another for or concede subjective domination. See *reciprocity (mode of intersubjectivity)*.

subjectivity The meaning-giving which occurs when the *projects* which a person chooses become contexts of meaning for the objects of his or her consciousness. In this way, and only in this way, meaning comes into the world.

subject / object reversal A shift from or to experiencing oneself as the centre of reference around which the world is organized (that is, as a subject), to or from a state of experiencing oneself as an object in the world organized and evaluated by another person, or group of persons. These transformations result from the *internal subject / object relation between consciousnesses* and cannot be derived from the other person's status as object.

temporality Time as organized and experienced through one's *projects*.

transcendence This is the process of going beyond a given state of affairs, and refers either to *consciousness* or to *conscious being*. The former is always transcendent, with one object of consciousness continuously succeeding another. The latter is conditional on a person's choice and situation-in-the-world. See *freedom*.

Works of Simone de Beauvoir

The first section lists, in order of first publication, all of Beauvoir's books. English editions listed are those used in this text. The second and third sections, which list articles by Beauvoir and interviews with her, are in no way complete.

Books

L'Invitée (novel). Paris: Gallimard, 1943.
She Came to Stay, trans. Yvonne Moyse and Roger Senhouse. London: Flamingo, 1984.

Pyrrhus et Cinéas (essay). Paris: Gallimard, 1944.

Les Bouches inutiles (play). Paris: Gallimard, 1945.
Who Shall Die? trans. Claude Francis and Fernande Gontier. Florissant, Mo.: River Press, 1983.

La Sang des autres (novel). Paris: Gallimard, 1945.
The Blood of Others, trans. Yvonne Moyse and Roger Senhouse. Harmondsworth: Penguin, 1964.

Tous les hommes sont mortels (novel). Paris: Gallimard, 1946.
All Men are Mortal, trans. Leonard M. Friedman. London: Norton, 1992.

Pour une morale de l'ambiguïté (essay). Paris: Gallimard, 1947.
The Ethics of Ambiguity, trans. Bernard Frechtman. New York: Citadel Press, 1970.

L'Amérique au jour le jour (essay). Paris: Morihien, 1948.
America Day by Day, trans. Patrick Dudley. London: Duckworth, 1952.

L'Existentialisme et la sagesse des nations (collected essays). Paris: Nagel, 1948.

Le Deuxième Sexe (essay). 2 vols, Paris: Gallimard, 1949.
The Second Sex, trans. H. M. Parshley. Harmondsworth: Penguin, 1972.

Les Mandarins (novel). Paris: Gallimard, 1954.
The Mandarins, trans. Leonard M. Friedman. London: Flamingo, 1984.

Privilèges (collected essays). Paris: Gallimard, 1955.
Must We Burn Sade? trans. Annette Michelson. London: Peter Nevill, 1953.

La Longue Marche (essay). Paris: Gallimard, 1957.
The Long March, trans. Austryn Wainhouse. London: André Deutsch/ Weidenfeld and Nicolson, 1958.

Mémoires d'une jeune fille rangée (memoirs). Paris: Gallimard, 1958.
Memoirs of a Dutiful Daughter, trans. James Kirkup. Harmondsworth: Penguin, 1963.

La Force de l'âge (memoirs). Paris: Gallimard, 1960.
The Prime of Life, trans. Peter Green. Harmondsworth: Penguin, 1965.

Brigitte Bardot and the Lolita Syndrome (essay). London: André Deutsch/ Weidenfeld and Nicolson, 1960.

La Force des choses (memoirs). Paris: Gallimard, 1963.
Force of Circumstance, trans. Richard Howard. Harmondsworth: Penguin, 1968.

Une mort très douce (biography). Paris: Gallimard, 1964.
A Very Easy Death, trans. Patrick O'Brian. Harmondsworth: Penguin, 1969.

Les Belles Images (novel). Paris: Gallimard, 1966.
Les Belles Images, trans. Patrick O'Brian. London: Flamingo, 1985.

La Femme rompue (short stories). Paris: Gallimard, 1968.
The Woman Destroyed, trans. Patrick O'Brian. London: Flamingo, 1984.

La Vieillesse (essay). Paris: Gallimard, 1970.
Old Age, trans. Patrick O'Brian. Harmondsworth: Penguin, 1977.

Tout compte fait (memoirs). Paris: Gallimard, 1972.
All Said and Done, trans. Patrick O'Brian. Harmondsworth: Penguin, 1977.

Les Écrits de Simone de Beauvoir (previously unpublished writings, including 'Deux chapitres inédits de *L'Invitée*'), ed. C. Francis and F. Gontier. Paris: Gallimard, 1979.

Quand prime le spirituel (short stories). Paris: Gallimard, 1979.
When Things of the Spirit Come First: Five Early Tales, trans. Patrick O'Brian. London: Flamingo, 1983.

La Cérémonie des adieux suivi de *Entretiens avec Jean-Paul Sartre* (biography and conversations). Paris: Gallimard, 1981.
Adieux: A Farewell to Sartre, trans. Patrick O'Brian. Harmondsworth: Penguin, 1985.

Lettres à Sartre, vol. 1: *1930–1939*; vol. 2: *1940–1963*, ed. and annotated Sylvie Le Bon de Beauvoir. Paris: Gallimard, 1990.
Letters to Sartre, trans. and ed. Quintin Hoare. London: Radius, 1991.

Journal de guerre: Septembre 1939–Janvier 1941, ed. Sylvie le Bon de Beauvoir. Paris: Gallimard, 1990.

Articles

'*La Phénoménologie de la perception* de M. Merleau-Ponty', *Les Temps Modernes*, 1.2 (Nov. 1945), pp. 363–7.

'Eye for Eye', trans. Mary McCarthy, *Politics* (July–Aug. 1947), pp. 134–40.

'Brigitte Bardot and the Lolita Syndrome', *Esquire* (Aug. 1959), pp. 32–8.

Introduction to Gisèle Halimi, *Djamila Boupacha*, Paris: Gallimard, 1962. English edn trans. Peter Green, London: André Deutsch / Weidenfeld and Nicolson, 1962.

'What Love Is – and Isn't', *McCall's* (Aug. 1965), pp. 71, 133.

'Merleau-Ponty and Pseudo-Sartreanism', trans. Veronique Zaytzeff and Frederick Morrison, *International Studies in Philosophy*, 21 (1989), pp. 3–48.

Interviews

'Sex, Society, and the Female Dilemma: A Dialogue between Simone de Beauvoir and Betty Friedan', *Saturday Review*, 14 June 1975, pp. 14–20, 56–7.

'Simone de Beauvoir: *The Second Sex*, 25 years Later', by John Gerassi, *Society* (Jan.–Feb. 1976), pp. 79–85.

'Beauvoir elle-même', by Catherine David, *Le Nouvel Observateur*, 22 Jan. 1979, pp. 82–5, 88–9.

'Simone de Beauvoir: An Interview', by Margaret A. Simons and Jessica Benjamin, trans. Véronique Zaytzeff, *Feminist Studies*, 5.2 (Summer 1979), pp. 330–45.

'Interview with Simone de Beauvoir', by Alice Jardine, *Signs*, 5.2 (Winter 1979), pp. 224–36.

Simone de Beauvoir, by Josée Dayan and Malka Ribowska. Paris: Gallimard, 1979.

Simone de Beauvoir Today: Conversations, 1972–1982, by Alice Schwarzer, trans. Marianne Howarth. London: Chatto and Windus, 1984.

'Encountering Simone de Beauvoir', by Hester Eisenstein, *Women and Politics*, 11.1 (1991), pp. 61–74.

Index

Adieux: A Farewell to Sartre, 36, 135
adolescence, 69–72, 138
African-American thought, 94, 97–9
Alain, 15–16, 20, 27
Alain-Fournier, 20
Alcott, Louisa May, 11
Algerian War, 35, 141–2, 143, 144
Algren, Nelson, 121
All Men Are Mortal, 34, 44–51, 100
All Said and Done, 35, 136, 141
America Day by Day, 35, 40, 73, 97–8, 107, 121, 160, 162
Anthony, Susan B., 128
Aquinas, Thomas, 10, 11, 12, 17, 19, 123, 124
Aragon, Louis, 20
Aristotle, 12, 19, 38–9, 124
Aron, Raymond, 14, 23, 26, 28, 29
Audry, Colette, 120, 132, 162
avant-garde, the, 20, 22
A Very Easy Death, 35

bad faith, 68–70, 72, 78–9, 82, 88, 94, 138, 140, 165
  of immanence, 68–70, 79, 93, 103, 105, 165
  of transcendence, 68, 78–9, 82, 88, 90–1, 157–8, 159, 165
Bair, Deirdre, 32, 144
Balzac, Honoré de, 14
Barnes, Hazel, 96, 156, 159

de la Barre, Poulain, 128
Baruzi, Jean, 22–3, 25
Bataille, Georges, 28
Belles Images, Les, 36, 136–8, 139
Benjamin, Jessica, 3
Bergoffen, Debra, 73, 113
Bergson, Henri, 16, 18, 19
Blood of Others, The, 34, 92–7, 100
body, *see* embodiment
le Bon de Beauvoir, Sylvie, ix
Bost, Jacques, 121
Bouches inutiles, Les, 34
Brentano, Franz, 57–60, 166
Breton, André, 20, 28, 64
Brunschvicg, Cécile, 24
Brunschvicg, Léon, 13, 23–5, 28, 152
Butler, Judith, 117, 133–4, 163

Camus, Albert, 5, 16, 34, 111
Cartesianism, 12, 16, 27, 56, 59, 80, 132
Champigneulle, Jacques, 14, 18
Cixous, Hélène, 124
collective intentionality, 107–8, 165
colonialism, 35, 63, 99, 123, 141–2, 164
concrete (the) and the particular, 38–41, 42–4, 48–50, 60, 61, 80, 82, 85, 88, 102, 105, 112, 123, 127, 130, 141, 158, 159–60, 167

consciousness and conscious being, 21, 44, 53–60, 62–3, 65–74, 77–92, 96, 101–2, 104–5, 106, 107, 113, 124, 146–8, 158, 165
consumerism, 136–8, 145

Descartes, René, 16, 17, 18, 26, 58
desire, 50, 72–4, 102–6, 113, 130, 137
'Deux chapitres inédits de *L'Invitée*', 65–7, 81, 154, 156
Diderot, Denis, 128, 131
Djamila Boupacha, 35, 141–2
Le Doeuff, Michèle, 2, 117, 163
double-touching, 81, 157
Douglass, Frederick, 98

economics, 94, 95, 102–3, 145–7, 160
Einstein, Albert, 25
Eliot, George, 11
embodiment, 48, 58, 62, 65–8, 75–82, 101, 105, 116, 133, 136, 140, 146–8, 156, 157–8, 165
empiricism, 18, 19, 23, 48, 59, 78, 79–80, 100, 168
Engels, Friedrich, 29, 125
epistemology, 49, 53, 61
essence at the heart of human existence, 41, 44, 165–6
ethical theory, 100–15
Ethics of Ambiguity, The, 4, 31, 35, 69–70, 73, 97, 100, 104–8, 110, 112, 113, 116, 120, 121, 124
Everley, Christine, 159
L'Existentialisme et la sagesse des nations, 35

Fallaize, Elizabeth, 92–3, 105, 159
feminism, 1, 7, 24, 35, 36, 117, 118, 120, 125–6, 141
Firestone, Shulamith, 117, 163
Fitche, Johann, 104
Force of Circumstance, 4, 35, 50, 131, 141, 143, 144
Foucault, Michel, 136
freedom, 27–8, 62–3, 66, 69–70, 72, 101–13, 115, 121, 140, 146, 148, 166, 167
freedom-in-situation, 62, 70, 101–2, 105–9, 166

interdependence of, 93–4, 107–9
ontological, 62–3, 101–4, 106–7, 166
Freud, Sigmund, 20, 27, 28, 70

Gaarder, Jostein, 44
Gallimard, 31–3
Gandillac, Maurice de, 14
Garric, Robert, 16–17, 18, 25
gaze (the), 88–9, 91–2, 94, 96, 98, 146–7, 166
gender and philosophy, 1–6, 13–14, 28, 39, 60, 71, 87, 109–10, 113–15, 117, 118–20, 124, 158
Gerassi, Fernando, 29

Halimi, Gisèle, 35, 141–2
Hamelin, 19
Hegel, Georg, 4, 15, 28, 29, 33, 47, 85–6, 104, 118, 124, 127, 128, 158
Heidegger, Martin, 29, 71, 85, 127, 152
Hobbes, Thomas, 114
holistic union, 82, 85, 89–91, 95, 113, 166
Holmes, Oliver Wendel, 147
Holveck, Eleanore, 39, 41
Hume, David, 23, 25, 44, 53, 54–5, 57, 58, 59, 63, 65, 71, 114
Husserl, Edmund, 15, 29, 53, 57, 60, 118, 158
Huxley, Aldous, 70

Imitation of Christ, The, 10, 11
immanence, 60–3, 65–70, 79–81, 91, 106, 130, 143, 147, 166
Individual Others, 63, 94, 145, 146
see also Other; Social Other
intentionality, 57–60, 62–3, 72–4, 77, 98, 101–2, 106
two modes of, 72–4, 101, 109, 110, 113, 156, 166
internalization, 98, 107, 139, 147
internal subject/object relation between consciousnesses, 86–99, 158, 159–60, 166
intersubjective social theory, 89, 93–9, 166

intersubjectivity, 75, 76, 82–99, 101, 105–15, 116, 121, 125–6, 130, 136, 144–5, 156, 158, 159, 160, 166
irrationalism, 20, 28

Jaspers, Karl, 29, 71

Kant, Immanuel, 18, 19, 23, 25, 26, 27, 28, 38–9, 52–3, 54–5, 60–1, 78, 80, 104, 154
Kempis, Thomas à, 10, 12
Kierkegaard, Sören, 29, 43, 54, 61–2, 71, 117
Kojève, Alexandre, 28
Kruks, Sonia, 112, 125

Lacan, Jacques, 28
lack, 57–60, 102–6, 124, 146, 166
Laporte, 25
Leibniz, Gottfried, 13, 19, 23, 24–5, 26, 38–9, 53, 152
Lenin, Vladimir, 128
Lettres au Castor et à quelques autres, 36
Levinas, Emmanuel, 124
Lévi-Strauss, Claude, 25, 118, 164
literary-philosophical method, 30, 34, 35, 37–51, 52, 75–6, 92, 117, 135, 159
'Littérature et métaphysique', 37–44, 80
Long March, The, 35
Luther, Martin, 47

Mackie, J. L., 101, 114
Macquarrie, John, 62
Marcel, Gabriel, 71
Maheu, René, 14, 15, 23, 25, 26
Malraux, André, 17
Mandarins, The, 31, 35, 135, 136
Marcuse, Herbert, 145
Marx, Karl, 27, 28, 29, 70
meaning, *see* value
Memoirs of a Dutiful Daughter, 7, 9, 31, 35, 56
Mercier, Mlle, 13, 17–18, 23, 25, 26
Merleau-Ponty, Maurice, 3, 5, 21–2, 23, 25, 28, 36, 38, 39, 40, 43, 59, 72, 73–4, 77, 78, 89, 96, 118, 156, 159

methodological holism, 95–9, 160, 166
methodological individualism, 95–9, 160, 166
methodological intersubjectivity, 94–9, 166
Mill, John Stuart, 83–5, 87, 89, 128, 131, 158
Millett, Kate, 117, 162–3
modes of intentionality, 72–4, 101, 113, 156, 167
Moi, Toril, 14
Montaigne, 4
mortality, 45–51
mysticism and mystification, 21, 22–3, 41, 42, 43, 68, 82–3, 108, 123, 160

narrative self, 57, 63–7, 68, 72, 146–8, 167
Nietzsche, Friedrich, 19, 22, 23, 28, 44, 61, 128
Nizan, Paul, 14, 26, 29, 152
non-conscious being, 37, 58, 62, 67, 87, 101, 167
non-self-identity, 66–72, 105, 167
nothingness, *see* lack

objectification, 87, 88–92, 94, 96, 99, 106, 107, 120, 128, 146, 147, 160, 167
Old Age, 26, 54, 107, 115, 119, 122, 136, 138, 139, 140, 141–8
ontology, 17, 26, 37, 56, 57–63, 72, 95, 101, 103, 104, 107, 112, 125, 145, 167
Other, the, 33, 63, 75, 92–4, 96–8, 118, 121, 124–6, 127, 129, 130, 131–2, 134, 145–7, 158
see also Individual Others; Social Other
other minds (the problem of), 82–92

Parshley, H. M., 3, 163
perception, 53, 55, 57, 59, 75, 78, 79–80, 103, 146, 156, 157
phenomenology, 4, 8, 11, 29, 40, 43, 53–60, 67–8, 70, 72, 159, 167

philosophical universalism, 37, 39–44, 45, 46–51, 52, 60–1, 78, 80, 105, 109, 132
Pilardi, Jo-Ann, 117
Plato, 19, 43
point of view, 38–44, 45, 46–51, 58, 71, 77–8, 80, 104–5, 124, 167
politics, 16, 35
Politzer, Georg, 26
postmodernism, 3, 39, 49, 72, 117
Prime of Life, The, 2–3, 7, 31–2, 35, 63, 70, 141, 142, 143
Privilèges, 35
project, 80, 82, 102–5, 106–7, 110, 111–12, 113, 130, 147, 167
Protagoras, 114
Proust, Marcel, 147
Pyrrhus et Cinéas, 34, 39, 62, 63, 100–4, 106, 110, 111–12, 115, 116, 124

Queer Theory, 133
Queneau, Raymond, 28

Rabelais, François, 4
racism, 97–9, 121, 142
rationalism, 18, 23, 27, 28, 40, 46, 48, 53, 82, 123
rationality, 102–4
reciprocity (mode of intersubjectivity), 33, 42, 108, 110, 113–15, 124, 138, 139, 147–8, 167
Rousseau, Jean-Jacques, 26
Russell, Bertrand, 84–5, 158

St John of the Cross, 22
St Paul, 128
Saint-Simon, 4
Sartre, Jean-Paul, 1–2, 4, 5, 8, 14, 15, 16, 17, 23–4, 25, 26, 27, 28, 31, 32, 34, 36, 62, 68, 70, 71, 73, 77, 118, 120, 121–2, 124, 135, 144, 152, 155, 157, 158
Schopenhauer, Arthur, 19
Schwarzer, Alice, ix, 119, 163
science, 19, 23, 42–3, 44, 45, 49, 128

Second Sex, The, 3, 31, 32, 52, 54, 72, 87, 94, 97, 99, 107, 108, 111, 112, 115, 116–34, 139, 141, 142, 145, 148, 160, 162
Sévigné, Madame de, 147
She Came to Stay, 29, 33, 34, 35, 38, 43, 56, 62, 75–83, 85–92, 93, 94, 96–7, 99, 125, 148, 156, 157, 158–9
Simons, Margaret A., ix, 2, 3, 40, 73, 97, 149, 152, 160, 163
Singer, Linda, 109, 115, 149
Smith, Adam, 94
social science, 84, 94–9, 102–4, 123, 128, 166–7
Social Other, 17, 63, 92–9, 118, 159
   see also Individual Others; Other
social solipsism, 82–5, 86–91, 95, 98, 110, 158, 167
spatiality, 48, 82, 105, 168
Spinoza, Benedict de, 4, 18, 25, 26, 38–9
Staël, Mme de, 128
Stone, Bob, 109
subjection (mode of intersubjectivity), 108, 110, 113–14, 124, 168
subjectivity, 11, 39, 81–2, 105, 108, 130, 137, 139, 163, 168
subject/object relation, 87, 88–92, 94, 95–9, 107, 108, 110, 114, 166
subject/object reversal, 88–9, 96–9, 108, 160, 168
subject/object split, 57, 81, 88, 92–3
surrealism, 20–21, 22, 64

temporality, 50, 80, 105, 157, 168
Temps Modernes, Les, 16, 35, 37, 131
theology, 9–12, 16, 17, 25, 55, 64
transcendence, 60–3, 65–70, 78–82, 96, 102, 103, 106, 107, 109, 130, 137, 168

value (and meaning), 45, 48, 49, 50, 69, 101–8, 110, 112, 113, 130, 146–8, 161

Warnock, G. L., 114
Warnock, Mary, 43

Weil, Simone, 15, 21
Weiss, Louise, 24
When Things of the Spirit Come First, 31, 32, 33, 36, 63
Who Shall Die?, 100, 113
Wittgenstein, Ludwig, 3, 161
Wittig, Monique, 117, 132–4
Wollstonecraft, Mary, 128

Woman Destroyed, The, 36, 136, 138–40
women as philosophers, 1–6, 12–14, 27–8, 30–2, 33, 34, 60, 71, 87, 109–10, 113–15, 118–20, 158, 159–60
Woolf, Virginia, 29, 44, 128
Wright, Richard, 97–9, 121, 160